SEX DETERMINATION IN MOUSE AND MAN

Anne Goroch

SEX DETERMINATION IN MOUSE AND MAN

PROCEEDINGS OF
A ROYAL SOCIETY DISCUSSION MEETING
HELD ON 9 AND 10 MARCH 1988

ORGANIZED AND EDITED BY
ANNE McLAREN, F.R.S., AND
M. A. FERGUSON-SMITH, F.R.S.

LONDON
THE ROYAL SOCIETY
1988

Printed in Great Britain for the Royal Society
at the
University Press, Cambridge

ISBN 0 85403 369 6

First published in the *Philosophical Transactions of the Royal Society of London*, series B, volume 322 (no. 1208), pages 1–157.

British Library Cataloguing in Publication Data

Sex determination in mouse and man.
1. Mammals. Sex differences
I. McLaren, Anne II. Ferguson-Smith, M.A.
III. Royal Society IV. Philosophical
Transactions of the Royal Society of London.
Series B.
599′.03′6

ISBN 0-85403-369-6

Published by the Royal Society
6 Carlton House Terrace, London SW1Y 5AG

PREFACE

When 'Sex Determination in Mouse and Man' was proposed in early 1985 as a suitable topic for a Discussion Meeting of the Royal Society, it seemed to the organizers that research in these two species was converging in an exciting way towards an understanding of the factors that initiate the early stages of sex differentiation.

In our own species, observations on the presence of specific Y sequences in so-called XX males and their absence in XY females suggested that the cloning and characterization of the Y-specific factor necessary for initiation of testis formation was imminent. In the mouse there was recent evidence of the important role of the Sertoli cells in the early development of the testis and the possibility that these cells were the recipient of the primary sex-determining signal. At that time there was also controversy about the possibility that the H-Y antigen was the primary signal for male differentiation. Autosomal mutations in the mouse were being described that influenced sex determination in XY embryos. Clearly the field was moving rapidly and the next three years up to the date of the Discussion Meeting were likely to provide answers to some of the outstanding questions on the mechanisms of mammalian sex determination and differentiation and, in particular, on the nature of the Y sequences responsible for initiating testis development in XX males.

And so it has proved. The paper describing the cloning of a possible candidate for the testis-determining gene by Page and his colleagues was published on Christmas Eve 1987 (*Cell* **51**, 1091). There has been enough time for those attending the Discussion Meeting in March 1988 to consider the implications of this development in their own work. Thus 11 of the 14 contributors to this volume refer specifically to Page's paper. However, it would be a mistake to assume that all is now understood. Page's zinc finger protein has yet to be formally confirmed as the primary sex-determining signal and, because of this, he modestly refers in his contribution to the locus of his gene as *ZFY*, although others might presume its gonad-determining role by naming the locus *GDY*. The observation of a homologous gene, *ZFX*, on the differential segment of the X has been sufficient to raise controversy between those who think it likely that the dose of the zinc finger protein is the important factor in primary sex determination (males having two doses in mammals and birds, and females having only one active dose) and those who believe that a Y-dominant factor is more likely. Fortunately, these hypotheses are testable and, no doubt, appropriate experiments are underway as these words are being written.

The organizers and participants were excited by many other new developments which were reported at the Meeting. Many aspects of sex determination were considered and the wide ranging discussion was not confined to mouse and man. For example, there was great interest in the recent observation that marsupials differ from eutherian mammals in that several sex characteristics that arise secondarily to gonadal sex-hormone secretion in mouse and man, are primary sex characteristics controlled directly by sex-chromosome genes in marsupials. It will be fascinating to discover how these differences have evolved. Similarly, there is much interest in the mechanism of temperature-dependent sex determination in alligators and turtles; can this be related to a dosage theory? Sex determination in several small mammals seems to be dependent on an unnecessarily complex sex-chromosome mechanism, but what theory can account for the observation that the X*YY exceptional wood lemming is a fertile female? Discussion continues on the role of the H-Y antigen in development. If H-Y is no longer the primary testis determinant, can it have a function elsewhere in the pathway to testis determination?

The reader will obtain much of the feeling of excitement expressed at the Meeting from this collection of papers and from the fragments of discussion following them. This was a timely meeting, and it is to be hoped that the publication of this volume will be a stimulus to the next phase of research on sex determination in mouse and man.

October 1988

M. A. Ferguson-Smith
Anne McLaren

CONTENTS

[Seven plates]

Phil. Trans. R. Soc. Lond. B **322**, 3–9 (1988) [3]
Printed in Great Britain

Somatic and germ-cell sex in mammals

By Anne McLaren, F.R.S.

MRC Mammalian Development Unit, University College London, Wolfson House, 4 Stephenson Way, London NW1 2HE, U.K.

The phenotypic sex of an individual mammal is determined by the sex of its gonads, i.e. testes or ovaries. This in turn is determined by the presence or absence of a small region of the Y chromosome, located near the X–Y pairing region in man and on the short arm of the Y chromosome in the mouse. The testis-determining region of the Y appears to exert its primary effect by directing the supporting-cell lineage of the gonad to differentiate as Sertoli cells, acting at least in part cell-autonomously.

The phenotypic sex of a germ cell, i.e. whether it undergoes spermatogenesis or oogenesis, is determined at least in the mouse by whether or not it enters meiotic prophase before birth. This depends not on its own sex chromosome constitution, but on its cellular environment. A germ cell in or near normal testis cords (made up mainly of Sertoli cells) is inhibited from entering meiosis until after birth; one that escapes this inhibition will develop into an oocyte even if it is in a male animal and is itself XY in chromosome constitution.

The sex-determining switch

Most animals have two sexual forms (e.g. female and male, or male and hermaphrodite), with rather few intermediates. The developmental decision between the two forms depends on a switch, which may be environmental, chromosomal or genic. For those animals (*Caenorhabditis*, *Drosophila*) for which the genetic basis of sex determination has been most thoroughly worked out, the switch activates a succession of sex-determining genes. The final gene in the series then call into play the various genetic loci concerned with the differentiation of sexual organs and structures.

In this symposium, Judith Kimble gives a brief review of how this whole system works in *Caenorhabditis*, with a passing glance at *Drosophila*. For both these groups, the switch consists of the X:autosome ratio; i.e., for a diploid chromosome set, two X chromosomes rather than one. Some genetic evidence exists that the sex-determining switch in birds too may be based on the X:autosome ratio (Sittmann 1984).

Mark Ferguson describes an environmental sex-determining switch used by some reptiles, namely the temperature at which the fertilized eggs are reared.

In mammals, a Y-linked gene is used as a switch. The central role of the Y chromosome in mammalian sex determination was first established in 1959. In that year Jacobs & Strong described the first human sex chromosome abnormality, an XXY chromosome constitution in a male patient; a few months later Ford *et al.* (1959) reported an XO chromosome constitution in a female patient; and Welshons & Russell (1959) reported that XO mice, like XX, were fertile females. As Welshons & Russell wrote ‘Since a fertile female can be of the X/X or X/O constitution, it follows that the Y-chromosome of the mouse is male-determining. This may apply to other, perhaps all, mammals, including man.’ This result was unexpected because in *Drosophila* XO individuals were known to be male and XXY individuals female.

The mammalian sex-determining genes that are activated by the Y genic switch are likely to be located on autosomes or on the X chromosome rather than on the Y. Ulrich Wolf's paper discusses various models for the genetic control of sex determination; Karl Fredga gives an example of X chromosomal involvement, as well as discussing some unusual variations on the basic XX/XY pattern; Eva Eicher deals with autosomal genes concerned with sex determination in the mouse.

Testis determination and sex hormones

One distinctive feature of mammals is that sexual differentiation is mostly controlled, not by direct gene action, but by hormones. In the male, these sex hormones are produced largely by the testis. In a classic paper published in 1947, Jost showed that male rabbit foetuses deprived of their testes before birth develop female secondary sexual characteristics. An analogous situation is seen in testicular feminization (*Tfm*), in which female characteristics develop because the male target organs are unable to respond to the male sex hormones produced by the testis (Lyon & Hawkes 1970). Thus for most, if not all, of our sexual phenotype, sex determination is equivalent to testis determination. An intriguing exception is presented in the paper by Marilyn Renfree and Roger Short. Some sexual characteristics in marsupials appear to be determined directly by the sex chromosomes, by-passing the gonads (O *et al.* 1988); whether this will also hold true for eutherian mammals remains to be seen.

The hormonal links between testis and male phenotype have been exhaustively studied. In contrast, little or nothing is known of the links between the Y chromosomes and the testis, either at the molecular level or in terms of developmental process. One hypothesis that has been widely quoted is the 'H-Y hypothesis' (Wachtel *et al.* 1975), which postulated that the male-specific H-Y antigen, known to be controlled by the Y chromosome, acted as a diffusible inducer to switch cells of the indifferent gonad into the testicular pathway. Although initially very attractive (no other function for H-Y antigen was known, and no other inducer of testis determination had been proposed), this hypothesis is no longer tenable. Ellen Goldberg's paper reviews the history and present status of male-specific antigens in relation to testis determination.

Sex-reversed mice

In the mouse, much of what we know about testis determination stems from the discovery by Cattanach *et al.* (1971) of a mutation generating XX males. This sex-reversed (Sxr) condition turned out to be due to a rearranged Y chromosome (Singh & Jones, 1982), in which the region containing the testis-determining gene (*Tdy*) appears to have been duplicated and transposed to the distal end of the long arm, beyond the region where the X and Y chromosomes pair. Because in every male meiosis a cross-over occurs between an X and a Y chromatid (Burgoyne 1982), one copy of the transposed region will be transferred to one of the X chromatids. When a sperm carrying the X with the transposed region attached fertilizes an egg, the resulting XX embryo develops as a male; hence the transposed region is now referred to as the Sxr region. However, the masculinizing effect of *Tdy* may be in part or whole negated by the preferentially expressed X-autosome translocation T16H. T16H/XSxr embryos may develop as fertile females in spite of the presence of Sxr (McLaren & Monk 1982). T16H/XSxr females and XX Sxr males express H-Y antigen (Simpson *et al.* 1984), so not only *Tdy* but also

Hya, the gene responsible for H-Y expression, must be located within the Sxr region. A variant form of the Sxr region, termed Sxr′, has been reported (McLaren *et al.* 1984), which retains *Tdy* but appears to have lost *Hya*. XXSxr′ mice are male, but do not express H-Y antigen. Because testis determination occurs in the absence of H-Y antigen, the H-Y hypothesis cannot be sustained.

But if H-Y antigen is not involved, what is the mechanism of testis determination? Alfred Jost's paper outlines what the development of the testis actually involves, at the cellular level; and Paul Burgoyne presents what we know of male-specific gene expression during early testis development.

Colin Bishop's paper describes molecular studies on the Sxr region, and establishes that the transition from Sxr to Sxr′ involved a small deletion. He and his colleagues have shown by *in situ* hybridization that the homologous region to Sxr on the normal Y chromosome is located on the very minute short arm (Roberts *et al.* 1988), a conclusion in full agreement with our own genetic findings (McLaren *et al.* 1988).

The human Y chromosome

In man, the location of the testis-determining region on the short arm of the Y chromosome was first established by Jacobs & Ross (1966). The gene responsible for expression of H-Y antigen is now known to be on the long arm of the Y (Simpson *et al.* 1987), so in man as in the mouse, H-Y antigen cannot be the testis inducer. Immediately distal to the testis-determining region lies the region of X–Y pairing, where the single obligatory cross-over occurs during male meiosis. Genes located in or beyond this region are not completely sex-linked, but show recombination with sex ranging up to 50 % near the telomere. They are therefore termed pseudoautosomal because in the extreme case they cannot be distinguished by linkage testing from autosomal genes.

Jean Weissenbach discusses how these different regions of the human Y chromosome have been mapped, with particular reference to the pseudoautosomal region; Malcolm Ferguson-Smith's paper illustrates the hazards of having the testis-determining region directly adjacent to the region of X–Y recombination; Peter Goodfellow describes in more detail the boundary region, comprising the proximal part of the pseudoautosomal and the distal part of the testis-determining region; and David Page tells how he and his colleagues have cloned a gene that seems likely to be *TDF*, the human testis-determining gene.

Determination of germ-cell sex

The emphasis of the present meeting is on sex determination of the somatic component of the gonad. We often take for granted that male gonads contain male germ cells and female gonads contain female germ cells; it is therefore worth considering briefly how germ-cell sex is determined.

By germ-cell sex, I mean whether a primordial germ cell embarks on spermatogenesis, as in a normal testis, or oogenesis as in an ovary. The decision for most mammals is taken well before birth. In the mouse, all the germ cells in the ovary enter meiotic prophase up to a week before birth: there is thus no stem-cell population in the female, and no more germ cells are ever made. The germ cells in the testis enter mitotic arrest at the same stage of gestation as the ovarian germ cells enter meiosis. The male germ cells start dividing again immediately after birth and the first wave to enter meiotic prophase do so about a week later.

Whether a mouse germ cell embarks on oogenesis or spermatogenesis does not in any way depend on its own chromosome constitution. Its chromosomes may determine how well it does, how far it gets, but they do not determine in which direction it goes.

In a foetal testis, both XX and XO germ cells go into mitotic arrest rather than entering meiosis; XX die shortly after birth because of the presence of the second X chromosome, XO do better but few survive into the adult because they lack a Y chromosome gene required for normal spermatogenesis (Levy & Burgoyne 1986). Like *Hya*, this gene has been lost in the transition from Sxr to Sxr′ (Burgoyne *et al.* 1986), raising the possibility that H-Y antigen may itself play a role in spermatogenesis. In an XXSxr foetal testis, a few germ cells enter meiosis and develop as oocytes (McLaren 1980), probably because the testis is not entirely normal in its somatic development. They do rather better than the majority that take the male pathway, but they do not survive into the adult.

In the ovary of an XY female mouse, the XY germ cells may form oocytes that can be fertilized and give rise to normal progeny (Robin Lovell-Badge, personal communication). Even when the Y chromosome is entirely normal, as in a female XX↔XY chimera, the XY germ cells can enter meiosis and give rise to oocytes. T16H/XSxr females are fully fertile (McLaren & Monk 1982): both X chromosomes are known to be expressed during oogenesis, so evidently the presence of the testis-determining gene attached to an active X is fully compatible with normal oogenesis. In *Drosophila* too, sex-determining genes appear to control sex in somatic tissues only, and do not affect germ cells (Baker & Belote 1983); but in *Caenorhabditis*, as Judith Kimble makes clear in her paper, most sex-determining genes affect both somatic and germ-line tissues.

If it is not the chromosomes of the germ cells that determine their sex, it must be their environment, i.e. the environment provided by the gonad or its precursor, the genital ridge, in which they develop. What happens if we disturb that environment, or put them into a different environment? Disturbing the ovarian environment has little effect; if the germ cells survive, they enter meiosis on schedule and develop as oocytes. But if the genital ridge of a male mouse embryo is transplanted to the kidney or cultured *in vitro* from a sufficiently early age ($10\frac{1}{2}$ days *post coitum*, before Sertoli cell differentiation), some of the germ cells become diverted into the female pathway and undergo oogenesis (McLaren 1985). We can also examine germ cells outside the gonad, because during the course of their migratory phase, some germ cells fail to enter the gonads and end up either in the directly adjacent mesonephric region, or in the nearby adrenal primordium. In the adrenal, all the germ cells enter meiosis before birth and develop as oocytes even if the embryo is male; in the mesonephric region of a male embryo, some germ cells enter meiosis before birth but others enter mitotic arrest as they would in the testis (Zamboni & Upadhyay 1983; A. McLaren, unpublished observations). The XY germ cells in the male adrenal not only enter meiosis before birth, but having done so they follow the female pathway and develop into large growing oocytes surrounded by zona pellucidas. So for germ-cell sex, it seems that germ cells are female (that is they follow the female pathway of development) because they have entered meiosis before birth, rather than entering meiosis before birth because they are female.

The findings on germ cells in the mesonephric region and adrenal suggest that some diffusible signal coming from the testis is retaining the germ cells in the mitotic cycle, and inhibiting their entry into meiosis before birth. In the absence of the signal all germ cells, whether XX or XY, enter meiosis before birth and undergo oogenesis. Because the only differentiated cells in the testis at the critical stage of development are the Sertoli cells, the signal may be presumed to emanate from the Sertoli-cell population. The situation is formally similar to that described by Judith Kimble for *Caenorhabditis*, where the distal tip cell produces a signal that allows all germ cells within a certain range to continue in the mitotic cycle, but those out of range of the signal all enter meiosis.

Such analogies should not be pushed too far, yet surely the recent discovery of the germ-line proliferation gene (*glp*−1) in *Caenorhabditis* (Austin & Kimble 1987) must reinforce our view that students of sex determination in mouse and man have much to learn from the extensive and elegant analyses that have proved possible in the nematode.

References

Austin, J. & Kimble, J. 1987 glp-1 is required in the germ line for regulation of the decision between mitosis and meiosis in *C. elegans*. *Cell* **51**, 589–599.

Baker, B. S. & Belote, J. M. 1983 Sex determination and dosage compensation in *Drosophila melanogaster*. *A. Rev. Genet.* **17**, 345–393.

Burgoyne, P. S. 1982 Genetic homology and crossing over in the X and Y chromosomes of mammals. *Hum. Genet.* **61**, 85–90.

Burgoyne, P. S., Levy, E. R. & McLaren, A. 1986 Spermatogenic failure in male mice lacking H-Y antigen. *Nature, Lond.* **320**, 170–172.

Cattanach, B. M., Pollard, C. E. & Hawkes, S. G. 1971 Sex-reversed mice: XX and XO males. *Cytogenetics* **10**, 318–337.

Ford, C. E., Jones, K. W., Polani, P. E., de Almeida, J. C. & Briggs, J. H. 1959 A sex-chromosome anomaly in a case of gonadal dysgenesis (Turner's syndrome). *Lancet* i, 711–713.

Jacobs, P. A. & Ross, A. 1966 Structural abnormalities of the Y chromosome in Man. *Nature, Lond.* **210**, 352–354.

Jacobs, P. A. & Strong, J. A. 1959 A case of human intersexuality having a possible XXY sex-determining mechanism. *Nature, Lond.* **183**, 302–303.

Jost, A. 1947 Recherches sur la différenciation sexuelle de l'embryon de lapin. *Archs Anat. microsc. Morph. Exp.* **36**, 271–315.

Levy, E. R. & Burgoyne, P. S. 1986 The fate of XO germ cells in the testes of XO/XY and XO/XY/XYY mouse mosaics: evidence for a spermatogenesis gene on the mouse Y chromosome. *Cytogenet. Cell Genet.* **42**, 208–213.

Lyon, M. F. & Hawkes, S. G. 1970 X-linked gene for testicular feminization in the mouse. *Nature, Lond.* **227**, 1217–1219.

McLaren, A. 1980 Oocytes in the testis. *Nature, Lond.* **283**, 688–689.

McLaren, A. 1985 Relation of germ cell sex to gonadal differentiation. In *The origin and evolution of sex* (ed. H. O. Halvorson & A. Monroy), vol. 7, pp. 289–300. New York: Alan R. Liss.

McLaren, A. & Monk, M. 1982 Fertile females produced by inactivation of an X chromosome of *sex-reversed* mice. *Nature, Lond.* **300**, 446–448.

McLaren, A., Simpson, E., Epplen, J. T., Studer, R., Koopman, P., Evans, E. P. & Burgoyne, P. S. 1988 Location of the genes controlling H-Y antigen expression and testis determination on the mouse Y chromosome. *Proc. natn. Acad. Sci. U.S.A.* (In the press.)

McLaren, A., Simpson, E., Tomonari, K., Chandler, P. & Hogg, H. 1984 Male sexual differentiation in mice lacking H-Y antigen. *Nature, Lond.* **312**, 552–555.

O, W.-S., Short, R. V., Renfree, M. B. & Shaw, G. 1988 Primary genetic control of somatic sexual differentiation in a mammal. *Nature, Lond.* **331**, 716–717.

Roberts, C., Weith, A., Passage, E., Michot, J. L., Mattei, M. G. & Bishop, C. E. 1988 Molecular and cytogenetic evidence for the location of *Tdy* and *Hya* on the mouse Y chromosome short arm. *Proc. natn. Acad. Sci. U.S.A.* (In the press.)

Simpson, E., Chandler, P., Goulmy, E., Disteche, C. M., Ferguson-Smith, M. A. & Page, D. C. 1987 Separation of the genetic loci for the H-Y antigen and for testis determination on the human Y chromosome. *Nature, Lond.* **326**, 876–878.

Simpson, E., McLaren, A., Chandler, P. & Tomonari, K. 1984 Expression of H-Y antigen by female mice carrying Sxr. *Transplantation* **37**, 17–21.

Singh, L. & Jones, K. W. 1982 Sex reversal in the mouse (*Mus musculus*) is caused by a recurrent nonreciprocal crossover involving the X and an aberrant Y chromosome. *Cell* **28**, 205–216.
Sittmann, K. 1984 Sex determination in birds: progeny of nondisjunction canaries of Durham (1926). *Genet. Res.* **43**, 173–180.
Wachtel, S. S., Ohno, S., Koo, G. C. & Boyse, E. A. 1975 Possible role for H-Y antigen in the primary determination of sex. *Nature, Lond.* **257**, 235–236.
Welshons, W. J. & Russell, L. B. 1959 The Y chromosome as the bearer of male determining factors in the mouse. *Proc. natn. Acad. Sci. U.S.A.* **45**, 560–566.
Zamboni, L. & Upadhyay, S. 1983 Germ cell differentiation in mouse adrenal glands. *J. exp. Zool.* **228**, 173–193.

Discussion

M. A. FERGUSON-SMITH, F.R.S. (*Department of Pathology, University of Cambridge, U.K.*). Does Dr McLaren not agree that the recent observations by Page *et al.* (1987) that there is likely to be a functional homologue of *TDF* on the X chromosome in man, strongly suggest that sex is primarily determined by the number of active *TDF* loci rather than by a dominant Y-linked factor? In this scheme, X-inactivation results in one dose of TDF in females and two in males. This brings man back into line with *Drosophila* and *Caenorhabditis*.

Reference

Page, D. C., Mosher, R., Simpson, E. M., Fisher, E. M. C., Mardon, G., Pollack, J., McGillivray, B., de la Chapelle, A. & Brown, L. G. 1987 The sex-determining region of the human Y chromosome encodes a finger protein. *Cell* **51**, 1091–1104.

ANNE MCLAREN. Although I can appreciate the attraction of bringing man 'back into line with *Drosophila* and *Caenorhabditis*', there seems little scientific justification at present for preferring a dosage rather than a dominant-male hypothesis for sex determination in mammals. I see no reason to expect the 'switch' mechanism to be evolutionarily stable: Hodgkin (1987) has pointed out that, even within *Caenorhabditis*, it only needs a mutation or two to shift the switch from X:autosome ratio to dominant male to dominant female to temperature dependence. Until further evidence is forthcoming (as it surely soon will be), I prefer to keep an open mind with regard to the four possible roles that Page *et al.* (1987) postulate for the putative *TDF* homologue that they have detected on the mammalian X chromosome.

Reference

Hodgkin, J. 1987 Primary sex determination in the nematode *C. elegans*. In *The mammalian Y chromosome: molecular search for the sex-determining factor* (ed. P. N. Goodfellow, I. W. Craig, J. C. Smith & J. Wolfe) (*Development* **101** (suppl.)), pp. 5–16. Cambridge: Company of Biologists.

M. ADINOLFI (*Paediatric Research Unit, Guy's Hospital, London, U.K.*). Dr McLaren has mentioned that Sertoli cells produce a factor that induces mitotic arrest. I wonder if Dr McLaren can tell us more about the physicochemical properties and characteristics of this factor? As she knows, it has been suggested that Sertoli cells release H-Y antigen capable of triggering the differentiation of the primordial gonads into testes. Paul Polani, Jo Zenthon and I have tried to repeat these experiments with little success. We have incubated mouse primordial gonads in serum-free media from mouse Sertoli cells cultured *in vitro*. The gonads were then transplanted under the kidney capsule of adult mice. When analysed histologically, we were able to observe a sort of arrest of the differentiation of the genotypically XX primordial gonads, but no evidence of testicular structures. I wonder if this effect may be attributed to the mitotic arresting factor Dr McLaren has mentioned?

ANNE MCLAREN. Because of the evidence that Burgoyne presents in this meeting, it is not surprising that Professor Adinolfi and his colleagues were unable to induce testis-cord formation in embryonic XX gonads by incubating them with Sertoli-cell-conditioned medium.

The arrest of differentiation of the XX gonads could have been due to the effect of anti-Müllerian hormone (AMH) known to be produced by Sertoli cells. Vigier *et al.* (1987), have recently shown that exposure to purified AMH *in vitro* causes depletion of germ cells in embryonic rat ovaries, and it is well known that follicle cells do not survive in the absence of oocytes. The gene for AMH has recently been cloned (Cate *et al.* 1986; Picard *et al.* 1986).

References

Cate, R. L., Mattaliano, R. J., *et al.* 1986 Isolation of the bovine and human genes for Müllerian inhibiting substance and expression of the human gene in animal cells. *Cell* **45**, 685–698.

Picard, J.-Y., Benarous, R., Guerrier, D., Josso, N. & Kahn, A. 1986 Cloning and expression of cDNA for anti-Müllerian hormone. *Proc. natn. Acad. Sci. U.S.A.* **83**, 5464–5468.

Vigier, B., Watrin, F., Magre, S., Tran, D. & Josso, N. 1987 Purified bovine AMH induces a characteristic freemartin effect in fetal rat prospective ovaries exposed to it *in vitro*. *Development* **100**, 43–55.

Phil. Trans. R. Soc. Lond. B **322**, 11–18 (1988) [11]
Printed in Great Britain

Genetic control of sex determination in the germ line of *Caenorhabditis elegans*

By Judith Kimble

Laboratory of Molecular Biology, Graduate School and Department of Biochemistry, College of Agricultural and Life Sciences, University of Wisconsin, Madison, Wisconsin 53706, *U.S.A.*

The nematode *Caenorhabditis elegans* normally exists as one of two sexes: self-fertilizing hermaphrodite or male. Development as hermaphrodite or male requires the differentiation of each tissue in a sex-specific way. In this review, I discuss the genetic control of sex determination in a single tissue of *C. elegans*: the germ line. Sex determination in the germ line depends on the action of two types of genes: – those that act globally in all tissues to direct male or female development and those that act only in the germ line to specify either spermatogenesis or oogenesis. First, I consider a tissue-specific sex-determining gene, *fog-1*, which promotes spermatogenesis in the germ line. Second, I consider the regulation of the hermaphrodite pattern of germ-line gametogenesis where first sperm and then oocytes are produced.

Introduction

One of the great successes of modern developmental genetics has been the identification and characterization of regulatory genes that control sex determination. Sex is normally determined by the chromosomal complement of an individual. For example, in mammals, XX animals are female and XY animals are male. However, in organisms as diverse as worms and mice, mutations have been isolated that override the chromosomal signal and therefore cause sexual differentiation that is independent of the chromosomal constitution of the animal. Genetic studies have emphasized genes that control the sexual phenotype of an entire organism. These 'global' sex-determining genes regulate sexual development in all tissues of the animal. However, the differentation of an animal as male or female involves the regulation of each cell or tissue to differentiate according to a particular sex-specific pathway. In this short review, I discuss progress that has been made in the free-living nematode *Caenorhabditis elegans* to elucidate the genetic regulation of sex determination in a single tissue: the germ line. This regulation depends on both global and tissue-specific sex-determining genes.

Over the past two decades, *C. elegans* has been subjected to intensive genetic and descriptive analyses (see Wood (1988) for review). With its simple anatomy and short life cycle ($3\frac{1}{2}$ days), this tiny worm proves to be particularly useful for studies of developmental regulation. Genetic analyses of sex determination, pioneered by Jonathan Hodgkin at the MRC Laboratory of Molecular Biology in Cambridge, England, have led to the identification and genetic characterization of several 'global' sex-determining genes (see Hodgkin (1987*a*) for review). In addition, genes that control the sexual differentiation of a single tissue, the germ line, have recently been discovered (Doniach 1986*a*; Schedl & Kimble 1988; Barton & Kimble 1988; this laboratory, unpublished results).

Normally in *C. elegans*, XX animals are self-fertilizing hermaphrodites (somatic 'females' that make sperm first and then produce oocytes continuously) and XO animals are males (figure

1). These two sexes differ substantially in morphology, biochemistry, and behaviour (table 1). Oocytes can either be self-fertilized by hermaphrodite sperm or cross-fertilized by male sperm. Sperm and oocytes are distinct cell types: sperm are small cells specialized for motility, whereas oocytes are large cells specialized for embryogenesis (Kimble & Ward 1988).

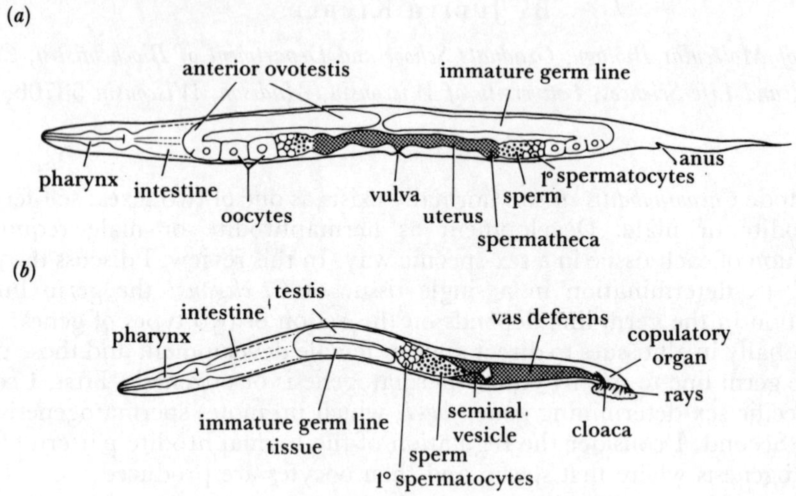

FIGURE 1. Schematic diagrams of (*a*) a young adult hermaphrodite and (*b*) a male. Notice the sexually dimorphic gonads (two ovotestes in the hermaphrodite, one testis in the male) and tails (a whip-like tail in the hermaphrodite, a tail specialized for copulation in the male). The somatic gonad of each is indicated by shading, the rest of the tubular gonad is germ line.

TABLE 1. SEXUAL DIMORPHISM IN *C. ELEGANS*

	hermaphrodite	male
chromosomes	XX; 5AA = 12	XO; 5AA = 11
hypodermis	vulva	copulatory bursa, spicules, rays
nerve	neurons for egg-laying	neurons for mating
muscle	muscles for egg-laying	muscles for mating
intestine	yolk synthesis	
somatic gonad	two ovotestes, uterus, spermathecae	one testis, seminal vesicle, vas deferens
germ line	sperm, then oocytes	sperm
total somatic nuclei	959	1031
total germ-line nuclei	about 2500	about 1000

The initial signal for sex determination in *C. elegans* is the ratio of X chromosomes to sets of autosomes (A) (Nigon 1951; Madl & Herman 1979). This signal controls the activity of several global sex-determining genes. Certain of these genes, e.g. *sdc-1* (Villeneuve & Meyer 1987), regulate both sexual development and dosage compensation, whereas others, e.g. the *fem* and *tra* genes, regulate only the sexual phenotype (for review see Hodgkin (1987*a*)).

The mutant phenotypes of those sex-determining genes considered further in this review are summarized in table 2. The phenotype of loss-of-function (*lf*) mutations is used to deduce the wild-type function of a gene; the phenotype of gain-of-function (*gf*) mutations may be due to a novel, poisonous, increased, unregulated or inappropriate activity. Although most *lf* mutations are recessive and most *gf* mutations are dominant, among the mutations that regulate *C. elegans* sex determination, both dominant *lf* and recessive *gf* mutations are known.

TABLE 2. PHENOTYPES OF MUTANTS DISCUSSED IN THIS PAPER

gene	mutant phenotype[a] XX	XO
wild type	female soma, sperm then oocytes	male
tra-1(lf)[b]	pseudomale soma, sperm, then oocytes	pseudomale soma, sperm, then oocytes
tra-2(lf)[c]	pseudomale soma, sperm only	male
tra-3(lf)[c]	pseudomale soma, sperm, then oocytes	male
fem-1(lf)[d], *fem-2(lf)*[e], *fem-3(lf)*[f]	female	female
her-1(lf)[g]	female soma, sperm, then oocytes	female soma, sperm, then oocytes
fog-1(lf)[h]	female	male soma, oocytes only
fog-2(lf)[i]	female	male
tra-2(gf)[j]	female	male
fem-3(gf)[k]	female soma, sperm only	male

[a] 'female' refers to female development in both soma and germline; 'male' refers to male development in both soma and germline

[b] Hodgkin & Brenner (1977); Hodgkin (1987*b*); Kimble & Schedl (1988); T. Schedl, unpublished results.

[c] Hodgkin & Brenner (1977).

[d] Nelson *et al.* (1978); Doniach & Hodgkin (1984).

[e] Kimble *et al.* (1984); Hodgkin (1986).

[f] Hodgkin (1986); Barton *et al.* (1987).

[g] Hodgkin (1980); Trent *et al.* (1988).

[h] Doniach (1986*a*); Barton & Kimble (1988).

[i] Schedl & Kimble (1988).

[j] Doniach (1986*b*); Schedl & Kimble (1988).

[k] Barton *et al.* (1987).

Among the global sex-determining genes of *C. elegans*, some are required for hermaphrodite development and others are required for male development. The phenotype of *lf* mutations in any of three *tra* genes (for sexual *tra*nsformation) is masculinization of XX animals; therefore the *tra* genes normally direct female development. The phenotype of *lf* mutations in any of three *fem* genes (for *fem*inization) is feminization of both XX and XO animals; therefore the *fem* genes normally specify male development in the hermaphrodite germ line (sperm) and in males. The phenotype of *her-1(lf)* (for *her*maphroditization) is sexual transformation of XO animals into hermaphrodites; therefore *her-1* normally directs male development.

In addition to global sex-determining genes, there exist germ-line-specific sex-determining genes: *fog* and *mog* genes (for *f*eminization (or *m*asculinization) *o*f the *g*ermline). Mutants that specifically affect germ-line sex determination have been isolated both in mutant screens and by genetic selection (Kimble *et al.* 1986; Doniach 1986*a*; Schedl & Kimble 1988; Barton & Kimble 1988; this laboratory, unpublished results). The idea behind the genetic selections used to isolate germ-line-specific sex determination mutants is shown in figure 2. Basically an XX hermaphrodite is self-sterile if it produces only sperm or only oocytes, but it is self-fertile if sperm and then oocytes are made. Therefore mutants that feminize the hermaphrodite germline so that only oocytes are made (or masculinize it so that only sperm are made) can be used to select for suppressor mutations that reinstate self-fertility. In this way, either masculinizing or feminizing suppressors can be isolated. Mutations in the *fog* and *mog* genes result in sexual transformation in the germ line, but do not affect somatic tissues. The functions of these tissue-specific sex-determining genes are discussed below.

The regulatory relationships among the sex-determining genes have been investigated by examination of the phenotypes of double mutants (see, for example, Hodgkin 1987*a*). In

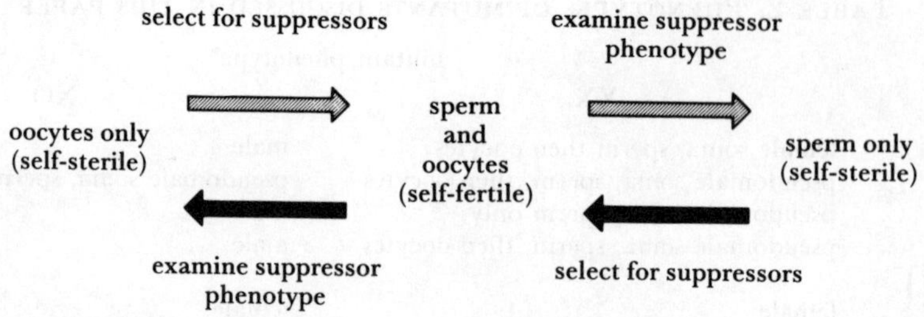

FIGURE 2. Basic idea behind genetic selections for mutants that affect germ-line sex determination. See text for explanation. These selections have been used to isolate mutations in new genes (*fog-1*, Barton & Kimble (1988); *fog-2*, Schedl & Kimble (1988); *fog-3*, M. K. Barton and T. Schedl, unpublished results), to isolate rare gain-of-function mutations in known genes (*tra-1*, M. K. Barton, unpublished results; *tra-2*, Schedl & Kimble (1988); *fem-3*, Barton *et al.* (1987)), and to isolate transposon insertions into sex-determining genes for cloning (*fem-3*, Rosenquist & Kimble (1988); *tra-2*, Okkema & Kimble (1988)).

somatic tissues, a cascade of negative regulators appears to control the activity of a master switch-gene, *tra-1*, to determine the somatic sexual phenotype (Hodgkin 1980, 1987*b*). However, in the germ line, it is the activity of the *fem* genes that plays the critical role in the decision between spermatogenesis and oogenesis (Nelson *et al.* 1978; Doniach & Hodgkin 1984; Kimble *et al.* 1984; Hodgkin 1986). A *fem(-1, -2 or -3)*; *tra-1* double mutant has a male soma but a female germ line. Although the state of *tra-1* can influence sexual fate in the germ line, its role is not understood (Hodgkin 1987*b*; Schedl *et al.* 1988).

The global genes that are central to sex determination in the germ line are *tra-2, fem-1, fem-2* and *fem-3*. Hodgkin has proposed that *tra-2* negatively regulates the activity of the *fem* genes (Hodgkin 1986). A highly simplified pathway of sex regulation, tailored for consideration of sex determination in the germ line, is provided in table 3*a*. The *tra-1* gene is not included in this pathway because its role in germ-line sex determination has not yet been established. Although *tra-3* is included, its role in germ-line sex determination is variable and probably minor. Therefore emphasis is placed on the role of *tra-2*.

In the simplified pathway shown in table 3*a*, *tra-2* (and *tra-3*) control the activity of the *fem* genes. If *tra-2* is active, then *fem* genes are inactive and female development ensues; conversely if *tra-2* is inactive, the *fem* genes are active and male development occurs. Regulators appear to have evolved to control the *tra-2* gene in response to the X:A ratio or tissue-specific cues. For example, in males the *her-1* gene negatively regulates *tra-2* in response to the X:A ratio; consequently the *fem* genes are active and male development occurs (table 3*b*). Moreover, the *fem* genes may in turn regulate downstream genes in specific tissues. For example, the *fem* genes regulate *tra-1,* which appears to have its primary female-directing function in the soma (Hodgkin 1987*b*; T. Schedl, unpublished results).

In the rest of this review, I consider two questions. Firstly, how do the global male- or female-directing genes specify sexual differentiation of a particular cell type (e.g. sperm)? And secondly, how is male development (spermatogenesis) turned on in the germ line of a somatically female animal and then turned off to permit oogenesis?

TABLE 3. GENETIC REGULATION OF SEX DETERMINATION IN THE GERM LINE

(See text for explanation. (*a*) Simplified pathway of genetic control of sex determination (adapted from Hodgkin (1986)). (*b*) The onset of male spermatogenesis depends on the X:A ratio, which acts through *her-1* to control *tra-2* on XO males (adapted from Hodgkin (1980)). (*c*) The onset of hermaphrodite spermatogenesis depends on the germ-line-specific regulatory gene, *fog-2*. This may act by controlling *tra-2* in XX (or (XO) hermaphrodites (adapted from Schedl & Kimble (1988)). (*d*) The switch to oogenesis from spermatogenesis in hermaphrodites appears to involve inactivation of *fem-3*. (i) One model for inactivation of *fem-3* invokes a germ-line-specific negative regulator of *fem-3*. (ii) Another model invokes some regulator to inactivate *fog-2* so that *tra-2* might inactivate *fem-3*. That regulator might be an unknown gene, or it might require negative feedback by, for example, *fog-2*.)

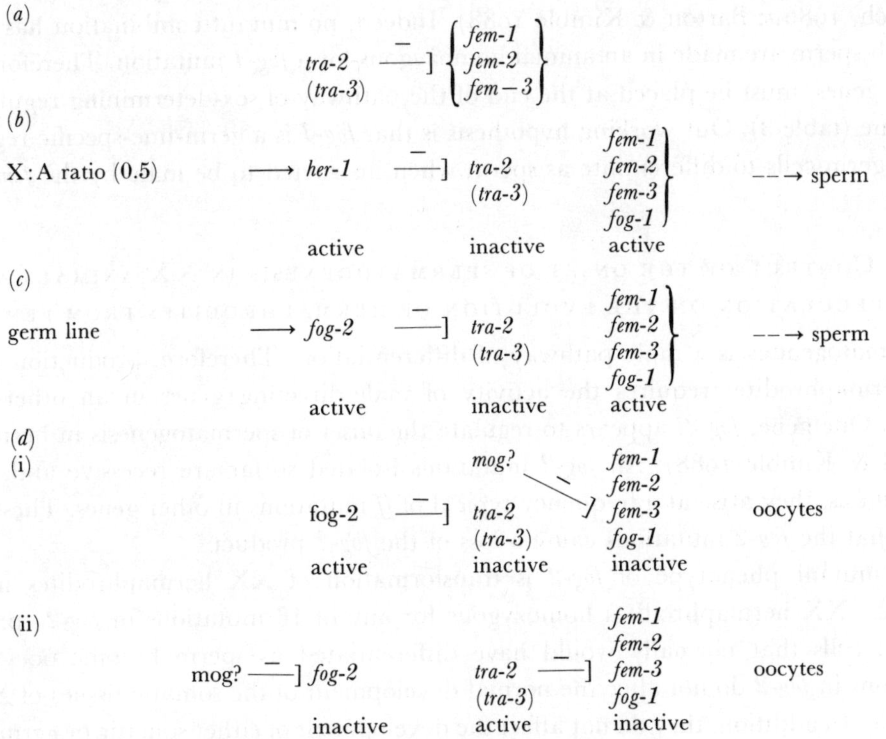

GENETIC CONTROL OF CELL TYPE IN THE GERM LINE

The global sex-determining genes direct male or female development in all tissues of the animal. It is clear that specification of a particular male cell type (e.g. sperm, vas deferens) must require additional regulation. One germ-line-specific sex-determining gene, *fog-1*, appears to regulate the male differentiation of germ cells to become sperm (Doniach 1986*a*; Barton & Kimble 1988). In *fog-1* mutants, whether XX or XO, germ cells that would normally differentiate as sperm become oocytes instead. No effect on somatic tissues is observed in *fog-1* mutants. These *fog-1* mutations are semi-dominant. Whereas *fog*-homozygotes make no sperm, *fog-1*/+ heterozygotes make fewer sperm in hermaphrodites and make some sperm and then oocytes in males.

Despite the semidominance of *fog-1* mutations, they are probably due to a loss of *fog-1* function (Barton & Kimble 1988). One argument that *fog-1* mutations are *lf* is based on mutation frequency. After ethyl methane sulphonate (EMS) mutagenesis, the *fog-1* mutations are isolated at the same frequency as *lf* mutations in other genes. A second argument is based on studies in which production of sperm or oocytes was examined in a duplication strain to alter the dose of *fog-1*. The phenotype of an animal carrying one wild-type copy and two mutant copies of *fog-1* is identical to that of a *fog-1*/+ heterozygote. Also, the phenotype of an animal carrying two wild-type copies and one mutant copy of *fog-1* is identical to that of a wild-type animal. These studies show that the *fog-1* phenotype is dictated by the number of wild-type, rather than mutant, copies of *fog-1*. Therefore the semidominance of *fog-1* is not likely to be due to a novel or unregulated activity. Instead, it seems to indicate a sensitivity of sperm production to the dose of *fog-1*.

The *fog-1* gene is essential to specification of sperm. No sperm are made in double mutants that are homozygous for *fog-1* and either *her-1(lf)*, *tra-1(lf)*, *tra-2(lf)*, *tra-3(lf)* or *fem-3(gf)* (Doniach, 1986*a*; Barton & Kimble 1988). Indeed, no mutant combination has been found in which sperm are made in an animal homozygous for a *fog-1* mutation. Therefore *fog-1*, like the *fem* genes, must be placed at the end of the pathway of sex-determining regulators in the germ line (table 3). Our working hypothesis is that *fog-1* is a germ-line-specific regulator that directs germ cells to differentiate as sperm when instructed to be male by the *fem* genes.

Control of the onset of spermatogenesis in XX animals and speculation on the evolution of hermaphrodites from females

Spermatogenesis is a male pathway of differentiation. Therefore, production of sperm in XX hermaphrodites requires the activity of male-directing genes in an otherwise female animal. One gene, *fog-2*, appears to regulate the onset of spermatogenesis in hermaphrodites (Schedl & Kimble 1988). All *fog-2* mutations isolated so far are recessive and, after EMS mutagenesis, they arise at a frequency typical of *lf* mutations in other genes. These properties imply that the *fog-2* mutations cause a loss of the *fog-2* product.

The mutant phenotype of *fog-2* is transformation of XX hermaphrodites into females (table 2.) XX hermaphrodites homozygous for any of 16 mutations in *fog-2* produce only oocytes: cells that normally would have differentiated as sperm become oocytes instead. Mutations in *fog-2* do not alter the normal development of the somatic tissues of XX animals as female. In addition, they do not affect the development of either somatic or germ-line tissues of XO animals as male. The specific effect of *fog-2* mutations on the hermaphrodite germ line suggests that wild-type *fog-2* is required for the onset of spermatogenesis only in the hermaphrodite. It is clear that *fog-2* is not required to specify sperm *per se* because spermatogenesis in XO *fog-2* mutant males occurs normally.

An attractive model for the function of *fog-2* is that it negatively regulates *tra-2* in the germ line to permit the *fem* genes to direct spermatogenesis (figure 3*c*). This suggestion derives from the phenotype of *tra-2*; *fog-2* double mutants. The *tra-2(lf)* single mutant causes sexual transformation of XX animals into pseudomales. All tissues of these *tra-2* pseudomales are masculinized, though sexual transformation is not complete. Similarly *tra-2*; *fog-2* double mutants are masculinized. In the germ line, where the activity of *fog-2* might be expected to have some effect, the double mutant makes sperm but not oocytes. Therefore in the absence of *tra-2*, the state of *fog-2* is not critical.

The possibility that *tra-2* is negatively regulated to permit spermatogenesis in hermaphrodites is also suggested by the mutant phenotype of gain-of-function (*gf*) alleles of *tra-2*. XX *tra-2(gf)* animals are female, whereas XO animals are male (Doniach 1986*b*; Schedl & Kimble 1988). The *tra-2(gf)* phenotype is therefore identical to that of *lf* alleles of *fog-2*. One plausible hypothesis is that *tra-2(gf)* is defective in its regulation by *fog-2*.

The activity of *fog-2* does not appear to be sensitive to the X:A ratio. This conclusion comes from the phenotype of *her-1 fog-2* double mutants. The *her-1* single mutant causes sexual transformation of X0 animals into hermaphrodites (Hodgkin 1980). The *her-1 fog-2* double mutant, however, is female (Schedl & Kimble 1988). Therefore, even in XO animals, the state of *fog-2* is critical to the onset of hermaphrodite spermatogenesis.

Both *fog-2(lf)* and *tra-2(gf)* mutations transform *C. elegans* into a male–female strain. Therefore the evolution of *tra-2* regulation by *fog-2* may have been the primary step in the evolution of *C. elegans* self-fertilizing hermaphrodites from a related *Caenorhabditis* species such as *C. remanei* that reproduces as a male–female strain. It is intriguing that *her-1* and *fog-2* are both on chromosome V. Given that both genes appear to function as negative regulators of *tra-2*, perhaps *her-1* and *fog-2* encode related proteins with *her-1* under regulation by the X:A ratio and *fog-2* under tissue-specific control.

Control of the hermaphrodite switch from spermatogenesis to oogenesis

Once spermatogenesis has been initiated in the hermaphrodite germ line, the switch to oogenesis requires further regulation. The mutant phenotype of *fem-3(gf)* alleles may provide insight into the mechanism of this switch.

The wild-type *fem-3* gene is required for specification of the male fate. Both XX and XO mutants lacking *fem-3* activity are sexually transformed into females (hermaphrodites with no sperm) (Hodgkin 1986; Barton *et al.* 1987). Therefore *fem-3* is required both for spermatogenesis in XX hermaphrodites and for male development of all tissues in XO males.

A *fem-3(gf)* hermaphrodite makes sperm continuously and in great excess; it makes no oocytes. The somatic tissues of *fem-3(gf)* XX animals, however, are not sexually transformed: the soma remains female. This germ-line-specific masculinization by *fem-3(gf)* suggests that, in wild-type hermaphrodites, *fem-3* activity is regulated to permit the onset of oogenesis (table 3*d*).

The mechanism by which *fem-3* is inactivated is not known. One possibility is that a germ-line-specific regulator of *fem-3* activity exists (table 3*d*, (i)). Another possibility is that a negative regulator of *fog-2* exists so that *tra-2* can then negatively regulate *fem-3* to permit the switch to oogenesis (table 3*d*, (ii)). Either model predicts the existence of a gene which, when mutant, causes XX animals to produce sperm and to be unable to switch to oogenesis. At least three such genes, the *mog* genes, have been identified (J. Kimble and T. Schedl, unpublished results). However, the *mog* genes have not yet been characterized genetically.

Conclusions

Sex determination in the germ line of the nematode, *C. elegans*, is subject to two kinds of tissue-specific control. These include germ-line-specific regulatory genes, e.g. *fog-1* and *fog-2*, and germ-line-specific regulation of global sex-determining genes as detected by gain-of-function mutations in *fem-3* and *tra-2*. Models are presented by which these genes may regulate the germ line to achieve spermatogenesis and the oogenesis.

This work was supported by the National Institutes of Health through grants GM31816 and

HD00630, and by the March of Dimes Birth Defects Foundation by Basil O'Connor Starter Research Grant no. 5-514.

References

Barton, M. K. & Kimble, J. 1988 *fog-1*, a germline-specific sex determination gene required for spermatogenesis in *C. elegans*. (Submitted.)

Barton, M. K., Schedl, T. B. & Kimble, J. 1987 Gain-of-function mutations of *fem-3*, a sex determination gene in *Caenorhabditis elegans*. *Genetics* **115**, 107-119.

Doniach, T. 1986*a* Genetic analysis of sex determination in the nematode *Caenorhabditis elegans*. Ph.D. thesis, MRC Laboratory of Molecular Biology, Cambridge, England.

Doniach, T. 1986*b* Activity of the sex-determining gene *tra-2* is modulated to allow spermatogenesis in the *C. elegans* hermaphrodite. *Genetics* **114**, 53–76.

Doniach, T. & Hodgkin, J. 1984 A sex-determining gene, *fem-1*, required for both male and hermaphrodite development in *Caenorhabditis elegans*. *Devl Biol.* **106**, 223–235.

Hodgkin, J. 1980 More sex-determination mutants of *Caenorhabditis elegans*. *Genetics* **96**, 649-664.

Hodgkin, J. 1986 Sex determination in the nematode *C. elegans*: analysis of *tra-3* suppressors and characterization of *fem* genes. *Genetics* **114**, 15–52.

Hodgkin, J. 1987*a* Sex determination and dosage compensation in *Caenorhabditis elegans*. *A. Rev. Genet.* **21**, 133–154.

Hodgkin, J. 1987*b* A genetic analysis of the sex-determining gene, *tra-1*, in the nematode *Caenorhabditis elegans*. *Genes Dev.* **1**, 731–745.

Hodgkin, J. A. & Brenner, S. 1977 Mutations causing transformation of sexual phenotype in the nematode *Caenorhabditis elegans*. *Genetics* **86**, 275–287.

Kimble, J., Barton, M. K., Schedl, T., Rosenquist, T. A. & Austin J. 1986 Controls of postembryonic germline development in *C. elegans*, pp. 97–110. In *Symposium of the Society for Developmental Biology*, vol. 44 (ed. J G. Gall). New York: Alan R. Liss.

Kimble, J., Edgar, L. & Hirsh, D. 1984 Specification of male development in *Caenorhabditis elegans*. *Devl Biol.* **105**, 234–239.

Kimble, J. & Schedl, T. 1988 Developmental genetics of *Caenorhabditis elegans*. In *Developmental genetics, a primer in developmental biology* (ed. G. M. Malacinski). Macmillan Publishing.

Kimble, J. & Ward, S. 1988 Germline development and fertilization. In *The nematode Caenorhabditis elegans* (ed. W. B. Wood). Cold Spring Harbor, New York: Cold Spring Harbor Laboratory. (In the press.)

Madl, J. E. & Herman, R. K. 1979 Polyploids and sex determination in *Caenorhabditis elegans*. *Genetics* **93**, 393–402

Nelson, G. A., Lew, K. K. & Ward, S. 1978 Intersex, a temperature-sensitive mutant of the nematode *Caenorhaditis elegans*. *Devl Biol.* **66**, 386–409

Nigon, V. 1951 Polyploidie expérimentale chez un nématode libre, *Rhabditis elegans* Maupas. *Bull. biol. Fr. Belg.* **25**, 187–225

Rosenquist, T. A. & Kimble, J. E. 1988 Molecular cloning and transcript analysis of a sex-determination gene in *C. elegans*. *Genes Dev.* (In the press.)

Schedl, T., Graham, T., Barton, M. K. & Kimble, J. 1988 Analysis of the role of *tra-1* in sex determination of the somatic gonad and germ line of *C. elegans*. (In preparation.)

Schedl, T., & Kimble, J. 1988 *Fog-2*, a germline-specific sex determination gene required for hermaphrodite spermatogenesis in *C. elegans*. *Genetics*. (In the press.)

Trent, C., N., Wood, W. B., & Horvitz, H. R. 1988 A novel dominant transformer allele of the sex-determining gene *her-1* of *Caenorhabditis elegans*. (In preparation.)

Villeneuve, A. M. & Meyer, B. J. 1987 *sdc-1*: a link between sex determination and dosage compensation in *C. elegans*. *Cell* **48**, 25–37.

Wood, W. B. (ed.) 1988 *The nematode Caenorhabditis elegans*. Cold Spring Harbor, New York: Cold Spring Harbor Laboratory. (In the press.)

Phil. Trans. R. Soc. Lond. B **322**, 19–39 (1988) [19]
Printed in Great Britain

Environmental regulation of sex determination in reptiles

BY D. C. DEEMING AND M. W. J. FERGUSON
Department of Cell and Structural Biology, The University of Manchester,
Coupland III Building, Manchester, M13 9PL, U.K.

[Plates 1 and 2]

The various patterns of environmental sex determination in squamates, chelonians and crocodilians are described. High temperatures produce males in lizards and crocodiles but females in chelonians. Original experiments on the effects of incubation at 30 °C (100% females) or 33 °C (100% males) on development in *Alligator mississippiensis* are described. These include an investigation of the effect of exposing embryos briefly to a different incubation temperature on the sex ratio at hatching, and a study of the effects of 30 °C and 33 °C on growth and development of alligator embryos and gonads. A 7-day pulse of one temperature on the background of another was insufficient to alter the sex ratio dramatically. Incubation at 33 °C increased the rate of growth and development of alligator embryos. In particular, differentiation of the gonad at 33 °C was enhanced compared with 30 °C. A hypothesis is developed to explain the mechanism of temperature-dependent sex determination (TSD) in crocodilians. The processes of primary sex differentiation are considered to involve exposure to a dose of some male-determining factor during a specific quantum of developmental time during early incubation. The gene that encodes for the male-determining factor is considered to have an optimum temperature (33 °C). Any change in the temperature affects the expression of this gene and affects the dose or quantum embryos are exposed to. In these cases there is production of females by default. The phylogenetic implications of TSD for crocodilians, and reptiles in particular, are related to the life history of the animal from conception to sexual maturity. Those animals that develop under optimal conditions grow fastest and largest and become male. A general association between the size of an animal and its sex is proposed for several types of vertebrate.

INTRODUCTION

The determination of vertebrate sex is controlled by genetic or environmental factors or both. Mammals and birds exhibit genetic sex determination (GSD), which is characterized by the gender of the individual being fixed at conception. Environmental sex determination (ESD) is common in other vertebrates and some invertebrates (Bull 1980, 1983), and is characterized by the establishment of sex only after the embryonic or larval stage of the animal has been exposed to various environmental factors during development. Temperature-dependent sex determination was first observed (Charnier 1966) in an agamid lizard and has subsequently been observed in other reptiles. The temperature of egg incubation is the major environmental factor determining the sex of the individual and sex appears to be fixed at hatching (Pieau 1971, 1972; Yntema 1976, 1979; Ferguson & Joanen 1983: Webb & Smith 1984). Temperature also influences primary sex determination of some fish, whereas in some hermaphroditic fish (see Harrington 1967, 1968) and amphibians (see Witschi 1929; Gallien 1974; Houillon & Dournon 1978) temperature induces a change in the sexual phenotype of the adult.

Environmental regulation of reptilian sex determination is described and reviewed here. First, the incidence and patterns of temperature-dependent sex determination in reptiles are reviewed. Second, original experiments that examine the effects of temperature on sex determination and development in eggs of *Alligator mississippiensis* are described. Third, we speculate on possible mechanisms of reptilian sex determination and their phylogenetic implications.

Temperature-dependent sex determination in reptiles

Many studies of the phenomenon of temperature-dependent sex determination (TSD) in reptiles have observed the relation between temperature and sex ratio in natural nests (Ferguson & Joanen 1982, 1983; Bull 1985; Schwarzkopf & Brooks 1987), whereas others have been laboratory investigations examining the effects of constant incubation temperature on sex determination (Pieau 1971, 1972; Yntema 1976, 1979; Bull & Vogt 1979, 1981; Bull 1987*a*, *b*). Laboratory experiments involving a switch in the incubation temperature of eggs from one that induces 100% males to one that induces 100% females and vice versa have defined the temperature-sensitive period (TSP) for sex determination. The TSP is the earliest period of incubation when the sex ratio can be significantly switched. In many cases the TSP for a switch from a high to a low temperature is later than the TSP for a low to high switch (Ferguson & Joanen 1983; Webb *et al.* 1987; Bull 1987*a*), contrary to what one would intuitively predict given that higher temperatures accelerate external development of the embryo.

Squamata

The phenomenon of temperature-dependent sex determination (TSD) is poorly reported in the lizards and snakes despite the fact that it was first described for the lizard *Agama agama* (see Charnier 1966): an incubation temperature of 29 °C produced 100% males compared with 98% females at 26–27 °C. The gekkonid lizard *Eublepharis macularius* shows a similar pattern to *Agama* (see Warner 1980; Bull 1987*a*, 1987*b*). A long TSP has been described for *Eublepharis*, occurring between morphological stages 32–37 during the first half of incubation (Bull 1987*a*). A different pattern of sex determination has been observed in *Gekko japonicus* (Tokunaga 1985). Females are induced at low and high temperatures, with males occurring at intermediate temperatures. Temperature-dependent sex determination is absent in the lacertid *Lacerta viridis* (Raynaud & Pieau 1972). The iguanid lizard *Dipsosaurus dorsalis* has GSD but incubation temperature has a small influence on the sex ratio (Muth & Bull 1981).

Most snakes exhibit genetic sex determination and possess heteromorphic sex chromosomes (Baker *et al.* 1972; Bull 1980). Skewed sex ratios do, however, occur in some populations of snakes (Shine & Bull 1977; Gutzke *et al.* 1985). Incubation temperature does not affect the sex ratio of the snake *Nerodia fasciata* (Osgood 1980) and TSD comparable to that observed in lizards has not been reported. A form of TSD occurs in *Pituophis melanoleucus*, which has differential mortality of the eggs: low temperatures kill male embryos whereas higher temperatures kill females (see Burger & Zappalorti 1988).

Chelonia

In contrast to squamates (and crocodilians), incubation of chelonian eggs at high temperatures induces female hatchlings; low temperatures induce males in both field and laboratory investigations of most species studied (table 1). In at least four species, however,

TABLE 1. THE DOCUMENTED INCIDENCE OF TSD IN THE ORDER CHELONIA

suborder: Cryptodira	
family: Carettochelyidae	
Carettochelys insculpta	Webb *et al.* (1986).
family: Chelydridae	
Chelydra serpentina	Yntema (1976, 1979, 1981); Wilhoft *et al.* (1983); Packard *et al.* (1984, 1987).
Macroclemys temmincki	Bull (1980).
family: Chelonidae	
Caretta caretta	Yntema & Mrosovsky (1980, 1982); Stoneburner & Richardson (1981); Mrosovsky *et al.* (1984); Standora & Spotila (1985); Limpus *et al.* (1985).
Chelonia mydas	Mrosovsky & Yntema (1980); Miller & Limpus (1981); Wood & Wood (1982); Morreale *et al.* (1982); Mrosovsky *et al.* (1984); Standora & Spotila (1985); Spotila *et al.* (1987).
Eretmochelys imbricata	Dalrymple *et al.* (1985).
Lepidochelys olivacea	Dimond & Mohanty-Hejmadi (1983); McCoy *et al.* (1983); Standora & Spotila (1985).
family: Dermochelyidae	
Dermochelys coriacea	Mrosovsky *et al.* (1984); Standora & Spotila (1985); Rimblot *et al.* (1985); Rimblot-Baly *et al.* (1986–1987).
family: Emydidae	
Chinemys reevesii	Hou Ling (1985).
Chrysemys picta	Bull & Vogt (1979, 1981); Bull *et al.* (1982); Gutzke & Paukstis (1983, 1984); Paukstis *et al.* (1984); Vogt & Bull (1984); Schwarzkopf & Brooks (1985, 1987).
Emys orbicularis	Pieau (1971, 1972, 1973, 1974, 1982); Pieau & Dorizzi (1981); Pieau *et al.* (1982).
Graptemys ouachitensis	Bull & Vogt (1979, 1981); Bull *et al.* (1982); Vogt & Bull (1984); Bull (1985).
G. geographica	Bull & Vogt (1979); Bull *et al.* (1982); Vogt & Bull (1984); Bull (1985).
G. pseudogeographica	Bull & Vogt (1979); Bull *et al.* (1982); Vogt & Bull (1984); Bull (1985).
Pseudemys scripta	Bull *et al.* (1982).
family: Kinosternidae	
Sternotherus odoratus	Bull & Vogt (1979); Vogt *et al.* (1982).
Kinosternon flavescens	Bull (1980); Vogt *et al.* (1982).
family: Testudinidae	
Testudo graeca	Pieau (1971, 1972).
suborder: Pleurodira	
family: Pelomedusidae	
Podocnemis expansa	Alho *et al.* (1985).

temperature has little effect on sex determination: *Trionyx spiniferus* (Trionychidae), *Emydura macquarii*, *E. signata* (suborder Pleurodira: Chelidae) and *Clemmys inscupta* which as yet is the only emydid turtle not to exhibit TSD (Vogt & Bull 1982; Thompson 1983, 1988; Bull *et al.* 1985). Thus both TSD and GSD exist among turtles, even among closely related species.

A second pattern of TSD is characterized by the induction of females at high and low incubation temperatures, with males at intermediate temperatures. This occurs in at least two families of turtle (Chelydridae and Kinosternidae) and is well documented for *Chelydra serpentina* (Yntema 1976, 1979, 1981; Wilhoft *et al.* 1983) and *Sternotherus odoratus* (Vogt *et al.* 1982). In *C. serpentina* incubation at 22 °C, 24 °C or 26 °C induced male development but at higher temperatures (28 °C and 30 °C) females were produced. Eggs incubated at 20 °C were not viable but transfer to 26 °C (male-producing) after 83–88 days allowed the eggs to hatch and produced 100% females (Yntema 1976). Low-temperature females have not been observed in wild nests of *C. serpentina* (Wilhoft *et al.* 1983). By contrast, eggs of *S. odoratus* can produce 81% females at 23.5 °C with males predominating at 25 °C and females predominating again at 28.0–30.5 °C (Vogt *et al.* 1982). This pattern also occurs in *Macroclemmys temincki* and *Kinosternon flavescens* (Bull 1980) although more data are necessary (Vogt *et al.* 1982).

Temperature-sensitive periods have been established for *C. serpentina* and they vary according to the direction of the temperature shifts (Yntema 1979; Wilhoft *et al.* 1983). For shifts from 20 °C to 26 °C the TSP is between Yntema (1968) stages 13–17; for 26 °C to 30 °C stages 16–20; for 30 °C to 26 °C stages 12–15 and for shifts from 26 °C to 20 °C stages 12–18. Less time at 30 °C is required to feminize a clutch of eggs than is required at 26 °C to masculinize it (Yntema 1979). In the laboratory, exposure to 30 °C for at least 4 h per day was sufficient to induce females (Wilhoft *et al.* 1983).

Laboratory studies using eggs of *Chrysemys picta* have shown that females can be induced at temperatures that normally produce males. Extremely dry nest environments (not more than −1100 kPa) at a temperature of 25 °C induce females despite the masculinizing effect of the temperature (Gutzke & Paukstis 1983; Paukstis *et al.* 1984). Nest humidity may therefore affect sex determination.

Crocodylia

Heteromorphic sex chromosomes are absent in all crocodilian species (Cohen & Gans 1970) and TSD is prevalent (Ferguson 1985; Deeming & Ferguson 1988). Macroscopic and histological examinations of the gonads of crocodilian hatchlings have shown that sex is fully determined at the time of hatching and no hermaphrodites, sex reversals or intersexes occur (Ferguson & Joanen 1983; Webb & Smith 1984).

One pattern of TSD is present in *Alligator mississippiensis* (Ferguson & Joanen 1982, 1983), *Caiman crocodilius* (Lang *et al.* 1988), *Crocodylus niloticus* and *Crocodylus siamensis* (Hutton 1987; Lang 1987). Artificial incubation of eggs at low temperatures (not more than 30 °C in *A. mississippiensis*; not more than 31 °C in *C. niloticus*; not more than 31.5 °C in *C. crocodilus*) induces 100% females; high temperatures (not less than 33 °C) induce 100% males. At intermediate temperatures both sexes are produced although there is a strong female bias; the incidence of males increases with increasing incubation temperature (Ferguson & Joanen 1983; Joanen *et al.* 1987). In temperature shifts from 30 °C to 33 °C the TSP occurs between days 14 and 21 of a total incubation period of 65 days, but in shifts from 33 °C to 30 °C it occurs between days 28 and 35 (Ferguson & Joanen 1983).

A second pattern of TSD is present in *Crocodylus johnstoni* (Webb *et al.* 1983, 1987; Webb & Smith 1984), *Crocodylus porosus* (Webb *et al.* 1987; Webb 1988) and *Crocodylus palustris* (Lang *et al.* 1988). In *C. johnstoni*, female hatchlings can be induced at any viable incubation temperature (Webb *et al.* 1983; Webb & Smith 1984). Males could only be produced within a narrow range of temperatures (31.0 °C–32.5 °C) but the highest sex ratio that could be achieved in the laboratory was 36% males (Webb & Smith 1984). In contrast to

A. mississippiensis, high temperatures (33 °C and 34 °C) induced females that had large oviducts, ovaries with a distinct cortical region and a small clitiropenis (Webb & Smith 1984). High-temperature females have also been reported in *C. porosus* although the pattern of TSD in this species has similarities with that in *A. mississippiensis*: high temperatures (32 °C and 33 °C) induce 100 % males (Webb *et al.* 1987). Similarly, in *C. palustris* incubation of eggs below 31.5 °C induces 100 % females and at 32.5 °C, 100 % males. Males occur in varying proportions at intermediate temperatures but incubation at 33 °C produces only 47 % males (Lang *et al.* 1988). Temperature-shift experiments on eggs of *C. johnstoni* have been done despite the difficulties in interpretation associated with the absence of any temperature that induces 100 % males (Webb *et al.* 1987). Switches from low temperatures (29 °C, 30 °C, and 31 °C) to 32 °C were found to be effective in producing males despite the fact that at constant temperatures these are female-inducing conditions. Over half of the incubation period was temperature sensitive though the morphological age at which femaleness could be maintained increased with greater incubation temperatures (Webb *et al.* 1987). Shift experiments in *C. porosus* and *C. palustris* showed similar results to *A. mississippiensis* (Webb *et al.* 1987; Lang *et al.* 1988). Possibly the primitive pattern of TSD is high- and low-temperature females, with intermediate-temperature males; in some species selection for viable incubation temperatures has merely eliminated either the high (e.g. crocodilians) or low (e.g. chelonians) temperature category (Deeming & Ferguson 1988).

Temperature-sensitive sex determination is not a phenomenon restricted to laboratory experiments. In the natural habitat of *A. mississippiensis* in Louisiana, U.S.A., three basic types of nest mound were described (Ferguson & Joanen 1982, 1983). Wet marsh nests were the coolest and most humid and produced 100 % female hatchlings. Levée nests were the warmest and driest and produced 100 % males. The dry marsh nest was intermediate in temperature and humidity, and produced both sexes. Nest maps revealed that males only developed in the warmest parts of the nest. Nests of *C. palustris* that attain 31.5–32.0 °C by 30 to 40 days of incubation contain more males than cooler nests (Lang *et al.* 1988). In *C. johnstoni* the hatchling sex ratio is biased towards females, and only 33 % of immature animals and 17 % of adults are male (Webb *et al.* 1983). Natural nests that produce 100 % males have been observed in *C. johnstoni* (Smith 1987), despite the fact that this is not attainable under laboratory conditions (Webb *et al.* 1987). Induction of males is correlated to the total length of incubation, with males emerging after 72–82 days (Smith 1987). The adult population structure of all wild crocodilians is heavily biased towards females (Ferguson & Joanen 1982, 1983; Webb *et al.* 1983, 1987; Ferguson 1985; Hutton 1987).

Temperature not only influences the sex of crocodilian hatchlings but also the rate of embryonic development (Ferguson 1985; Webb *et al.* 1987; Webb 1988). The difference in the incubation period for eggs incubated at 30 °C (93 days) and 33 °C (78 days) is 15 days in *C. porosus* (Webb 1988) but only 8 days in *A. mississippiensis* (74 and 66 days respectively) (Joanen *et al.* 1987). Hatchling size in crocodilians is related to incubation temperature (Ferguson & Joanen 1982, 1983; Webb *et al.* 1987; Joanen *et al.* 1987). Eggs of *A. mississippiensis* incubated at extremes of temperature (29.4 °C and 32.8 °C) produced larger hatchlings than those incubated at intermediate temperatures (30.6 °C and 31.7 °C). Hatchlings from high incubation temperatures also have more residual abdominal yolk compared with hatchlings from lower temperatures (Ferguson & Joanen 1982, 1983; Webb *et al.* 1987). Post-hatching growth rates, under constant conditions, were also related to incubation temperature. Hatchlings from intermediate incubation temperatures grew faster than those from the extremes. Males always grew faster than females from the same incubation temperature (Joanen *et al.* 1987). The length, but not the mass, of hatchlings of *C. niloticus* and *C. porosus* was influenced by incubation temperature: male hatchlings were shorter, but by three months of age they were significantly larger than females (Hutton 1987; Webb 1988). Incubation temperature also affects post-hatching thermoregulation, at least in *C. siamensis*, with males consistently selecting higher temperatures for thermoregulation (Lang 1987). In addition, the pigmentation pattern of *A. mississippiensis* hatchlings is affected by incubation temperature. Males from eggs incubated at 33 °C are darker than females from eggs incubated at 30 °C (Deeming & Ferguson 1988).

Original experiments on TSD in *Alligator mississippiensis*

Surprisingly, despite the wealth of data on the patterns and incidence of TSD in reptiles, no-one previously has investigated its mechanism. We have examined three aspects of the effect of incubation temperature on general development, and in particular sex determination, in embryos of *Alligator mississippiensis*: (1) the effects of a pulsed change in incubation temperature; (2) the effects of a male- (33 °C) and a female- (30 °C) inducing temperature on the growth of embryos in terms of mass and morphometric measurements; (3) the effects of male (33 °C) and female (30 °C) temperatures on gonadal growth and differentiation. These new findings are used with other data to develop a hypothesis concerning the mechanisms of TSD in crocodilians.

'*Shift twice*' *pulsed temperature experiments*

Previous experiments to determine the time of sex determination have concentrated upon defining temperature-sensitive periods (Yntema 1979; Bull & Vogt 1981; Ferguson & Joanen 1982, 1983; Bull 1987*a*), though some shift-twice experiments have also been done (Yntema 1981; Bull & Vogt 1981; Pieau & Dorizzi 1981), in which embryos are exposed to short pulses of one incubation temperature on the background of another. The effects on sex determination of exposing embryos of *A. mississippiensis* to this type of experimental treatment have been examined. The experimental design and results are illustrated in figure 1.

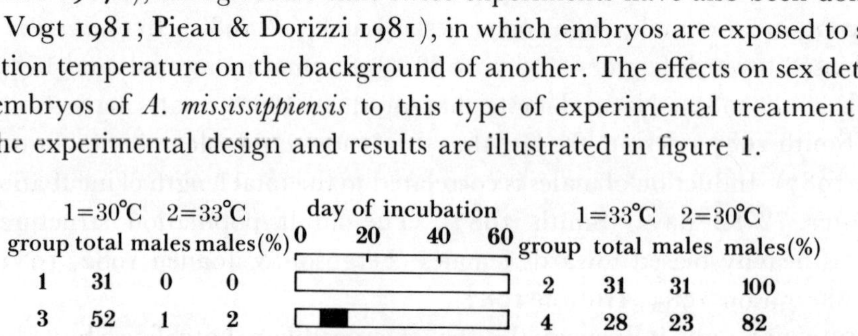
1=30°C 2=33°C
group total males males(%)
day of incubation
0 20 40 60
1=33°C 2=30°C
group total males males(%)
1 31 0 0
3 52 1 2
5 57 8 14
7 27 0 0
9 28 0 0
11 26 0 0
13 31 0 0
15 29 0 0
2 31 31 100
4 28 23 82
6 29 27 93
8 55 50 91
10 53 48 91
12 28 26 93
14 30 28 93
16 32 32 100
temperature 1
temperature 2

FIGURE 1. Details of a 'shift-twice' experiment done on eggs of *Alligator mississippiensis*. The eggs in each group were incubated either at 30 °C (exclusively female-producing) or 33 °C (exclusively male-producing) and exposed to 7-day periods of the other temperature. Groups 1 and 2 are controls. Macroscopic sexing was done on day 60 of incubation and confirmed in several animals by histological examination (Ferguson & Joanen 1983). The number and percentage of males in each group was recorded.

A 7-day pulse of one incubation temperature on the background of a second temperature was insufficient to alter radically the sex ratio associated with the original temperature (figure 1). A shift from 30 °C to 33 °C was very poor at producing male embryos; only in the third week of incubation (14–21 days) did 33 °C induce any males to develop. A 7-day pulsed reduction in temperature from 33 °C to 30 °C during the second to the seventh weeks of incubation could induce a few females only. The highest percentage of females was induced during the second week (7–14 days) pulse (figure 1).

Temperature and growth

Unlike avian eggs, which require a specific incubation temperature for normal development, reptilian eggs can successfully develop at a range of temperatures (28–34 °C in *A. mississippiensis* (Ferguson 1985)). It is not clear what effect temperature has on the growth and development of many reptiles although it is assumed that higher temperatures accelerate development. Indeed, higher temperatures do produce higher growth rates in *Python molurus*, two species of crocodile and many turtles (Vinegar 1973; Webb *et al.* 1987; Ewert 1985). This section describes an experiment that studied the non-sexual effects of temperature on embryonic development in *A. mississippiensis*.

Eggs of *A. mississippiensis* were incubated at 30 °C or 33 °C (± 0.01 °C) in 100% humidity. At particular times during incubation eggs were removed from the incubator, opened and the embryos removed and fixed in formal saline (100 g l^{-1}) or Karnovsky's fixative until they were measured. Embryos were staged by using the criteria of Ferguson (1985) and wet mass was determined after fixation. Various morphometric parameters of the embryos were measured with a Wild M8 dissecting microscope eye-piece graticule or Vernier scale calipers. Parameters measured included total length of the animal, head length, eye length and the length of the trunk (measured as the distance between the limbs).

Incubation at 33 °C accelerated embryonic development and growth as assessed by all parameters measured. Embryos incubated at 33 °C reached morphological stage 20 approximately 5 days earlier than at 30 °C (figure 2*a*). Embryonic growth was also accelerated by the higher temperature (figure 2*b*). The total length of the animal and the length of the trunk were greater at 33 °C from early in incubation (figure 3*a*, *b*). For any morphological stage (particularly later in incubation), however, embryo mass was smaller at 33 °C than at 30 °C. Head length increased more rapidly during incubation at 33 °C than at 30 °C (figure 4*a*). Eye length showed a similar pattern although its rate of growth declined later in incubation (figure 4*b*). The ratio of eye length to head length was similar at the two temperatures (figure 4*c*), indicating that although increased incubation temperature accelerates external development it does not stimulate asynchronous growth of different parts of the embryo.

The effect of temperature on gonad development

Three distinct phases in the development of the gonad–kidney complex have been described in *A. mississippiensis*: the period of genital ridge formation, the period of bisexuality and the period of visible sex differentiation (Forbes 1940). The origin and route of migration of the germ cells is unknown in any crocodilian (Ferguson 1985). The genital ridge arises from a thickening of the ventromedial coelomic epithelium surrounding the mesonephros, which proliferates and develops rete cords. This phase persists in embryos up to 40 mm crown–rump

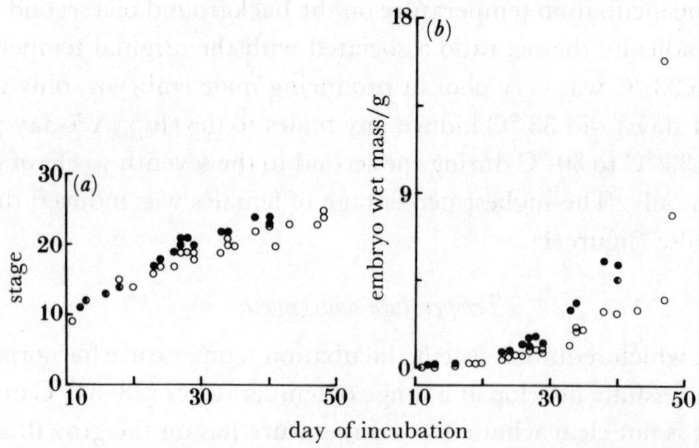

FIGURE 2. The development and growth of embryos of *A. mississippiensis* from eggs incubated at two incubation temperatures. (*a*) Relationship between morphological stage (Ferguson 1985) and days of incubation. (*b*) Growth of embryos measured as wet mass (in grams). Open circles, 30 °C; closed circles, 33 °C.

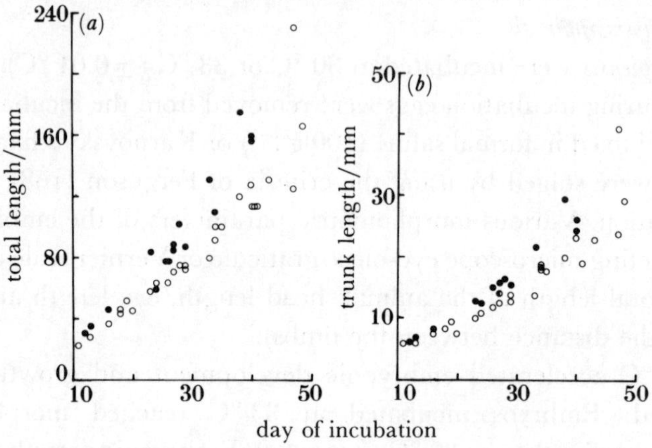

FIGURE 3. Two plots showing the effect of incubation temperature on the total length of the embryos of *A. mississippiensis* (*a*) and the length of the trunk, measured as distance between the limbs (*b*). Open circles 30 °C; closed circles, 33 °C.

length but no precise stages or time of incubation were recorded (Forbes 1940). The period of bisexuality is characterized by gonads that have distinct cortical and medullary parts but the sex of the individual is indeterminate. This phase persists in embryos up to a crown–rump length of 85 mm. Sexual differentiation then begins. Contrary to the report of Gutzke (1987), cortical tissues of the presumptive gonad differentiate into ovarian tissue compared with differentiation of the medulla to form testicular tissue (Forbes 1940).

There are several problems associated with the report by Forbes (1940). The eggs and embryos used in the study were from several sources and precise data on their incubation age or temperature were not available. The present study examines the effect of temperature on the development of the gonad in embryos of *A. mississippiensis* incubated at 30 °C and 33 °C (±0.01 °C). The gonad–kidney complex was dissected from the embryos that had been fixed in formal saline and measured, as described above. The gonad–kidney complex was prepared for histology, serially sectioned (5 μm), stained with haematoxylin and eosin, and examined by

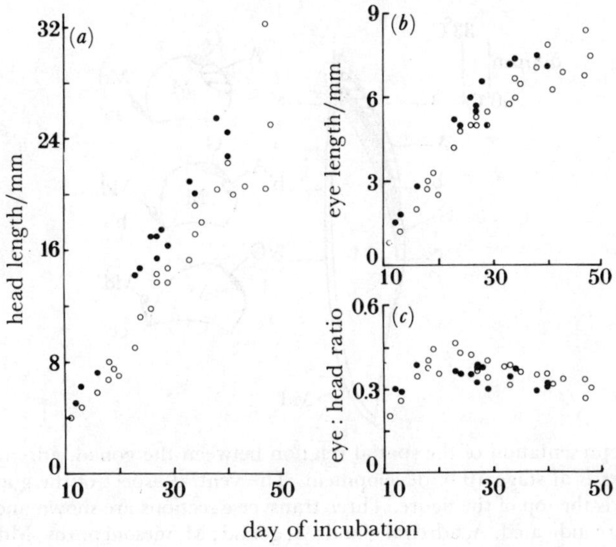

FIGURE 4. The effect of temperature on the growth of the head (*a*) and the eye (*b*) of embryos of *A. mississippiensis*. The relation between the eye:head ratio and time is plotted (*c*). Open circles, 30 °C; closed circles, 33 °C.

light microscopy. The length and thickness of the whole gonad and of the medulla were determined from the sections.

Incubation at 30 °C

At sixteen days of incubation (stage 13) the gonad was undetermined, with a thickened epithelium (continuous with the coelomic epithelium) covering a loosely arranged medulla. The gonad continued to grow and on day 24 (stage 17) there was a distinct change in the structure of the epithelium. The cells had a high nuclear:cytoplasmic ratio and a characteristic stalk-like appearance (figure 9, plate 1). Germ cells were sparse, and randomly arranged within the gonad. The medulla was densely cellular and not organized (figure 9). This general gonadal description remained similar up to day 40 (stage 23), when the cortical epithelium showed a larger number of germ cells (figure 9). By day 47 (stage 25) the gonad was differentiating into an ovary. The anterior portion of the ovary appeared to differentiate first, with posterior tissues beginning to form the medullary rest (Forbes 1940).

Incubation at 33 °C

Up to day 24 of incubation (stage 18) the appearance of the gonad was the same as at 30 °C, with the characteristic stalked epithelium and dense medulla (figure 9). Thereafter, there was a distinct organization of the medullary cells to form clumps and rounded masses (figure 9). By day 34 of incubation (stage 22) the gonad was well organized and differentiating into a testis (figure 9). On day 40 (stage 23) the gonad had a well-organized medullary region, the epithelium had lost its stalked appearance and was much flatter (figure 9). Germ cells were present in the medulla from the earliest stages, although they were difficult to observe as they bore a greater resemblance to medullary cells than to epithelial cells.

The position of the gonad on the mesonephros was predictable (figure 5). At the cloacal end of the complex, the gonad lies on the mediolateral ventral surface of the mesonephros. Further

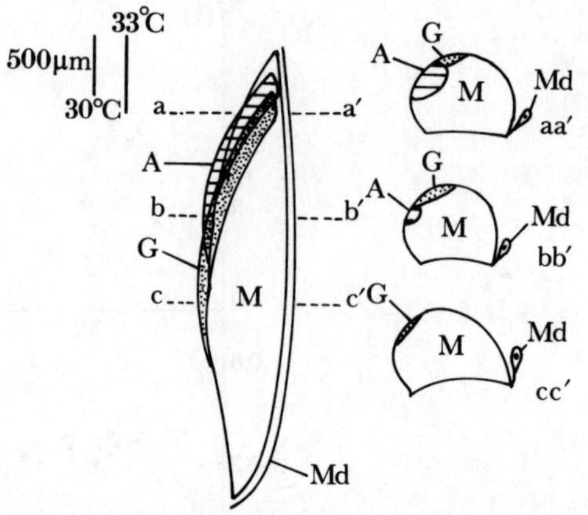

FIGURE 5. A diagrammatic representation of the spatial relation between the gonad, adrenal and mesonephros in embryos of *A. mississippiensis* at stage 19 of development. The ventral aspect of the gonad–kidney complex is shown; anterior is towards the top of the figure. Three transverse sections are shown and their positions on the gonad–kidney complex are indicated. A, adrenal gland; G, gonad; M, mesonephros; Md, Müllerian duct. Two scale bars (approximate) are included, owing to the differing effects of temperature on growth of the gonad at any stage of development.

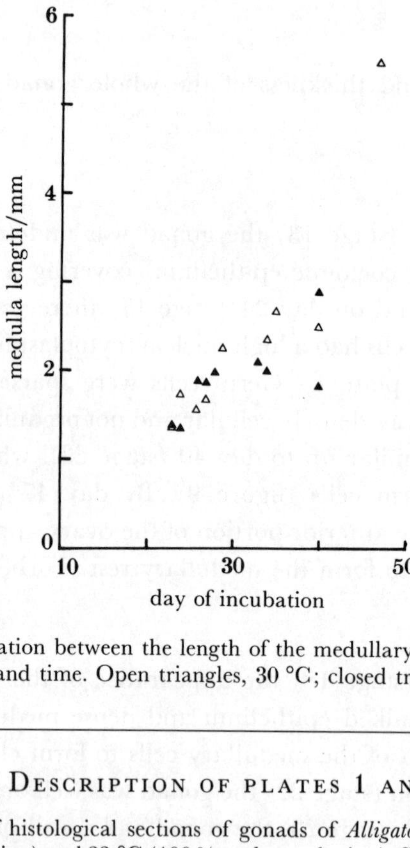

FIGURE 6. The relation between the length of the medullary region of the developing gonad and time. Open triangles, 30 °C; closed triangles, 33 °C.

DESCRIPTION OF PLATES 1 AND 2

FIGURE 9. Light micrographs of histological sections of gonads of *Alligator mississippiensis* embryos incubated at 30 °C (100% female-producing) and 33 °C (100% male-producing). Sections are from the centre of the gonad and are stained with haematoxylin and eosin. (*a*) Day 24, 30 °C, Ferguson (1985) stage 17. The medullary cells are loose and the epithelial cells have a characteristic 'stalked' appearance. (*b*) Day 34, 30 °C, stage 20. Similar to (*a*) but larger. (*c*) Day 40, 30 °C stage 23. The medulla is dense but does not show any signs of organization. (*d*) Day 24, 33 °C, stage 18. Note the stalked appearance of the epithelium. (*e*) Day 34, 33 °C, stage 22. The medulla is beginning to show signs of organization. (*f*) Day 40, 33 °C, stage 23. Note the flattened epithelium and the highly organized medulla. Scale bar 25 μm. A, adrenal gland; G, gonad; M, mesonephros.

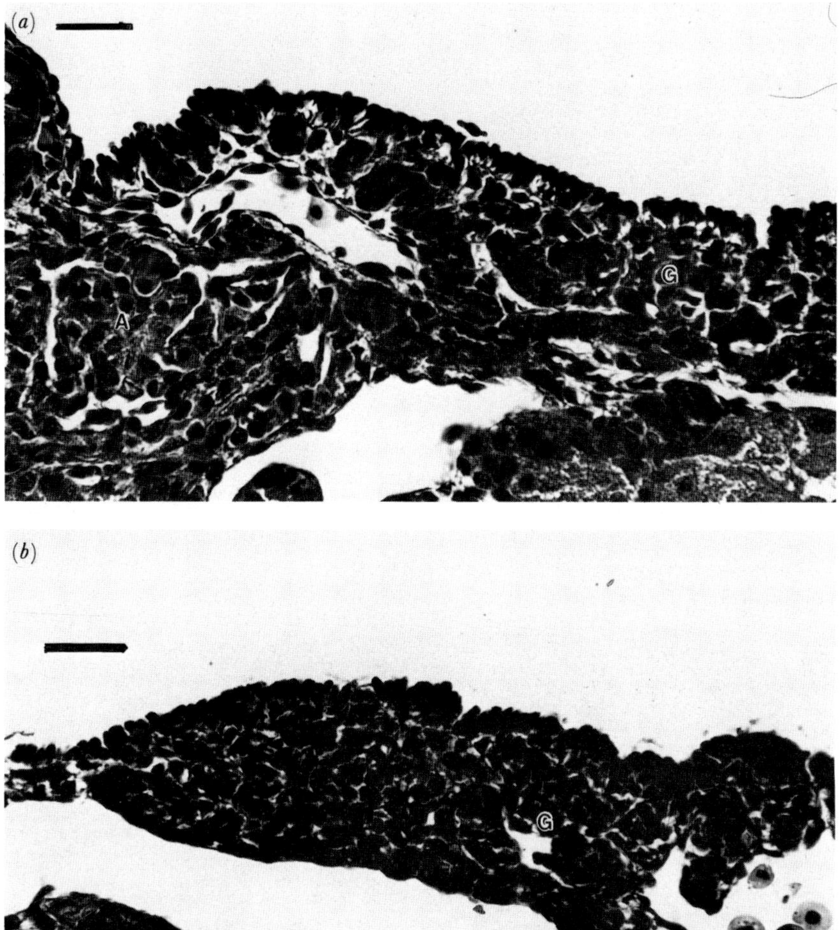

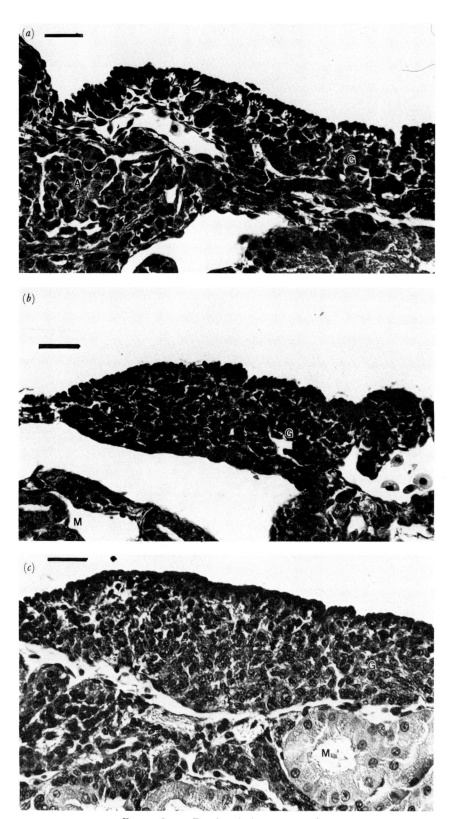

FIGURE 9 *a–c*. For description see opposite.

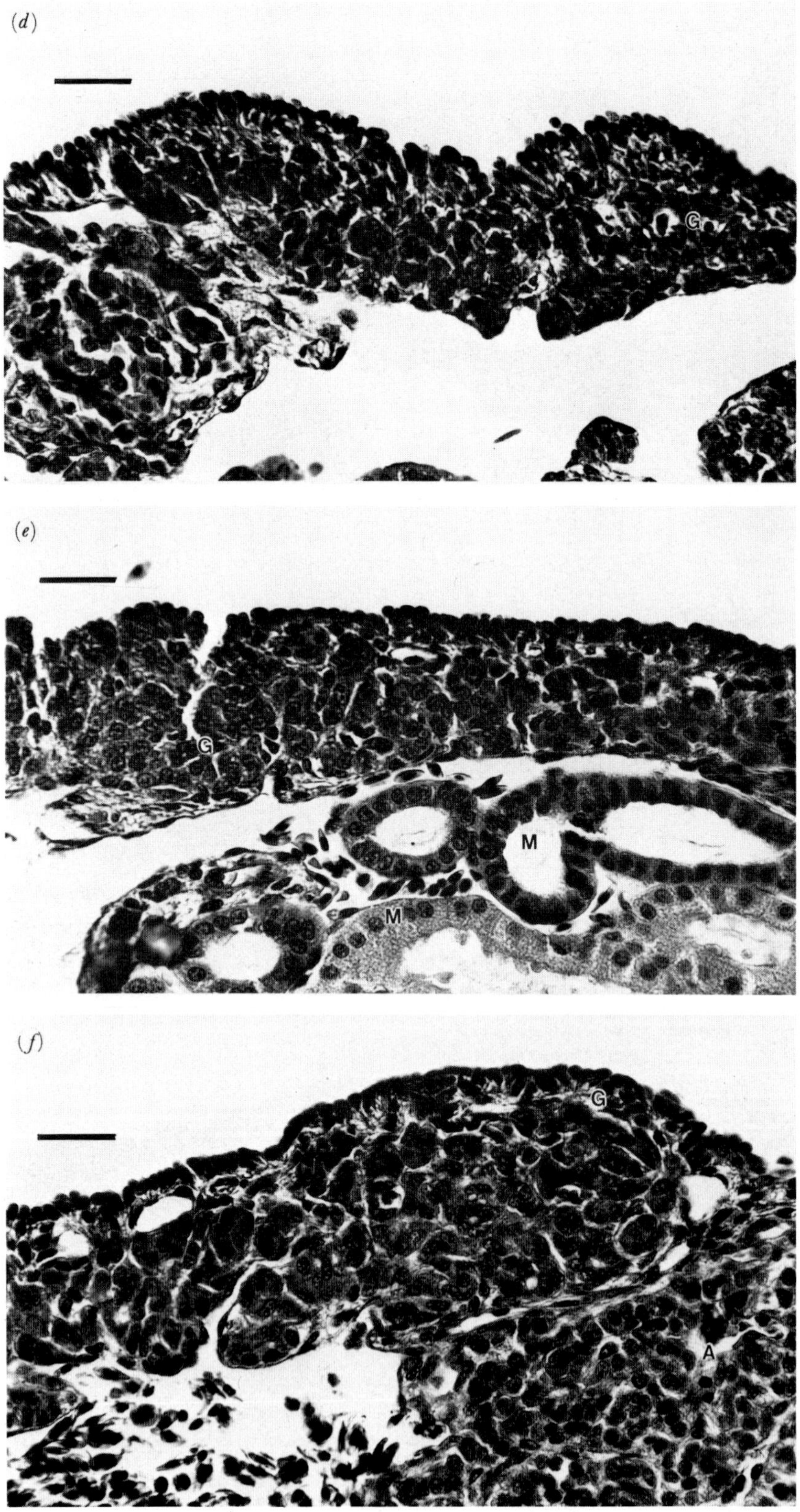

FIGURE 9 *d–f*. For description see p. 28.

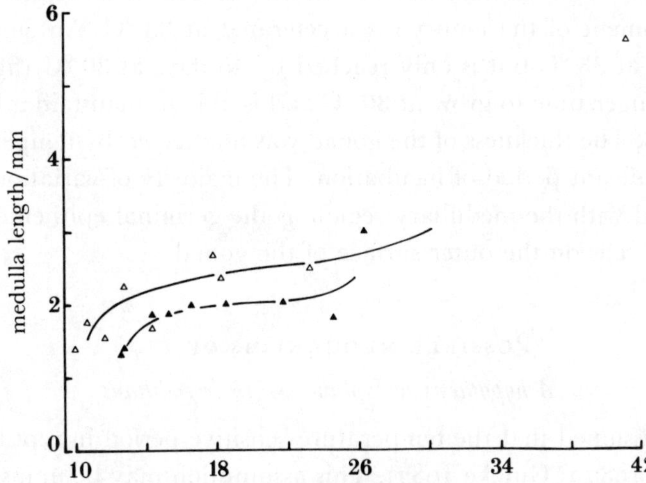

FIGURE 7. The relation between gonad size, measured as the length of the medulla, and the size of the embryo, measured as length of trunk. The two lines are fitted by eye. Open triangles, 30 °C; closed triangles, 33 °C.

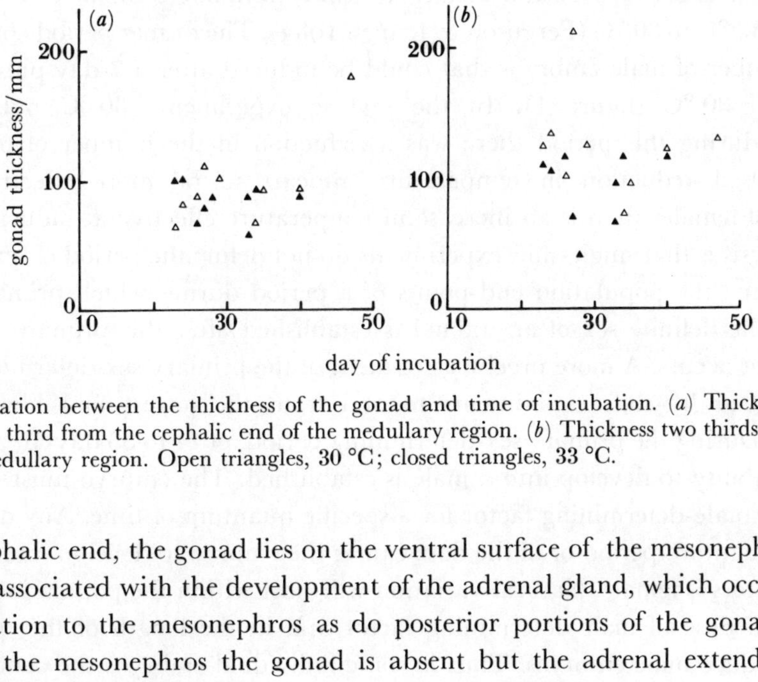

FIGURE 8. The relation between the thickness of the gonad and time of incubation. (*a*) Thickness of the gonad measured one third from the cephalic end of the medullary region. (*b*) Thickness two thirds from the cephalic end of the medullary region. Open triangles, 30 °C; closed triangles, 33 °C.

towards the cephalic end, the gonad lies on the ventral surface of the mesonephros (figure 5). This change is associated with the development of the adrenal gland, which occupies a similar position in relation to the mesonephros as do posterior portions of the gonad. Nearer the anterior tip of the mesonephros the gonad is absent but the adrenal extends further in a cephalic direction (figure 5.)

The point at which the germinal epithelium of the gonad arose from the coelomic epithelium was difficult to define. By contrast, the point at which the medulla arose was easily recognized and its overall length could be measured precisely. For this reason the length of the medulla was used as an assessment of gonadal growth. As incubation proceeded the length of the medullary region of the presumptive gonad increased (figure 6). When gonad length was compared with the length of the trunk, the rate of increase was very slow compared with the rapid elongation of the body (figure 7). For any given length of trunk the gonad was longer in embryos incubated at 30 °C than in those at 33 °C. This is associated with the fact that growth and development of the embryo is accelerated at 33 °C. An embryo mass of 5 g is attained by 33 days at 33 °C but is only reached by 45 days at 30 °C (figure 2). The gonad appears to have a longer time to grow at 30 °C and is able to maintain a better ratio to body length than at 33 °C. The thickness of the gonad was unaffected by temperature (figure 8*a*, *b*) or by time for a significant period of incubation. The majority of variation in thickness of the gonad was associated with the medullary region as the germinal epithelium only contributed one or two layers of cells on the outer surface of the gonad.

Possible mechanisms of TSD

A hypothesis to explain TSD in crocodilians

It has long been assumed that the temperature-sensitive period in reptiles is the time of sex determination (Bull 1987*a*; Gutzke 1987). This assumption may be unjustified in light of the present findings. The shift-twice experiment showed that the change in sex that is associated with a change in temperature is not simply a switch event at one particular embryonic age or stage. One week would appear to be insufficient to affect the processes of sex determination significantly. Conventional, single temperature-shift experiments on eggs of *A. mississippiensis* show that the TSP is between 14 and 21 days for shifts from 30 °C to 33 °C, and 28 to 35 days for shifts from 33 °C to 30 °C (Ferguson & Joanen 1983). The former period corresponds to the maximum number of male embryos that could be induced after a 7-day pulse of 33 °C on a background of 30 °C (figure 1). In the reverse experiment (30 °C pulse on a 33 °C background), during this period there was a reduction in the number of males produced. Indeed, a pulsed reduction in temperature appears to be more effective at allowing development of females than is an increase in temperature effective at inducing males.

Our hypothesis is that single-shift experiments do not define the period of sex determination but rather define the population end-points of a period during which primary sex is being determined. The definite sex of an animal is established after this primary period, when a secondary event occurs. A more precise assessment of the primary sex-determining period can only be achieved by shift experiments to and from the lowest and highest incubation temperatures. During the primary sex-determining period, of 14 to 35 days in *A. mississippiensis* embryos, the ability to develop into a male is established. The embryo must be exposed to a 'dose' of some male-determining factor for a specific quantum of time. Any disruption of the length of the quantum period or of the dose causes the embryo to develop into the default sex, which in alligators is female. Natural variation will exist within the population, both in terms of the required dose of male-determining factor and in the length of the quantum period necessary to induce male embryos. Thus in some individual embryos the conditions required to be a male are minimal, so 1-week pulses early in the quantum period allow these to develop into males, but the majority of embryos develop into females by default (figure 1). Starting off as 'male' during this period, however, is no guarantee that the embryo will remain male. Exposure to 30 °C on a background of 33 °C reduces both the dose and the quantum period, so that those individuals in the population requiring long exposure to the male-determining factor do not receive it, and so develop into females by default.

The nature of the factor that is active during the quantum period is not known. In *A. mississippiensis*, development and differentiation of the gonad is rapid at 33 °C relative to that at 30 °C. This may be a direct effect of temperature or an indirect effect of a male-determining factor that is inducing primary medullary organization. The size and relative development of the gonad in relation to the overall size of the embryo may also play some role in the process of secondary sex determination.

Although primary sex determination may occur during the quantum period, it is not the only phase of development concerned with sex determination. Embryos incubated at 33 °C can be converted into females even after a long period at the male-determining temperature (figure 1). In adult mammals and birds luteinizing hormone (LH) has an important role in maturation of both testes and ovaries: it is present during development of chick embryos (Woods 1987). If it is postulated that this single hormone is influencing gonadal differentiation during the development of two sexes in embryos of *A. mississippiensis*, then the second stage of sex determination may be associated with the presence and concentration of this hormone or its receptors during development. Incubation at different temperatures may affect hypothalamic control of LH secretion via luteinizing-hormone releasing hormone (LHRH), or may influence the presence of LH receptors on the two parts of the gonad, or both. The various non-sexual effects of temperature on development of crocodilians also suggests that incubation temperature is affecting the activity of the embryonic hypothalamus. The hypothalamus can detect temperature, pO_2, pCO_2, blood osmolality and pH in the adult and this ability presumably develops *in ovo*. Moreover, the hypothalamus not only controls LH secretion via LHRH but also growth (via growth-hormone releasing hormone), pigmentation (via melanocyte-stimulating hormone) and thermoregulation (via thyroid-hormone releasing hormone), which are all parameters influenced by the temperature of egg incubation in crocodilians. The implications of this hypothesis are dealt with by Deeming & Ferguson (1988).

Speculation on the cellular and molecular basis of TSD and its phylogenetic significance

The cellular basis of gonadal differentiation, particularly in reptiles, is poorly documented, yet our understanding of the mechanism of TSD, and sex determination in general, is reliant on such data. Several reports have shown the morphological and histological differences between the gonads of reptiles at hatching (Pieau 1971, 1972; Yntema 1979; Pieau & Dorizzi 1981; Ferguson & Joanen 1983; Webb & Smith 1984; Tokuanga 1985; Rimblot-Baly *et al.* 1986–1987), yet the present study is the first to describe the effects of two different temperatures on the gonadal development of any reptile. This highlights the problems associated with defining the mechanism of TSD in reptiles, yet despite the obvious lack of information several hypotheses have been advanced to explain the phenomenon.

One hypothesis is the presence of steroid hormones during development (Gutzke 1987). Exogenous testosterone and oestradiol applied to reptilian embryos that exhibit TSD can induce sex reversal (Gutzke & Bull 1986; Bull *et al.* 1988). Testosterone can be aromatized into oestrogen by embryos, inducing female development (Gutzke & Bull 1986). A theory of sex determination based on the relative proportions of steroid hormones has been developed to explain sex determination (Gutzke 1987). Similarly, the differing quantities of the enzyme aromatase during development at two temperatures has also been suggested to explain TSD (Bogart 1987).

The presence of H-Y antigen in the heterogametic sex in birds and mammals has led to suggestions that this may be important in TSD in turtles (Engel *et al.* 1981; Zaborski *et al.* 1982), although it is now considered to be less important (Gutzke 1987). Heat-shock proteins have been isolated in vertebrate tissues (Pelham 1985; Schlesinger 1986) and may have some role to play in the molecular basis of TSD. However, molecular analyses of different heat-shock proteins expressed during gonadal development in turtles have been disappointing (J. M. P. Joss, personal communication). Likewise, a hypothesis of sex determination based on differential gonadal growth as has been advanced for birds and mammals (Mittwoch 1971, 1973, 1983) clearly does not apply in alligators on the basis of the data presented in this paper. The idea that TSD induces differential mortality of eggs at different temperatures is contradicted by numerous studies (Bull 1980, 1983; Ferguson & Joanen 1983).

Recent work has isolated the gene for a mammalian testis-determining factor (TDF) on the Y chromosome and identified a homologue on the X chromosome (Page *et al.* 1987). These genes encode a DNA-binding protein or proteins regulating the expression of other genes. It may be that maleness in mammals and birds is associated with the presence of two doses of a single gene product, so that sex determination may be a dose-dependent phenomenon (Page *et al.* 1987). Using a cDNA probe for the human *TDF* gene, we have demonstrated hybridization to both male and female alligator DNA under conditions of high stringency, indicating the alligator *TDF* gene is very similar to that in man (figure 10).

Significantly, the temperatures that in reptiles cause the embryos to differentiate and develop fastest are also the ones that cause them to be male. It is easy to postulate that this is the optimal temperature for transcription, translation and enzyme activities, and that at this

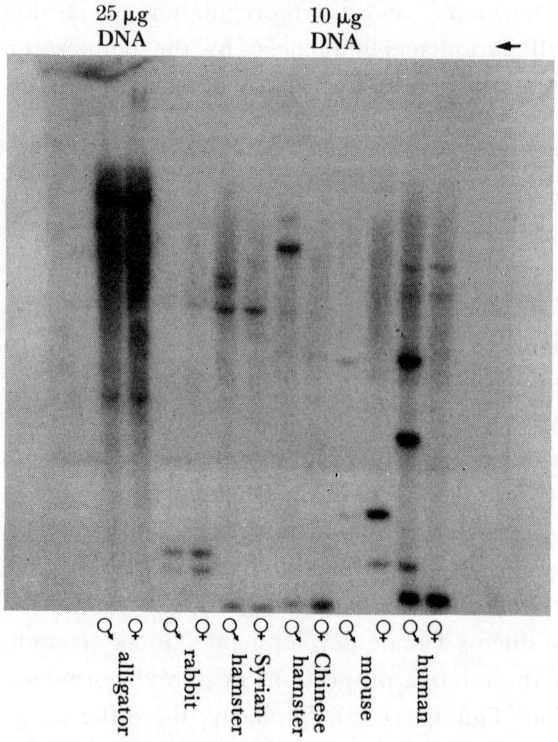

FIGURE 10. 'Ark blot' of DNA from male and female alligator, rabbit, Syrian hamster, Chinese hamster, mouse and man, hybridized with the PMF1 insert, 18 h at 55 °C, 1 M NaCl, 10% dextran sulphate and 1% SDS; washed 3 × 20 min, 65 °C, 0.2 × SSC (1 × SSC = 0.15 M sodium chloride + 0.015 M sodium citrate), 0.2% SDS and exposed for 3 days at −70 °C. Note that 25 µg of alligator DNA was loaded as opposed to 10 µg of mammalian DNA. Hybridization with the *TDF* probe to male and female alligator DNA is evident. This analysis was done by Dr. P. N. Goodfellow, Imperial Cancer Research Fund Laboratories, London.

temperature the dose of the sex-determinating gene product will be maximal, resulting in male differentiation. Temperatures above and below this maximum are sub-optimal and will result in a lower dose of the sex gene product, causing a higher percentage of females by default. Such a dose-dependent hypothesis would explain data from constant-temperature incubation, shift and pulse experiments from a variety of species, each with its own optimal temperature. Moreover, the DNA-binding protein encoded by the sex-determining gene may regulate gene expression at both gonadal and extra-gonadal sites. Thus it may regulate the release of various regulatory hormones from the hypothalamus. This would consolidate the male gender and ensure that animals that were incubated at the optimal temperature retained into adulthood optimal values for characteristics such as thermoregulation and growth. Additionally, factors that affect the processes of gene expression (e.g. pO_2, pCO_2, pH) would also affect the dose of the sex-gene product and so the sex of the animal, particularly at pivotal temperatures (i.e. those producing a 50% sex ratio due to variation in the dose and quantum period in a population of embryos). To the extent that external factors influence embryonic growth, and gonadal and sexual differentiation, reptiles are 'nature's sexual transgenics'.

The phylogenetic advantage of TSD in crocodilians may be in the association of sex with size. Embryos incubated in optimal conditions exhibit maximal pre- and postnatal growth, and more rapid differentiation (this paper; Joanen *et al.* 1987; Webb 1988). Large adult alligators are at a selective advantage if they are male: the largest males control the largest harems, produce sperm for longer periods and mate more frequently than smaller males (Ferguson 1985), thereby passing on more genes to the next generation. Incubation conditions vary, however, according to nest site and climate. As a consequence embryos with GSD would develop randomly into large or small males depending upon local incubation conditions. However, in reptiles sex is not determined until late in incubation, and those embryos that are exposed to an optimal incubation environment, and that therefore develop and differentiate fastest, become males. Thus TSD allows association of maleness with the most rapidly developing embryos and the greatest adult growth potential. This phylogenetic advantage is clearly within the confines of the theory of Charnov & Bull (1977). Indeed, association of size and sex appear to be universal in the animal kingdom. Most chelonians show sexual dimorphism and the females are the larger, a fact presumably associated with the limitations of the shell on egg production (Head *et al.* 1987). Whether the silverside fish (*Menidia menidia*) exhibits TSD or GSD is related to its north–south location and the length of its growing period (Conover & Heins 1986, 1987): high temperatures and short growing periods produce small males. In this species it is advantageous to be large and female, as potential fecundity is thereby increased. In certain coral-reef fish, social contact with smaller conspecifics induces large females to change sex into males (Ross *et al.* 1983; Ross 1987). High temperatures during larval development of amphibians also produce phenotypic males from genetic females (Gallien 1974; Houllion & Dournon 1978).

In birds and mammals, size and sex are also related. If reptilian TSD is a dose-dependent mechanism, then it is easy to envisage how genetic sex determination could have evolved. More uniform incubation conditions (brooding in birds, viviparity in mammals) would tend to equilibrate the dose in all embryos. The response to this could be inactivation of one set of homologous genes in females (X-chromosome inactivation) but persistence of two sets of sex-determining genes in the male (Y chromosome). This leads to male heterogamety in mammals and subsequent evolution of the sex gene on the Y chromosome to control testis differentiation more closely (Page *et al.* 1987). Another response, seen in birds, could be the loss of the sex-determining and other genes in the female (W chromosome) but the persistence of homologues in the male (Z chromosome), leading to female heterogamety. Birds and mammals may also have some non-sexual genes, e.g. secretion of hypothalamic releasing hormones, which are regulated by the DNA-binding protein transcribed by the sex-determining gene.

It is clear, therefore, that reptilian systems offer a unique opportunity to investigate the cellular and molecular mechanisms of sex determination and to manipulate them experimentally. Reptiles also hold the key to understanding the evolution of genetic sex-determining systems in birds and mammals.

We thank: Ted Joanen and Larry McNease of the Rockefeller Wildlife Refuge, Louisiana Department of Wildlife and Fisheries, U.S.A., for their invaluable assistance with obtaining eggs of *Alligator mississippiensis*; Grahame Webb, Jean Joss, Jeff Lang and Charlie Manolis for valuable discussion; and Marion Poulton, Janice Perks and Jill Garner for their invaluable assistance with the histological preparations. Charles Deeming is funded by the University of Manchester Research Support Fund.

References

Alho, C. J. R., Danni, T. M. S. & Padua, L. F. M. 1985 Temperature-dependent sex determination in *Podocnemis expansa* (Testinata: Pelomedusidae). *Biotropica* **17**, 75–78.

Baker, R. J., Mengden, G. A. & Bull, J. J. 1972 Karyotypic studies of thirty-eight species of north american snakes. *Copeia* **1972**, 257–265.

Bogart, M. H. 1987 Sex determination: a hypothesis based on steroid ratios. *J. theor. Biol.* **128**, 349–357.

Bull, J. J. 1980 Sex determination in reptiles. *Q. Rev. Biol.* **55**, 3–21.

Bull, J. J. 1983 *Evolution of sex determining mechanisms*. Menlo Park, California: Benjamin Cummings.

Bull, J. J. 1985 Sex ratio and nest temperatures in turtles: how well do laboratory experiments extrapolate to nature? *Ecology* **66**, 1115–1122.

Bull, J. J. 1987*a* Temperature-sensitive periods of sex determination in a lizard. Similarities with turtles and crocodilians. *J. exp. Zool.* **241**, 143–148.

Bull, J. J. 1987*b* Temperature dependent sex determination: reliability of sex diagnosis in hatchling lizards. *Can. J. Zool.* **65**, 1421–1424.

Bull, J. J., Gutzke, W. H. N. & Crews, D. 1988 Sex reversal by estradiol in three reptilian orders. *Gen. comp. Endocr.* (In the press.)

Bull, J. J., Legler, J. M. & Vogt, R. C. 1985 Non-temperature dependent sex determination in two suborders of turtles. *Copeia* **1985**, 784–786.

Bull, J. J. & Vogt, R. C. 1979 Temperature-dependent sex determination in turtles. *Science, Wash.* **206**, 1186–1188.

Bull, J. J. & Vogt, R. C. 1981 Temperature-sensitive periods of sex determination in emydid turtles. *J. exp. Zool.* **218**, 435–440.

Bull, J. J., Vogt, R. C. & McCoy, C. J. 1982 Sex determining temperatures in turtles: A geographic comparison. *Evolution* **36**, 326–332.

Burger, J. & Zappalorti, R. T. 1988 Effects of incubation temperature on sex determination in pine snakes: differential vulnerability of males and females. *Am. Nat.* (In the press.)

Charnier, M. 1966 Action de la température sur la sex-ratio chez l'embryon d'*Agama agama* (Agamidae, Lacertilien). *C. r. Séanc. Soc. Biol.* **160**, 620–622.

Charnov, E. L. & Bull, J. J. 1977 When is sex environmentally determined? *Nature, Lond.* **266**, 828–830.

Cohen, M. M. & Gans, C. 1970 The chromosomes of the order Crocodilia. *Cytogenetics* **9**, 81–105.

Conover, D. O. & Heins, S. W. 1986 Adaptive variation in environmental and genetic sex determination in a fish. *Nature, Lond.* **326**, 496–498.

Conover, D. O. & Heins, S. W. 1987 The environmental and genetic components of sex ratio in *Menidia menidia* (Pisces: Atherinidae). *Copeia* **1987**, 732–743.

Dalrymple, G. H., Hampp, J. C. & Wellins, J. 1985 Male biased sex ratio in a cold nest of a hawksbill sea turtle (*Eretmochelys imbricata*). *J. Herpetol.* **19**, 158–159.

Deeming, D. C. & Ferguson, M. W. J. 1988 The mechanism of temperature dependent sex determination in crocodilians: a hypothesis. *Am. Zool.* (In the press.)

Dimond, M. T. & Mohanty-Hejmadi, P. 1983 Incubation temperature and sex differentiation in a sea turtle. *Am. Zool.* **23**, 1017.

Engel, W., Klemme, B. & Schmid, M. 1981 H-Y antigen and sex determination in turtles. *Differentiation* **20**, 152–156.

Ewert, M. A. 1985 Embryology of turtles. In *Biology of the Reptilia*, vol. 14 (*Development. A.*) (ed. C. Gans, F. Billet & P. F. A. Maderson), pp. 75–267. New York: John Wiley.

Ferguson, M. W. J. 1985 The reproductive biology and embryology of crocodilians. In *Biology of the Reptilia*, vol. 14 (*Development. A.*) (ed. C. Gans, F. Billet & P. F. A. Maderson), pp. 329–491. New York: John Wiley.

Ferguson, M. W. J. & Joanen, T. 1982 Temperature of egg incubation determines sex in *Alligator mississippiensis*. *Nature, Lond.* **296**, 850–853.

Ferguson, M. W. J. & Joanen, T. 1983 Temperature dependent sex determination in *Alligator mississippiensis*. *J. Zool.* **200**, 143–177.

Forbes, T. R. 1940 Studies on the reproductive system of the alligator. IV. Observations on the development of the gonad, the adrenal cortex and the Mullerian duct. *Contr. Embryol.* **174**, 131–155.

Gallien, L. 1974 Intersexuality. In *Physiology of the Amphibia* (ed. B. Lofts), vol. II, pp. 523–549. New York: Academic Press.

Gutzke, W. H. N. 1987 Sex determination and sexual differentiation in reptiles. *Herp. J.* **1**, 122–125.

Gutzke, W. H. N. & Bull, J. J. 1986 Sex hormones reverse sex in turtles. *Gen. comp. Endocrinol.* **64**, 368–372.

Gutzke, W. H. N. & Paukstis, G. L. 1983 Influence of the hydric environment on sexual differentiation of turtles. *J. exp. Zool.* **226**, 467–470.

Gutzke, W. H. N. & Paukstis, G. L. 1984 A low threshold temperature for sexual differentiation in the painted turtle, *Chrysemys picta*. *Copeia* **1984**, 546–547.

Gutzke, W. H. N., Paukstis, G. L. & McDaniel, L. L. 1985 Skewed sex ratios for adult and hatchling bull snakes, *Pituophis melanoleucus*, in Nebraska. *Copeia* **1985**, 649–652.

Harrington, R. W. 1967 Environmentally controlled induction of primary male gonochrists from eggs of the self-fertilizing hermaphroditic fish, *Rivulus marmoratus* Poey. *Biol. Bull.* **132**, 174–199.

Harrington, R. W. 1968 Delimitation of the thermolabile phenocritical period of sex determination and differentiation in the ontogeny of the normally hermaphroditic fish, *Rivulus marmoratus* Poey. *Physiol. Zool.* **41**, 447–460.

Head, G., May, R. M. & Pendleton, L. 1987 Environmental determination of sex in reptiles. *Nature, Lond.* **329**, 198–200.

Houllion, C. & Dournon, C. 1978 Inversion du phénotype sexuel femelle sous l'action d'une température élevée chez l'amphibien urodèle *Pleurodeles waltlii* Michah. *C. r. hebd. Séanc. Acad. Sci., Paris* D **286**, 1475–1478.

Hou Ling 1985 Sex determination by temperature for incubation in *Chinemys reevesii*. *Acta Herp. sin.* **4**, 130.

Hutton, J. M. 1987 Incubation temperatures, sex ratios and sex determination in a population of Nile crocodiles (*Crocodylus niloticus*). *J. Zool.* **211**, 143–155.

Joanen, T., McNease, L. & Ferguson, M. W. J. 1987 The effects of egg incubation temperature on post-hatching growth of american alligators. In *Wildlife management: crocodiles and alligators* (ed. G. J. W. Webb, S. C. Manolis & P. J. Whitehead), pp. 533–537. Sydney: Surrey Beatty.

Lang, J. W. 1987 Crocodilian thermal selection. In *Wildlife management: crocodiles and alligators* (ed. G. J. W. Webb, S. C. Manolis & P. J. Whitehead), pp. 301–317. Sydney: Surrey Beatty.

Lang, J. W., Andrews, H. & Whitaker, R. 1988 Sex determination and sex status in *Crocodylus palustris*. *Am. zool.* (In the press.)

Limpus, C. J., Reed, P. C. & Miller, J. D. 1985 Temperature dependent sex determination in Queensland sea turtles: intraspecific variation in *Caretta caretta*. In *Biology of Australian frogs and reptiles* (ed. G. Grigg, R. Shine & H. Ehman), pp. 343–351. Sydney: Surrey Beatty.

McCoy, C. J., Vogt, R. C. & Censky, E. J. 1983 Temperature controlled sex determination in the sea turtle *Lepidochelys olivacea*. *J. Herpetol.* **17**, 404–406.

Miller, J. D. & Limpus, C. L. 1981 Incubation period and sexual differentiation in the green turtle *Chelonia mydas* L. In *Proceedings of the Melbourne Herpetological Symposium* (ed. C. B. Banks & A. H. Martin), pp. 66–73. Melbourne: The Geological Board of Victoria.

Mittwoch, U. 1971 Sex determination in birds and mammals. *Nature, Lond.* **231**, 432–434.

Mittwoch, U. 1973 *Genetics of sex determination*. New York: Academic Press.

Mittwoch, U. 1983 Heterogametic sex chromosomes and the development of the dominant gonad in vertebrates. *Am. Nat.* **122**, 159–180.

Morreale, S. J., Ruiz, G. J., Spotila, J. R. & Standora, E. A. 1982 Temperature dependent sex determination: current practices threaten conservation of sea turtles. *Science, Wash.* **216**, 1245–1247.

Mrosovsky, N., Dutton, P. H. & Whitmore, C. P. 1984 Sex ratios of two species of sea turtles nesting in Suriname. *Can. J. Zool.* **62**, 2227–2239.

Muth, A. & Bull, J. J. 1981 Sex determination in desert iguanas: does incubation temperature make a difference? *Copeia* **1981**, 869–870.

Osgood, D. 1980 Sex ratio and incubation temperature in a water snake. *Q. Rev. Biol.* **55**, 21.

Packard, G. C., Packard, M. J. & Boardman, T. J. 1984 Effects of the hydric environment on metabolism of embryonic snapping turtles do not result from altered patterns of sexual differentiation. *Copeia* **1984**, 547–550.

Packard, G. C., Packard, M. J., Miller, K. & Boardman, T. J. 1987 Influence of moisture, temperature and substrate on snapping turtle eggs and embryos. *Ecology* **68**, 983–993.

Page, D. C., Mosher, R., Simpson, E. M., Mardon, G., Pollack, J., McGillivray, B., de la Chapelle, A. & Brown, L. G. 1987 The sex determining region of the human Y chromosome encodes a finger protein. *Cell* **51**, 1091–1104.

Paukstis, G. L., Gutzke, W. H. N. & Packard, G. C. 1984 Effects of substrate water potential and fluctuating temperatures on sex ratios of hatchling painted turtles (*Chrysemys picta*). *Can. J. Zool.* **62**, 1491–1494.

Pelham, H. 1985 Activation of heat-shock proteins in eukaryotes. *Trends Genet.*, 31–34.

Pieau, C. 1971 Sur la proportion sexuelle chez les embryons de deux Chéloniens (*Testudo graeca* L. et *Emys orbicularis* L.) issus d'oeufs incubés artificiellement. *C. r. hebd. Séanc. Acad. Sci., Paris* D **272**, 3071–3074.

Pieau, C. 1972 Effets de la température sur le développement des glandes génitales chez les embryons de deux Chéloniens, *Emys orbicularis* L. et *Testudo graeca* L. *C. r. hebd. Séanc. Acad. Sci., Paris* D **274**, 719–722.

Pieau, C. 1973 Variation de l'activité enzymatique Δ5-3 β-hydroxystéroide déshydrogénasique dans les glandes génitales d'embryons d'*Emys orbicularis* L. (Chélonien) en fonction de la température d'incubation. *C. r. hebd. Séanc. Acad. Sci., Paris* D **276**, 197–200.

Pieau, C. 1974 Différentiation du sexe en fonction de la température chez les embryons d'*Emys orbicularis* L. (Chelonien); Effets des hormones sexuelles. *Annls Embryol. Morphol.* **7**, 365–394.

Pieau, C. 1982 Modalities of the action on sexual differentiation in field-developing embryos of the european pond turtle *Emys orbicularis*. *J. exp. Zool.* **220**, 353–360.

Pieau, C. & Dorizzi, M. 1981 Determination of temperature sensitive stages for sexual differentiation of the gonads in embryos of the turtle *Emys orbicularis*. *J. Morphol.* **170**, 373–382.

Pieau, C., Mignot, T., Dorizzi, M. & Guichard, A. 1982 Gonadal steroid levels in the turtle *Emys orbicularis* L.: a preliminary study in embryos, hatchlings and young as a function of the incubation temperature of eggs. *Gen. comp. Endocrinol.* **47**, 393–398.

Raynaud, A. & Pieau, C. 1972 Effets de diverse températures d'incubation sur le développement somatique et sexuel des embryons de lizard vert (*Lacerta viridis* Laur.). *C. r. hebd. Séanc. Acad. Sci., Paris* D **275**, 2259–2262.

Rimblot, F., Fretey, J., Mrosovsky, N., Lescure, J. & Pieau, C. 1985 Sexual differentiation as a function of the incubation temperature of eggs in the sea turtle *Dermochelys coriacea* (Vandelli, 1761). *Amphibia–Reptilia* **6**, 83–92.

Rimblot-Baly, F., Lescure, J., Fretey, J. & Pieau, C. 1986–1987 Temperature sensitivity of sexual differentiation in the leatherback *Dermochelys coriacea* (Vandelli, 1761). Data from artificial incubation applied to the study of sex ratio in nature. *Annls Sci. natur. Zool., Paris* **8**, 277–290.

Ross, R. M. 1987 Sex-change linked growth acceleration in a coral-reef fish, *Thalassoma duperrey*. *J. exp. Zool.* **244**, 455–461.

Ross, R. M., Losey, G. S. & Diamond, M. 1983 Sex change in a coral reef fish: dependence of stimulation and inhibition on relative size. *Science, Wash.* **221**, 574–575.

Schlesinger, M. J. 1986 Heat shock proteins: The search for functions. *J. Cell Biol.* **103**, 321–325.

Schwarzkopf, L. & Brooks, R. J. 1985 Sex determination in northern painted turtles: effects of incubation at constant and fluctuating temperatures. *Can. J. Zool.* **63**, 2543–2547.

Schwarzkopf, L. & Brooks, R. J. 1987 Nest site selection and offspring ratio in painted turtles, *Chrysemys picta*. *Copeia* **1987**, 53–61.

Shine, R. & Bull, J. J. 1977 Skewed sex ratios in snakes. *Copeia* **1977**, 228–234.

Smith, A. M. A. 1987 The sex and survivorship of embryos and hatchlings of the Australian freshwater crocodile *Crocodylus johnstoni*. Ph.D. thesis, Australian National University, Canberra.

Spotila, J. R., Standora, E. A., Morreale, S. J. & Ruiz, G. J. 1987 Temperature dependent sex determination in the green turtle (*Chelonia mydas*): effects on the sex ratio on a natural beach. *Herpetologica* **43**, 74–81.

Standora, E. A. & Spotila, J. R. 1985 Temperature dependent sex determination in sea turtles. *Copeia* **1985**, 711–722.

Stoneburner, D. L. & Richardson, J. I. Observations on the role of temperature in loggerhead turtle nest site selection. *Copeia* **1981**, 238–241.

Thompson, M. B. 1983 The physiology and ecology of the eggs of the Pleurodiran tortoise *Emydura macquarii* (Gray), 1831. Ph.D. dissertation, University of Adelaide, Australia.

Thompson, M. B. 1988 Influence of incubation temperature and water potential on sex determination in *Emydura macquarii* (Testudines: Pleurodira). *Herpetologia* **44**, 86–90.

Tokunaga, S. 1985 Temperature dependent sex determination in *Gekko japonicus* (Gekkonidae, Reptilia). *Dev. Growth Differ.* **27**, 117–120.

Vinegar, A. 1973 The effects of temperature on the growth and development of embryos of the indian python, *Python molurus* (Reptila: Serpentes: Boidae). *Copeia* **1973**, 171–173.

Vogt, R. C. & Bull, J. J. 1982 Genetic sex determination in the spiny softshell *Trionyx spiniferus* (Testudines: Trionychidae). *Copeia* **1982**, 699–700.
Vogt, R. C. & Bull, J. J. 1984 Ecology of hatchling sex ratio in map turtles. *Ecology* **65**, 582–587.
Vogt, R. C., Bull, J. J., McCoy, C. J. & Houseal, T. W. 1982 Incubation temperature influences sex determination in kinosternid turtles. *Copeia* **1982**, 480–482.
Warner, E. 1980 Temperature-dependent sex determination in a gekko lizard. *Q. Rev. Biol.* **55**, 21.
Webb, G. J. W. 1988 Effects of incubation temperature on crocodiles: insights into the evolution of reptilian oviparity. *Am. Zool.* (In the press.)
Webb, G. J. W., Beal, A. M., Manolis, S. C. & Dempsey, K. E. 1987 The effects of incubation temperatures on sex determination and embryonic development rate in *Crocodylus johnstoni* and *C. porosus*. In *Wildlife management: crocodiles and alligators* (ed. G. J. W. Webb, S. C. Manolis & P. J. Whitehead), pp. 507–531. Sydney: Surrey Beatty.
Webb, G. J. W., Buckworth, R. & Manolis, S. C. 1983 *Crocodylus johnstoni* in the McKinlay River, N. T. VI. Nesting Biology. *Aust. Wildl. Res.* **10**, 607–637.
Webb, G. J. W., Choquenot, D. & Whitehead, P. J. 1986 Nests, eggs and embryonic development of *Carettochelys insculpta* (Chelonia: Carettochelidae) from Northern Australia. *J. Zool.* B **1**, 521–550.
Webb, G. J. W. & Smith, A. M. A. 1984 Sex ratio and survivorship in a population of the Australian freshwater crocodile *Crocodylus johnstoni*. In *The structure, development and evolution of reptiles* (ed. M. W. J. Ferguson), pp. 319–355. London: Academic Press.
Wilhoft, D. C., Hotaling, E. & Franks, P. 1983 Effects of temperature on sex determination in embryos of the snapping turtle, *Chelydra serpentina*. *J. Herpetol.* **17**, 38–42.
Witschi, E. 1929 Studies on sex differentiation and sex determination in amphibians. II. Sex reversal in female tadpoles of *Rana sylvatica* following application of high temperature. *J. exp. Zool.* **52**, 267–291.
Wood, F. E. & Wood, J. R. 1982 Sex ratios in captive reared green turtles *Chelonia mydas*. *Copeia* **1982**, 482–485.
Woods, J. E. 1987 Maturation of the hypothalamic-adenohypophyseal-gonadal (HAG) axes in the chick embryo. *J. exp. Zool.* (suppl.) **1**, 265–271.
Yntema, C. L. 1968 A series of stages in the embryonic development of *Chelydra serpentina*. *J. Morph.* **125**, 219–252.
Yntema, C. L. 1976 Effects of incubation temperatures on sexual differentiation in the turtle *Chelydra serpentina*. *J. Morph.* **150**, 453–460.
Yntema, C. L. 1979 Temperature levels and periods of sex determination during incubation of eggs of *Chelydra serpentina*. *J. Morph.* **159**, 17–28.
Yntema, C. L. 1981 Characteristics of gonads and oviducts in hatchling and young of *Chelydra serpentina* resulting from three incubation temperatures. *J. Morph.* **167**, 297–304.
Yntema, C. L. & Mrosovsky, N. 1980 Sexual differentiation in hatchling loggerheads (*Caretta caretta*) incubated at different controlled temperatures. *Herpetologica* **36**, 33–36.
Yntema, C. L. & Mrosovsky, N. 1982 Critical periods and pivotal temperatures for sexual differentiation in loggerhead sea turtles. *Can. J. Zool.* **60**, 1012–1014.
Zaborski, P., Dorizzi, M. & Pieau, C. 1982 H-Y antigen expression in temperature sex-reversed turtles (*Emys orbicularis*). *Differentiation* **22**, 73–78.

Discussion

URSULA MITTWOCH (*University College London, U.K.*). Could Professor Ferguson please explain the sex dosage hypothesis, which he mentioned, in a little more detail? If male and female reptiles with environmentally controlled sex determination have the same genotype, gene dosage must likewise be the same for both sexes. The different effects of temperature on the development of alligators seem to be due to differences in the developmental rate, a fast rate leading to male sex differentiation, whereas a slower rate of development results in females.

M. W. J. FERGUSON. It is true that male and female alligator embryos develop at different rates as a consequence of being incubated at 33 °C for males and 30 °C for females. However, this difference in developmental rate primarily reflects differentiation rather than growth. Moreover, our hypothesis is not one of sex-gene dosage but rather the dosage of a product transcribed from a sex gene. We would postulate that this product may be a regulatory element such as that described recently for TDF namely a zinc finger protein. Our hypothesis is that at the male-determining temperature of 33 °C, gene transcription, translation and enzyme activity are optimal. At higher or lower temperatures, transcription, translation and enzyme activity are less than optimal but compatible with embryonic survival. Males result when there is a high dosage of the gene product above a certain threshold. Contrarywise, females develop when the gene product falls below a certain threshold. This hypothesis is similar to one put forward by Page concerning sex determination in mammals whereby males would get two doses of a sex-gene product, one from the X-chromosome and the other from the Y, whereas females would only get one dose of the sex-gene product, namely from one X-chromosome, the other gene being inactivated as part of the X inactivation mechanism.

U. WOLF (*Institute of Human Genetics, University of Freiburg, F.R.G.*). What about experimental sex inversion by steroid hormones in reptiles?

M. W. J. FERGUSON. As far as I am aware, only two experiments on reversal of temperature-dependent sex determination in reptiles by steroid hormones have been done. The first was by Bull and is cited in our paper. However, it must be emphasized that this study used a small number of eggs and had a very large mortality. Although sex reversal was demonstrated, the sex of all the dead embryos would need to be known to come to a firm conclusion. Second, there is an as yet unpublished study by Dr Dorizzi which she refers to in her comment on this paper. It would appear that steroids are capable of sex reversal in reptiles with temperature-dependent sex determination. However, I believe that this tells you little about the primary sex-determining mechanism.

MIREILLE DORIZZI (*Institut Jacques Monod, Paris, France*). I just want to add some information concerning the involvement of oestrogens on the differentiation of gonads – which are sensitive to temperature – in the turtle *Emys orbicularis*. If, during the thermosensitive period, oestrogens are injected into eggs incubated at 25 °C, a temperature yielding 100 % phenotypic males, gonads differentiate into ovaries instead of testes. If antioestrogens or aromatase inhibitors are injected into eggs incubated at 30 °C, a temperature leading to 100 % phenotypic females, testicular tubes differentiate. Therefore oestrogens inhibit the development of sex cords. When the production or the action of these steroids is prevented, testicular cords or tubes may differentiate.

P. ZABORSKI (*CNRS, Ivry-sur-Seine, France*). Would Professor Ferguson please add a comment concerning the dosage effect at the threshold (pivotal) temperature that produces both males and females with a sex ratio of 1:1.

M. W. J. FERGUSON. It has always been a puzzle as to how under temperature-dependent sex determination mechanisms, one can get a 50:50 sex ratio at one temperature. We hypothesize that the population of embryos exhibits variation in the threshold levels of the sex-gene product that they require to specify maleness. We also hypothesize that the population of embryos varies in the length of the quantum period of time that they need to be exposed to this factor to ensure male sexual determination. Thus at the incubation temperature that produces a 50:50 sex ratio, we would hypothesize that those embryos that become male have a lower threshold for the sex-gene product or require exposure to this product for a shorter period of time, or both, than do the embryos that develop into females. In this way, variation in the population of embryos can explain the 50:50 sex ratio. We are certain that this 50:50 sex ratio cannot be explained by minor fluctuations in incubator temperatures. All of the experiments we describe were done in incubators with 16 temperature recording probes (accurate to 0.001 °C) at different locations throughout the incubator. We are confident that there are no gradient effects of temperature influencing any of our data.

H. Sharma (71 *Barrack Road, Hounslow, U.K.*). Can Professor Ferguson set up a temperature gradient across the egg?

In the natural environment temperatures fluctuate by night and day. Has Professor Ferguson done experiments of changing temperatures at shorter intervals?

M. W. J. Ferguson. First, it is unknown how long it takes the egg contents to equilibrate to the temperature of the incubator and how much of a buffering capacity exists within the egg. It is also unknown to what extent the shell and egg-shell membranes buffer the embryo from fluctuations in ambient temperature. Experiments involving the placing of microthermocouples within different locations of the alligator egg, followed by different external thermal régimes, would be required to address such questions. Second, nest temperatures do fluctuate between day and night and also at different times during the season. However, these effects are not of critical importance for our hypothesis of sex determination. We believe that embryos require exposure to a threshold dose of a sex-gene product during a quantum time of embryonic development. If they exceed this threshold, the embryos become male; conversely, if they fall below it, they become female. We also hypothesize that transcription, translation and enzyme activity, all of which affect this sex-gene product, are different at different incubation temperatures. Therefore fluctuating temperatures will produce males when gene transcription, translation and enzyme activity are optimal and females at other times when they are not. Clearly the relative contributions of optimal to suboptimal during the fluctuating critical period will determine whether the embryos become male or female. This mechanism allows the embryo to integrate temperature changes over a period of developmental time. These fluctuating temperatures may also be important in later sexual differentiation, particularly in the release of various hormones and the expression of receptors for such hormones on the gonadal tissues. It is conceivable that the optimal temperature for hormone release and the optimal temperature for receptor expression may not be the same, in which case fluctuating temperatures could be advantageous. However, in the absence of data this is wild speculation.

Phil. Trans. R. Soc. Lond. B **322**, 41–53 (1988) [41]
Printed in Great Britain

Sex determination in marsupials: evidence for a marsupial–eutherian dichotomy

BY M. B. RENFREE AND R. V. SHORT, F.R.S.

Departments of Anatomy and Physiology, Monash University, Melbourne 3168, *Victoria, Australia*

[Plate 1]

In this paper, we review briefly the current state of knowledge about sexual differentiation in eutherian mammals, and then describe the situation in detail in two marsupial species: the North American opossum and the tammar wallaby.

The conventional explanation for the genesis of all male somatic sexual dimorphisms in mammals is that they are a consequence of the systemic action of testicular hormones. In the absence of testes, the embryo will develop a female phenotype.

We present evidence for the tammar wallaby that calls into question the universal applicability of this hormonal theory of mammalian sexual differentiation. We have shown that extensive somatic sexual dimorphisms precede by many days the first morphological evidence of testicular formation, which does not occur until around the third day of pouch life. Male foetuses, and pouch young on the day of birth, already have a well-developed gubernaculum and processus vaginalis, paired scrotal anlagen, and a complete absence of mammary anlagen, whereas female foetuses and newborn pouch young have a poorly developed gubernaculum and processus vaginalis, no scrotal anlagen, and well-developed mammary anlagen. Because it seems unlikely that the male gonad could begin hormone secretion until after the Sertoli and Leydig cells are developed, our results strongly suggest that some sexually dimorphic somatic characteristics develop autonomously, depending on their genotype rather than the hormonal environment to which they are exposed.

We have been able to confirm the hormonal independence of the scrotum, pouch and mammary gland by administering testosterone propionate daily by mouth to female pouch young from the day of birth; although the Wolffian duct was hyperstimulated, there was no sign of scrotal development, or pouch or mammary inhibition. When male pouch young were treated with oestradiol benzoate in a similar fashion, there was hyperstimulation of the Müllerian duct and inhibition of testicular migration and development, but no sign of scrotal inhibition or pouch or mammary development. Our results in the tammar wallaby are consistent with the earlier studies on the opossum, whose significance was not appreciated at the time.

Further evidence in support of this hormonal independence comes from earlier studies of spontaneously occurring intersexes in several species of marsupial, including the opossum and the tammar wallaby. An XXY individual had intra-abdominal testes and complete masculinization of the male reproductive tract internally, but externally there was a pouch and mammary glands and no scrotum. A similar picture was found in two XY individuals. On the other hand, an XO individual had hypoplastic ovaries, normal development of the female reproductive tract internally, and an empty scrotum. Thus the scrotum can develop in the absence of a testis, whereas the pouch and mammary glands can develop in the presence of one.

These results suggest a fundamental dichotomy between marsupials and eutherians in their sex-determining mechanisms. Although both subclasses probably require a Y-linked gene or genes for testis determination, marsupials appear to use other X-linked genes to control the development of structures such as the scrotum, pouch and mammary glands. In eutherians, on the other hand, scrotal and mammary development appears to be entirely under hormonal control. The lack of any genetic interchange between the X and the Y during meiosis in marsupials has presumably resulted in a much greater degree of genetic isolation of one sex chromosome from the other than is the case in eutherians, and the small size of the marsupial Y suggests that marsupials may have progressed further than eutherians in capture of genetic material by the X from the ancestral Y. Marsupials seem destined to play a vital role in the years to come in the mapping of sex-linked genes and determining their modes of action. Clearly they have much to tell us about the evolution of sex-determining mechanisms in all mammals.

Introduction

The conventional view of mammalian sexual differentiation has been that a gene or genes on the Y chromosome causes the indifferent gonad to develop into a testis, which then secretes two classes of hormone which are responsible respectively for masculinizing the Wolffian duct derivatives and the external genitalia to form the male reproductive tract, and bringing about atrophy of the Müllerian duct derivatives. In the absence of a Y chromosome, the indifferent gonad develops into an ovary which is endocrinologically quiescent to begin with, so that the Wolffian duct derivatives atrophy, the male external genitalia fail to develop, and the Müllerian ducts persist to form the female reproductive tract. All somatic sexual dimorphisms have therefore been assumed to be a consequence of gonadal hormone action (Ohno 1967; Jost *et al.* 1973).

Recent research has begun to fill in the fine details of this general conceptual framework. Page *et al.* (1987) have succeeded in cloning a 230 kilobase segment of the human Y chromosome which contains some or all of the testis-determining gene, and it now seems certain that the H-Y antigen is not involved in the process of testis determination (Simpson *et al.* 1987). The first morphological evidence of transformation of the indifferent gonad into a testis is the appearance of primordial Sertoli cells, which later aggregate to form the seminiferous cords (Magre 1985). These Sertoli cells appear to develop autonomously, under the influence of a Y-linked testis-determining gene (Burgoyne *et al.* 1988). They subsequently produce Müllerian-inhibiting substance (MIS), elsewhere referred to as anti-Müllerian hormone (AMH), a 144 kDa glycoprotein dimer of 575 amino acids, which has recently been isolated and sequenced with its regulatory gene (Cate *et al.* 1986). We have identified MIS activity by bioassay in the testes of newborn tammar wallabies from the time of first testicular formation, and have shown that it is undetectable in ovaries at comparable stages of development (Hutson *et al.* 1988). In addition to causing regression of the Müllerian ducts, MIS appears to inhibit the mitotic division of female but not of male primordial germ cells, and in culture it can bring about a transformation of cells of the indifferent female gonadal blastema into Sertoli cells; MIS is therefore probably responsible for the ovarian arrest and subsequent testicular transformation in the freemartin (Vigier *et al.* 1987). There is also growing evidence to suggest that MIS may play a role in the transabdominal migration of the testes to the internal inguinal ring, although subsequent descent into the scrotum appears to be androgen dependent (Hutson & Donahoe 1986; Hutson *et al.* 1988).

The female (XX) germ cells of eutherian mammals also appear to be under some degree of autonomous genetic control because they are incapable of producing normal spermatozoa even when in a testis (Short 1972; Burgoyne 1987). However, male germ cells can undergo oogenesis in an ovarian environment, and this subject will be discussed at length elsewhere in this symposium.

The Virginia opossum, *Didelphis virginiana*

A great deal of the early work on mammalian sexual differentiation was done in this species by workers in North America during the 1930s and 1940s (see review by Renfree *et al.* 1987; Short *et al.* 1988). These pioneering investigators established that in this marsupial, where the young weigh a mere 125 mg at birth following a 13-day gestation, the whole of sexual differentiation takes place after birth, during pouch life. First, the indifferent gonad develops into a testis on the third to fourth day; the ovary does not become recognizable as such until about the seventh day. It is claimed that nipples and mammary anlagen are present in both sexes at birth, but they subsequently regress in the male. The scrotum first becomes apparent in males on about day 10, and is said to form by fusion of the caudal ends of the developing pouch folds. The rest of the pouch then regresses in males, and persists in females, so it has been suggested that the pouch and scrotum share a partial homology.

The Wolffian duct starts to differentiate into the male reproductive tract from day 20 onwards, whereas in females it starts to regress at this time. The Müllerian duct begins to involute in males at around day 20 also, whereas in females it differentiates into the female reproductive tract. The testes begin their trans-abdominal migration soon after day 14 and enter the inguinal canal at about day 30, with testicular descent into the scrotum being complete by about day 80. Prostatic buds start to develop from the urogenital sinus of males at around day 16, coincident with the time at which the phallus of the male starts to enlarge more than that of the female, to form the characteristic bifid glans penis of the opossum.

There is nothing in the above description that is in any way out of keeping with the sequence of events that would be encountered in a eutherian mammal except, of course, the development of the pouch. However, two incidental observations whose significance was not appreciated by these early investigators should have alerted us to a major difference from the eutherian plan.

In 1925, Carl Hartman described an intersex opossum that had essentially a male external phenotype, except that the scrotum was empty, and there were some pouch rudiments still visible; nipples and mammary glands were absent (Hartman & League 1925). Internally, the animal had a normal, although infantile, female reproductive tract and no Wolffian duct derivatives. The gonads appeared to be hypoplastic ovaries containing numerous small cystic follicles, such as are sometimes found in normal females, but there were no oocytes present. Apart from the presence of the empty scrotum, the absence of mammary glands and the rudimentary pouch, the only other indications of masculinization were a normal male phallus, and the large size of the animal (1.75 kg) with a typical male-type head.

In retrospect, the remarkable feature of this animal is that internally it had a normal female phenotype, whereas externally it was male. The absence of Wolffian duct derivatives, and the persistence of Müllerian ducts, is proof that there could not have been a functional testis present during the first month of life when the internal and external genitalia was being formed. So how could the scrotum develop, and the pouch and mammary glands undergo atrophy in the absence of androgen? The answer to that question will gradually become apparent from the discussion that follows. The one unexplained feature is the presence of a normal penis; perhaps the sterile ovaries eventually produced sufficient androgen to masculinize the phallus later in life.

The second observation comes from the results of the work of R. K. Burns on androgen and oestrogen administration to newborn opossum pouch young, although its significance completely escaped him at the time (Burns 1961). In one of his illustrations (see figure 1), he

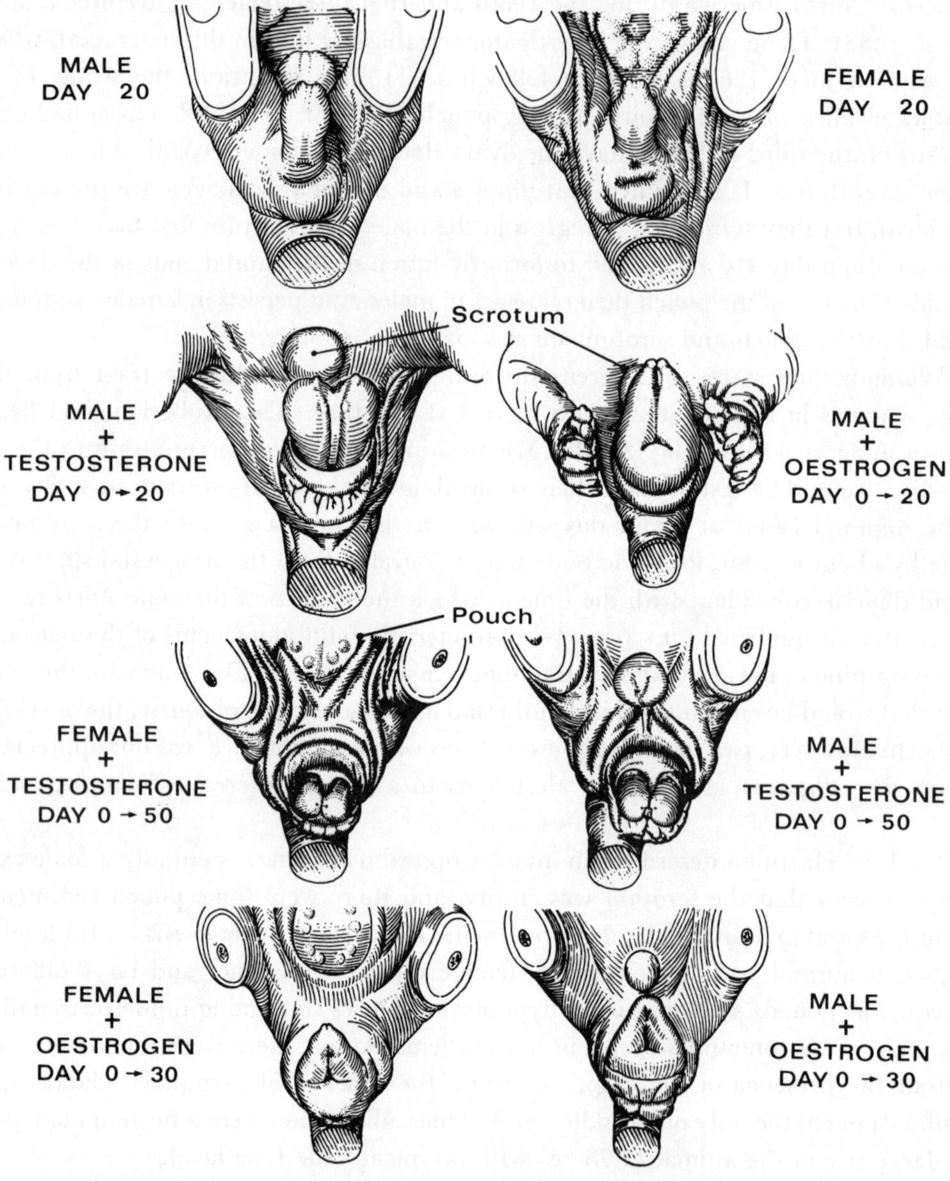

FIGURE 1. The effects of sex hormones on the external genitalia of young opossums (*Didelphis virginiana*). In the normal day-20 pouch young the phallus is slightly larger in the male, but otherwise similar. Sex is readily distinguished at this age by the scrotal sac in males and the presence of pouch folds and mammary rudiments in the female. When young are given testosterone propionate from birth to 20 or 50 days the phallus enlarges to form the penis in both males and females, but in the female the pouch and mammary anlagen appear unchanged and no scrotum develops. When young are given oestradiol dipropionate from birth to 20 or 30 days, the phallus assumes the typical female form regardless of sex. However, the scrotum is unchanged in the males. From Burns (1961).

clearly shows how testosterone propionate treatment of a newborn female from the day of birth for 50 days stimulated the development of a male phallus, but was completely without effect on the normal development of the pouch and mammary glands, and failed to induce scrotal development. Similarly, oestradiol dipropionate given for the first 30 days of life to a normal male suppressed penile development but failed to inhibit scrotal development, or induce pouch or mammary development. The conclusion should have been obvious: the mammary gland, pouch and scrotum develop independently of the steroidal environment. But Burns came to the conclusion that 'the hormones [androgen and oestrogen] produce genitalia of typical male or female form, regardless of the sex of the subject'. If he included scrotum, pouch and mammary gland in his definition of genitalia, then he was wrong.

Burns made another important discovery that has been widely acknowledged as an odd exception to the general rule that steroid hormones are incapable of sex-reversing the development of the mammalian (i.e. eutherian) gonad, but his observations have never been adequately explained, nor fully exploited. He showed that if newborn male opossums are treated with a relatively 'low' dose (0.2–0.3 μg d^{-1}) of oestradiol dipropionate from the day of birth for about 30 days, this will cause regression of the developing seminiferous tubules, suppression of interstitial tissue differentiation, and persistence of the germinal epithelium which subsequently gives rise to a proliferation of secondary sex cords. This new cortical zone contains a variable number of germ cells which have all the morphological characteristics of oocytes in meiotic prophase; they are often surrounded by cells that look like the early follicular cells of primordial follicles.

On the face of it, Burns had succeeded in producing almost complete gonadal sex reversal in a mammal with a steroid hormone, albeit at a grossly pharmacological dose. Unfortunately, the animals, 46 in all, were killed at the end of hormone treatment, so we do not know what would have happened to the gonads if the animals had been allowed to reach puberty. Could germ cells which were genetically XY really be transformed into functional oocytes that were capable of inducing normal follicular development up to the point of ovulation? These experiments, if repeated and extended, could shed some fascinating new light on the plasticity of germ-cell development in mammals.

In an attempt to repeat the work of Burns, Fadem & Tesoriero (1986) studied a related species, the pouchless gray opossum *Monodelphis domestica*, native to South America. They treated newborn pouch young of both sexes (average mass 100 mg) with testosterone propionate (20 μg) or oestradiol benzoate (1 μg) once or twice during the first week of life, and killed the animals at 22 weeks of age. They noted that it was only the oestradiol treatment of males that produced any significant effects, and then only if the animals were treated twice, on day 1 and day 3. They found that testicular development was inhibited by this relatively enormous dose of hormone (equivalent to 10 mg $kg^{-1} \times 2$), so that at autopsy the gonads were vestigial, and no longer recognizable morphologically as either male- or female-like. Not surprisingly, no germ cells were visible. No comments were made about the presence or absence of mammary glands in any of the animals, but one highly significant finding was that empty scrotal sacs were found in all the oestrogenized males, even though there was no phallic development, and the internal genitalia were entirely female in appearance. As in Burns' *Didelphis* study, this confirms that the development of the scrotum appears to be androgen-independent in this species.

Very recently, E. S. Robinson (personal communication) has been able to examine an intersex *Monodelphis* that had a 17,XO karyotype ($2n = 18$). This animal, which was stunted in appearance, had small, undifferentiated gonads with no detectable germ cells, a completely normal but hypoplastic female reproductive tract internally, and no phallic development, and yet it had a well-developed scrotum. It is not yet known whether any mammary glands were present. Once again, this animal provides beautiful confirmation of the androgen-independence of the scrotum, and suggests that a Y chromosome is not necessary for scrotal development.

Sex determination and differentiation in the tammar wallaby, *Macropus eugenii*

We have recently summarized the ontogeny of sexual differentiation in this species (Renfree *et al.* 1987). Our interest in sex determination and differentiation in the tammar was aroused through the incidental observation by one of us (M.B.R.) that foetuses could apparently be sexed in late gestation by the presence or absence of scrotal anlagen, at a time when the gonads were still at the indifferent stage of development. Alcorn (1975) had also observed scrotal and mammary anlagen in male and female tammars respectively immediately before and after birth, but did not comment on the significance of this. Our curiosity aroused, we decided to undertake a systematic investigation of sexual differentiation in this species.

We and our co-workers Dr Shaw and Dr O began by collecting 15 pouch young on the day of birth (mass at birth approximately 450 mg), recording their head length, body mass, and making a careful note of whether or not scrotal anlagen could be seen with the naked eye. Tissue was taken for karyotyping to determine genetic sex, and the hindquarters were fixed in formalin, embedded and serially sectioned (O *et al.* 1988). Our suspicions were fully confirmed. As Alcorn (1975) had previously claimed, it is possible to be 100% correct in assigning sex by visual inspection; scrotal bulges, lying on either side of the midline just anterior to the genital tubercle, were only present in males (figure 2). We could detect no histological or volumetric difference in gonadal structure or size between males and females; the first evidence of testicular differentiation does not become apparent microscopically until the third day of pouch life, although scanning electron microscopy suggests that there may be a difference in shape of the male and female gonads before this (O *et al.* 1988; Renfree *et al.* 1987).

The serial sections revealed clear sex differences not only in the presence or absence of scrotal anlagen but also in the size and shape of the gubernaculum and processus vaginalis (well developed in males, poorly developed in females) (see figure 3, plate 1), and in the presence or absence of mammary and pouch anlagen. Dr Shaw and Dr O quantified the degree of development of the Wolffian and Müllerian ducts, and found that they were identical in males and females, providing no evidence for the onset of any gonadal hormone secretion which, it could be argued, might precede morphological differentiation of the gonads.

To rule out the possibility that early gonadal hormone secretion might nevertheless be the cause of these sexual dimorphisms in scrotum, gubernaculum, processus vaginalis, pouch and mammary gland anlagen, we collected 19 embryos during the last 6 days of pregnancy; all the above-mentioned structures were sexually dimorphic as early as 5 days pre-partum.

We then did a series of hormone administration experiments, giving oestradiol benzoate orally at a dosage rate of 2 mg kg^{-1} d^{-1} (1 μg per pouch young per day) to newborn males for 25 days starting on the day of birth, and testosterone propionate to newborn females at a dosage rate of 40 mg kg^{-1} d^{-1} (20 μg per pouch young per day) using an identical protocol

FIGURE 3. Scanning electron micrograph of the internal genitalia of a male tammar pouch young aged 11 days *post partum*. Note the rounded-up testis, and prominent gubernaculum entering the processus vaginalis at the internal inguinal ring. The mesonephros is still large at this age, and the mesonephric duct (Wolffian duct) within the urogenital cord runs into the urogenital sinus near the base of the bladder (here shown cut off at the base for clarity).

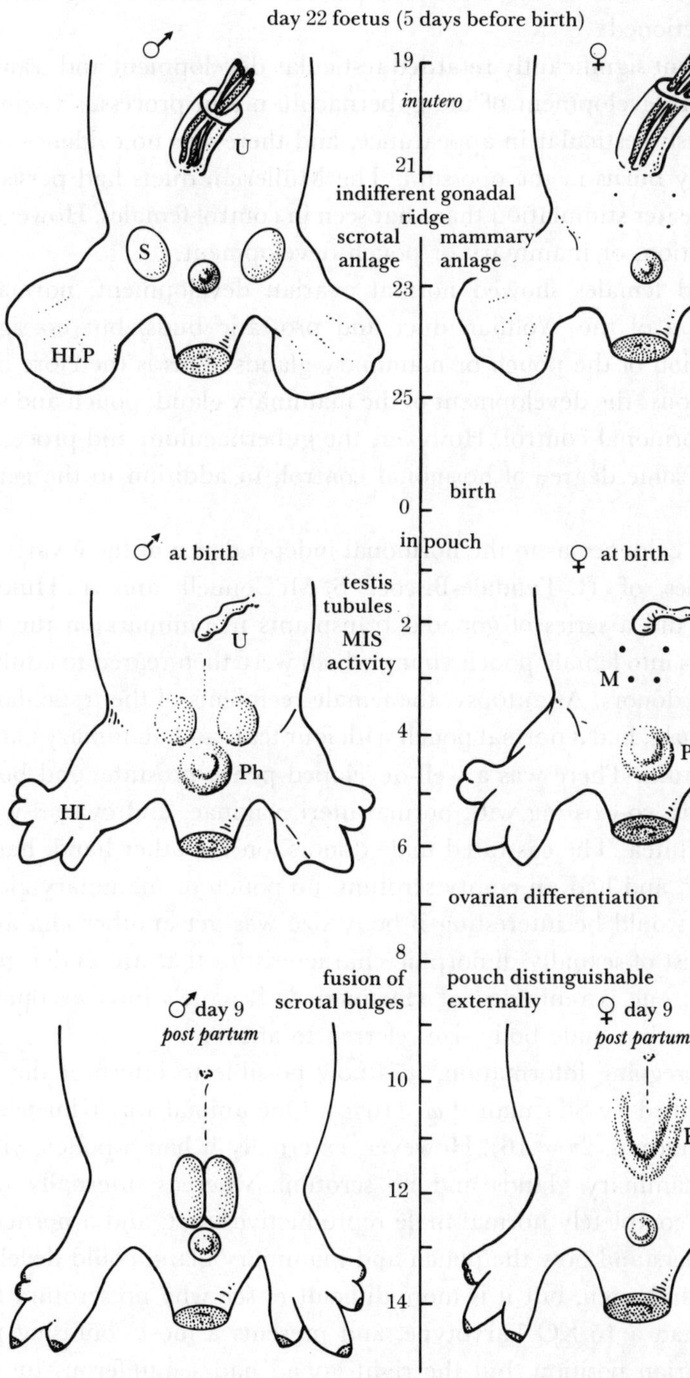

FIGURE 2. The ontogeny of scrotum and pouch in the foetal and neonatal tammar wallaby (*Macropus eugenii*) related to time of gonadal differentiation. Scrotal bulges and mammary anlagen are first observed in male and female foetuses respectively 5 days before birth (day 22; birth at day 26.5). In the males, the two scrotal anlagen gradually move to the midline where they fuse into a single scrotal sac by day 8 *post partum*. Pouch folds are just distinguishable at this time. Testis differentiation is first discernable on the third day *post partum* (d2) by histology and by Müllerian inhibiting substance (MIS) activity but the ovary lags behind this and is differentiated by about day 7. HLP, hind-limb paddle; HL, hind limb; M, mammary anlagen Ph, phallus; Po, pouch; S, scrotal anlagen: U, umbilicus.

(Shaw *et al.* 1988). At the end of the treatment period the pouch young were killed, and subsequently serially sectioned.

The oestrogen treatment significantly retarded testicular development and trans-abdominal migration, and impeded development of the gubernaculum and processus vaginalis, but the gonads were still obviously testicular in appearance, and there was no evidence of the type of sex-reversal described by Burns in the opossum. The Müllerian ducts had persisted, and the oestrogen had caused greater stimulation than that seen in control females. However, there was no sign of scrotal inhibition, or mammary or pouch development.

The androgen-treated females showed normal ovarian development, normal Müllerian development, stimulation of the Wolffian duct and prostatic buds, but no sign of scrotal development, or inhibition of the pouch or mammary glands. This is therefore in agreement with our other observations; the development of the mammary gland, pouch and scrotum does not seem to be under hormonal control. However, the gubernaculum and processus vaginalis do appear to be under some degree of hormonal control, in addition to the genetic control described above.

Further confirmatory evidence as to the hormonal independence of these various structures comes from the studies of H. Tyndale-Biscoe, S. McConnell and L. Hinds (personal communication). They did a series of gonadal transplants in tammars on the tenth day of pouch life, grafting testes into female pouch young which were then reared to adulthood, along with the castrated male donors. At autopsy, the female recipients of the testicular grafts were of normal female body mass, had a normal pouch with four teats and mammary glands, and had failed to develop a scrotum. There was a well-developed penis, prostate, and bulbo-urethral gland and a vas deferens, co-existing with normal uteri, vaginae, and ovaries with Graafian follicles but no corpora lutea. The castrated male donors, on the other hand, had achieved a normal male body mass, and had an empty scrotum, no pouch or mammary glands, and no penile development. It would be interesting if body size was yet another characteristic that could be added to the list of sexually dimorphic characteristics that are under genetic rather than hormonal control; one is reminded of Hartman & League's intersex opossum with a female reproductive tract but male body size referred to above.

In the light of the foregoing information, it is now possible to interpret the two intersex tammar wallabies described by Sharman *et al.* (1970). One animal was Klinefelter-like, with a 17,XXY karyotype (normal, $2n = 16$). However, externally it had a pouch with four well-developed teats and mammary glands and no scrotum, whereas internally it had intra-abdominal testes and a completely normal male reproductive tract, and a normal penis. It is not difficult now to understand how the pouch and mammary gland could develop normally in the face of so much androgen, but it is more difficult to see why no scrotum had formed.

The second animal had a 15,XO karyotype, and presents a most confusing picture. The gonads were in the ovarian position, but the right gonad had seminiferous tubules present, whereas the left gonad was clearly ovarian, although lacking primordial follicles. Internally the tract was like that of a normal female, but externally it seemed as if there was a hemi-pouch with two teats and two mammary glands on the ovarian side, and a hemi-scrotum on the testicular side. Perhaps this animal was a chromosomal mosaic, which might have accounted for the bilateral gynandromorphic effect; such an asymmetry would be very difficult to explain on hormonal grounds, but it is possible that the pouch and scrotal tissues could have differed in their genetic makeup.

Sharman *et al.* (1970) also described two other intersexes, a euro (*Macropus robustus*), and a brush-tailed possum (*Trichosurus vulpecula*), both of which had normal male karyotypes, intra-abdominal testes and normal male reproductive tracts internally, but externally they had normal pouches and mammary glands, and no scrotum. At present, these animals defy explanation genetically, although they confirm the hormonal independence of pouch, mammary gland and scrotum.

We can conclude that because scrotal, mammary and pouch development can occur independently of the presence or absence of a Y chromosome, these structures are more likely to be controlled by X-linked genes. Cooper *et al.* (1977) also hinted that the presence or absence of the Y cannot be wholly responsible for sex-determination in marsupials. Whether we are dealing with a simple X-dosage effect – one X for a scrotum, two for a pouch and mammary glands – remains to be determined, although the two XY intersexes with pouches and mammary glands but no scrotum would argue against such an explanation. However, D. W. Cooper (personal communication) suggests that if there is a small region of the X which must be expressed in double dose to produce a pouch and a mammary gland, then it is possible that these two animals carried a duplication of this region which would not have been detected except by G banding.

Discussion

The effects of steroid treatment on pouch and scrotum in American and Australian marsupials are entirely consistent with one another, and suggest the existence of a fundamental dichotomy between marsupials and eutherians in their sex-determining mechanisms. Tyndale-Biscoe's suggestion (Tyndale-Biscoe & Renfree 1987) that differentiation of the pouch and scrotum is determined by the particular chromosomal constitution of the cells of the anlagen, and that the Jost hypothesis may not apply in its entirety to sexual differentiation in marsupials is amply confirmed by all the recent evidence summarized here. This dichotomy presumably dates back to their divergence in the mid-Cretaceous period around 100 million years ago. Although both subclasses probably require a Y-linked gene or genes for testis determination, and rely on testicular androgens for Wolffian duct, prostatic and penile development, MIS for Müllerian duct inhibition, and a combination of the two hormones for testicular migration and descent into the scrotum, there the similarities end.

In eutherians, the androgen-dependent scrotum of the male is homologous with the vaginal labia of the female, which develop in the absence of androgen. In marsupials, because the rectal and urogenital passages all open into a common urogenital sinus with a single external orifice that is common to both sexes, there is no female counterpart of the scrotum. The scrotum of marsupials is not under the control of testicular hormones, and so it is presumably under autonomous genetic control. Because a scrotum can form in the absence of a Y chromosome, perhaps it is regulated by an X-linked gene, which must be inactivated in some way when two X chromosomes are present: hence the presence of a scrotum in XO or XY individuals, and the absence in XX and XXY individuals.

In most eutherians, mammary glands are present in adult males, but they are functionally inhibited by testicular androgen secretion. In some eutherians, e.g. rats and mice, mammary glands are absent in adult males, having been suppressed by androgen action during foetal life. In marsupials, mammary glands appear to be universally absent in all adult males. Testicular hormones are without effect on normal mammary development, so once again this control must be genetically determined. The presence or absence of a Y chromosome appears to be irrelevant for mammary development, so perhaps it also is regulated by an X-linked gene, which normally requires the presence of two X chromosomes for expression. Ancestral marsupials were thought to be pouchless (Tyndale-Biscoe & Renfree 1987) so the pouch may be a more recently derived characteristic. Because mammary gland and pouch development seem to go hand-in-glove, so to speak, the pouch is also likely to be regulated by an X-linked gene.

We already know of a number of fundamental differences between marsupials and eutherians in the behaviour of their sex chromosomes. Marsupials show paternal X inactivation, whereas in eutherians the X inactivation is random (VandeBerg *et al.* 1983). However, Cooper *et al.* (1977) make the interesting observation that X-inactivation is not complete, so an X-linked gene may be active, inactive or partly active, thus allowing the possibility of a double dosage of an X-linked gene or genes to be expressed in females. The marsupial Y is usually much smaller relative to the X than in eutherians, suggesting that marsupials may have progressed further than eutherians in the capture of genetic material by the X from the ancestral Y. This could also explain why the marsupial X and Y lack a homologous pairing segment and synaptonemal complex (Sharp 1982), preventing the obligatory crossover between the X and Y at meiosis that seems to occur in eutherians (Burgoyne 1982). Perhaps it is the small size of the marsupial Y, and this genetic isolation from the X, that has resulted in so many X-linked genes apparently being involved in sexual differentiation, although why marsupials have preferred genes to hormones for producing so many sexual dimorphisms is still a mystery.

The key to further elucidation of the genetic control of marsupial sexual differentiation lies in part in the examination of the karyotype and phenotype of a wider range of intersexes. Presumably some types of eutherian intersex will not be found in marsupials; XX males and XY females are unlikely to occur if there is no X–Y crossover at meiosis; if paternal X inactivation is obligatory, this will mean that all XO individuals can only arise by paternal non-disjunction. Because of the direct genetic control of so many somatic sexual dimorphisms in marsupials, it would seem to be important to karyotype the tissues of the pouch, scrotum and mammary gland as well as blood or bone marrow. Perhaps some of the perplexing marsupial gynandromorphs (Renfree *et al.* 1987) can be explained by tissue mosaicism in these regions.

It is amazing that it has taken us so long to appreciate that many sexually dimorphic characters in mammals may be genetically determined. So forceful and beguiling has been the hormonal theory of sexual differentiation, which dates back to the classical studies of Keller, Tandler and Lillie on the bovine freemartin at the beginning of this century, that nobody has looked for any alternative explanation. It will be interesting to see how many of the characters we have found in marsupials behave in a similar fashion in eutherian mammals. The gubernaculum, for example, the 'rudder of the testis', first described by John Hunter (1762), is clearly under dual genetic and hormonal control in marsupials. If this were true of eutherians also, it could provide a valuable new clue to our understanding of the aetiology of cryptorchidism. There is already a strong suggestion that male mouse embryos grow faster than females at an early stage of development, long before gonadal differentiation (Sellar & Perkin-Cole 1987), and this could possibly lead to the development of a simple, non-invasive method for embryo sexing in *in vitro* fertilization programmes.

In the years to come, marsupials seem likely to play an increasingly important role in elucidating the role of a multiplicity of sex-linked genes on both the X and Y chromosomes that are apparently involved in mammalian sex determination and sexual differentiation.

We thank our colleagues Dr Geoff Shaw and Dr Wai Sum O for their collaboration in many of the experiments summarized in this review. We also thank Dr Hugh Tyndale-Biscoe and Dr Ted Robinson for allowing us to quote their unpublished results, and Professor Des Cooper for helpful comments on the manuscript.

References

Alcorn, G. T. 1975 Development of the ovary and urinogenital ducts in the tammar wallaby *Macropus eugenii* (Desmarest, 1817). Ph.D. thesis, Macquarie University, Sydney.

Burgoyne, P. S. 1982 Genetic homology and crossing over in the X and Y chromosomes of mammals. *Hum. Genet.* **61**, 85–90.

Burgoyne, P. S. 1987 The role of the mammalian Y chromosome in spermatogenesis. *Development* **101**, 133–141.

Burgoyne, P. S., Buehr, M., Koopman, P., Rossant, J. & McLaren, A. 1988 Cell-autonomous action of the testis-determining gene: Sertoli cells are exclusively XY in XX↔XY chimaeric mouse testes. *Development* **102**, 443–450.

Burns, R. K. 1961 Role of hormones in the differentiation of sex. In *Sex and internal secretions*, 3rd edn, vol. 1 (ed. W. C. Young), pp. 76–158. Baltimore: Williams & Wilkins.

Cate, R. L., Mattaliano, R. J., Hession, C., Tizard, R., Farber, N. M., Cheung, A., Ninfa, E. G., Frey, A. Z., Gash, D. J., Chow, E. P., Fisher, R. A., Bertonis, J. M., Torres, G., Wallner, B. P., Ramachandram, K. L., Rogin, R. C., Manganaro, T. F., MacLaughlin, D. T. & Donahoe, P. K. 1986 Isolation of the bovine and human genes for Müllerian inhibiting substance and expression of the human gene in animal cells. *Cell* **45**, 685–698.

Cooper, D. W., Edwards, C., James, E., Sharman, G. B., VandeBerg, J. L. & Graves, J. A. M. 1977 Studies on metatherian sex chromosomes VI. A third state of an X-linked gene: partial activity for the paternally derived *Pgk*-A allele in cultured fibroblasts of *Macropus giganteus* and *M. parryi*. *Aust. J. biol. Sci.* **30**, 431–443.

Fadem, B. H. & Tesoriero, J. V. 1986 Inhibition of testicular development and feminization of the male genitalia by neonatal estrogen treatment in a marsupial. *Biol. Reprod.* **34**, 771–776.

Hartman, C. G. & League, B. 1925 Description of a sex-intergrade opossum, with an analysis of the constituents of its gonads. *Anat. Rec.* **29**, 283–297.

Hunter, J. 1762 Observations on the state of the testis in the foetus and on the hernia congenita. In *Medical commentaries*, part 1, p. 75. London: A. Hamilton.

Hutson, J. M. & Donahoe, P. K. 1986 The hormonal control of testicular descent. *Endocrine Rev.* **7**, 270–283.

Hutson, J. M., Shaw, G., O, W.-S., Short, R. V. & Renfree, M. B. 1988 The ontogeny of Müllerian inhibiting substance production and testicular differentiation, migration and descent in the pouch young of a marsupial. *Development*. (Submitted.)

Jost, A., Vigier, B., Prepin, J. & Perchellet, J. P. 1973 Studies on sexual differentiation in mammals. *Recent Prog. Horm. Res.* **29**, 1–35.

Magre, S. 1985 Différenciation des cellules de Sertoli et morphogénèse testiculaire chez le foetus de rat. *Archs Anat. microsc. Morph. exp.* **74**, 64–68.

O, W.-S., Short, R. V., Renfree, M. B. & Shaw, G. 1988 Primary genetic control of somatic sexual differentiation in a mammal. *Nature, Lond.* **331**, 716–717.

Ohno, S. 1967 Sex chromosomes and sex-linked genes. *Monogr. Endocr.* **1**, 154–171.

Page, D. C., Mosher, R., Simpson, E. M., Fisher, E. M. C., Mardon, G., Pollack, J., McGillivray, B., de la Chapelle, A. & Brown, L. G. 1987 The sex-determining region of the human Y chromosome encodes a finger protein. *Cell* **51**, 1091–1104.

Renfree, M. B., Shaw, G. & Short, R. V. 1987 Sexual differentiation in marsupials. In *Genetic markers of sex differentiation* (ed. F. P. Haseltine, M. E. McClure & E. H. Goldberg), pp. 27–41. New York: Plenum Press.

Sellar, M. J. & Perkin-Cole, K. J. 1987 Sex difference in mouse embryonic development at neurulation. *J. Reprod. Fert.* **79**, 159–161.

Sharp, P. J. 1982 Sex chromosome pairing during male meiosis in marsupials. *Chromosoma* **86**, 27–47.

Sharman, G. B., Robinson, E. S., Walton, S. M. & Berger, P. J. 1970 Sex chromosomes and reproductive anatomy of some intersex marsupials. *J. Reprod. Fert.* **21**, 57–68.

Shaw, G., Renfree, M. B., Short, R. V. & O, W.-S. 1988 Experimental manipulation of sexual differentiation in wallaby pouch young with exogenous steroids. *Development*. (Submitted.)

Short, R. V. 1972 Germ cell sex. In *Edinburgh Symposium on the Genetics of the Spermatozoon* (ed. R. A. Beatty & S. Gluecksohn-Waelsch), pp. 325–345. Copenhagen: Bogtrykkeriet Forum.

Short, R. V., Renfree, M. B. & Shaw, G. 1988 Sexual development in marsupial pouch young. In *The developing marsupial. Models for biomedical research* (ed. C. H. Tyndale-Biscoe & P. A. Janssens), pp. 200–210. Berlin: Springer-Verlag.

Simpson, E., Chandler P., Goulmy, E., Disteche, C. M., Ferguson-Smith, M. A. & Page, D. C. 1987 Separation of the genetic loci for the H-Y antigen and for testis determination on the human Y chromosome. *Nature, Lond.* **326**, 876–878.

Tyndale-Biscoe, C. H. & Renfree, M. B. 1987 *Reproductive physiology of marsupials.* (476 pages.) Cambridge University Press.

VandeBerg, J. L., Johnston, P. G., Cooper, D. W. & Robinson, E. W. 1983 X-chromosome inactivation and evolution in marsupials and other mammals. In *Isozymes: current topics in biological and medical research*, vol. 9 (*Gene expression and development*) (ed. M. C. Rattazi, J. G. Scandalios & G. S. White), pp. 201–218. New York: Alan R. Liss.

Vigier, B., Watrin, F., Magre, S., Tran, O. & Josso, N. 1987 Purified bovine AMH induces a characteristic freemartin effect in fetal rat prospective ovaries exposed to it *in vitro*. *Development* **100**, 43–55.

Discussion

MARY F. LYON, F.R.S. (*M.R.C. Radiobiology Unit, Didcot, U.K.*). The question is in regard to the anomalies in XXY and XO animals. As Professor Short said, marsupials show X-inactivation, and therefore what is the basis of these anomalies? X-inactivation in marsupial embryos has been relatively little studied; does Dr Renfree or Professor Short know whether inactivation could possibly occur later than in eutherians?

I know of one report by Johnston & Robinson (1985) on X-inactivation in kangaroo embryos. They found inactivation in cells of the embryos themselves, but both Xs remained active in some cells of the yolk-sac.

Reference

Johnston, P. G. & Robinson, E. S. 1985 *Genet. Res.* **45**, 205–208.

M. B. RENFREE AND R. V. SHORT. We do not know anything about the precise time-course of X inactivation in marsupials. It's interesting that paternal X inactivation appears to be the rule in marsupials. If this is obligatory rather than facultative, then XO individuals have presumably arisen as a result of paternal non-disjunction.

URSULA MITTWOCH (*University College London, U.K.*). Did Dr Renfree or Professor Short measure the volumes of the gubernaculum in newborn wallabies, and did they obtain a significant difference between males and females?

M. B. RENFREE. We did not measure the total volume of the gubernaculum as between male and female wallabies, but the sex differences in gubernacular length were readily apparent from an examination of serial sections of foetuses and newborn young.

ANNE GROCOCK (*Department of Human Anatomy, University of Oxford, U.K.*). Firstly, does the gubernaculum disappear with the oestrogen treatment? Secondly, why was testosterone used rather than dihydrotestosterone?

R. V. SHORT. The answer to the first question is no. The gubernaculum was inhibited by oestrogen treatment but did not disappear completely. Secondly, in collaboration with Dr Jean

Wilson we have shown that there is 5-α-reductase activity present in target tissues in the early stages of development, so the testosterone we administered could have been converted to dihydrotestosterone at its site of action.

M. W. J. Ferguson (*Department of Cellular and Structural Biology, University of Manchester, U.K.*). Professor Short referred in the discussion to our ideas about sex and growth in alligators, and commented that he agreed with these as Dr Tyndale-Biscoe in Australia had castrated male wallabies and shown that, as adults, they grew at the same rate as animals with intact testes, therefore suggesting that growth rate was sex-linked and independent of hormones.

I agreed with this interpretation based on alligator data, where the growth rate of animals up to 6 feet (1.83 m) in length was directly related to the temperature they were incubated at as eggs. That this was an egg-incubation effect and not a subsequent sex-determined effect could be demonstrated at temperatures of egg incubation which produce 50:50 sex ratios (31 °C in alligators). Animals resulting from such incubations grew at the same rate, independent of sex, faster than their 30 °C cohorts but slower than their 33 °C cohorts.

I also commented that from a phylogenetic standpoint it was not surprising to see differentiation of sex-associated characteristics e.g. secondary sexual structures in marsupials, eye pigmentation in quails, before the onset of overt embryonic gonadal differentiation and before any hormone release. The alligator data clearly show that several characters, e.g. pigmentation pattern, adult growth rate, preferred thermoregulatory temperature in the embryo, are determined by temperature of egg incubation as well as sex. If genetic sex determination in mammals evolved from temperature-dependent sex determination in reptiles, then clearly some of these temperature-associated characteristics could become controlled by sex genes in mammals. It was likely that there would be variation in different animals as to which characteristics became sex-gene linked, and so wide diversity might be predicted in mammals and birds.

Phil. Trans. R. Soc. Lond. B **322**, 55–61 (1988) [55]
Printed in Great Britain

Control mechanisms of testicular differentiation

By A. Jost and S. Magre
Laboratoire de Physiologie du Développement, Collège de France, Place Marcelin Berthelot,
75231 *Paris Cedex* 05, *France*

[Plates 1–4]

In this paper the importance of unknown factors responsible for the initial differentiation of a gonadal primordium is stressed. The hypothesis that in the absence of testis determining genes (TDG) the indifferent gonad is programmed to become an ovary is considered further. The TDG(s) are expressed only among cells already marked as gonadal cells, and they seem mainly to change the chronological sequence and intensity of expression of processes common to both sexes. The chronology of the normal events necessary for testicular differentiation and the fact that some of these events can be dissociated from one another under experimental conditions *in vitro*, suggest that many genes are involved in testicular differentiation and that the so-called testis-determining genes are probably regulatory genes.

Introduction

The embryonic development of organs like the lung or the pancreas, although intensively studied, is still incompletely understood. These organs originate from a bulging of a definite part of the primitive endodermal gut epithelium into the underlying mesodermal mesenchyme. Epithelial–mesenchymal interactions eventually end in the embryonic 'determination' of a pancreatic or a lung primordium whose fate is fixed for life. Characteristic proteins such as insulin, glucagon or lipase are synthesized.

The cellular influences that initiate the development of a definite organ in a definite region of the body are still unknown. It would seem that the cellular environment turns on some gene(s) in a definite area, and that 'organ-determining genes' come into play. These genes rapidly govern the morphological and physiological specialization of a localized part of the embryo.

The origin of the gonads, on the inner side of the mesonephroi, involves mesodermal cells, namely the coelomic epithelium and the underlying mesenchyme, and germ cells that have migrated into the region. The first recognizable gonadal primordium is the so-called undifferentiated (indifferent) gonad whose characteristics require some consideration.

The indifferent gonadal primordium and TDG(s) expression

Some 'organ-determining gene(s)' probably controls the initial formation of the gonadal primordium in a way similar to that conjectured for other organs. But unlike the lung or the pancreas, the fate of this primordium is not yet determined. It is a transitory structure than can become either an ovary or a testis or a hermaphroditic organ, or it can abort.

(*a*) *Sexual significance of the 'indifferent gonad'*

In the past, it had long been accepted that the indifferent gonad was hermaphroditic, i.e. composed of a male and of a female component, and that the final sex of the gonad resulted from the competition of two discrete and sexually opposite types of cell, male and female, under genetic control (Witschi 1951, 1957).

Several years ago, one of us (A.J.) introduced the concept that the unknown locally expressed 'gonad-determining gene(s)' actually initiated an 'ovary-determining' programme (Jost 1965, 1970). In males, this programme is upset when, at a definite time and for still unknown reasons, the testis-determining genes (TDGs) become activated. Morphogenesis and cytodifferentiation are accelerated according to the male pattern, for instance by calling into action genes that would have remained temporarily inactive in a developing ovary. Thus Voutilainen & Miller (1986) recently observed an early and time-dependent amount of mRNA for cholesterol side-chain cleavage enzyme and for 17 β-hydroxylase/17,20 lyase in the human foetal testis, whereas these mRNAs remained scarce in the ovary.

This concept is dramatically supported by the so-called 'undifferentiated sex races' of grass frogs, in which all individuals first develop gonads similar to ovaries until the time of metamorphosis. After that time the gonads of 50% of the individuals, the males, undergo a delayed masculinization, involving the disappearance of the large oocyte-like germ cells (Witschi 1930, 1942). It appears that the testis-differentiating gene(s) become active only at metamorphosis, permitting male gonads to differentiate along the ovarian line up to that time. Interestingly, the expression of the TDG seems to be controlled by environmental factors because masculinization is not delayed in the frogs living in mountains or in northern countries (Witschi 1930, 1942).

Another well-known example of delayed ovarian masculinization is afforded by ovaries of freemartins in cattle, which pass through three phases: (1) they first remain similar to presumptive ovaries at the time when testes differentiate in males; (2) next they become stunted for 6 weeks or more; (3) seminiferous cords and Leydig cells differentiate after the third month of foetal age (Jost *et al.* 1972, 1973). In that case testicular organogenesis in presumptive ovaries does not result from the presence of a Y chromosome (because no Y chromosome is present except in blood cells), but from the effect of humoral factors transmitted by blood exchange with the male twin.

(*b*) *Similarities and dissimilarities in testicular and ovarian development*

The developmental prospects for the gonadal primordium are in some measure similar in both sexes. Schematically, the gonads are organs that permit and control the differentiation of the germ cells, and on the other hand are endocrine glands that produce sex hormones. Seminiferous tubules in testes and ovarian follicles in ovaries are formed of homologous cells which both produce the Müllerian inhibitor (AMH or MIS) at one time or another (Vigier *et al.* 1984; Donahoe *et al.* 1987), and which control meiosis. In males, the aggregation of Sertoli cells around the germ cells is a very early event (Jost 1972; Magre & Jost 1980), and meiosis is prevented for a prolonged period of time. In females the follicle cells surround the oocytes only after the germ cells have entered meiosis, and meiotic prophase is arrested in the follicles. In both sexes the germ cells become isolated from direct contact with blood capillaries: they depend strictly on the surrounding cells, which govern the male or female gametogenesis in an unknown way.

On the other hand, in both sexes the sex hormones, testosterone and oestradiol, derive for the most part from cholesterol; the biosynthetic pathway is cut short in males, and androgens are released, whereas in the ovary androgens serve as precursors in a longer series of transformations.

To a large extent the tools used to make an ovary or a testis are similar, but the TDGs seem to change the chronological order completely, hastening, repressing or reinforcing the expression of genetically controlled processes, which in one way or another also occur in the developing ovary.

It is obvious that a concept expressed so bluntly is too schematical, and that it can be proposed only for the initial stages of gonadal development. Testes and ovaries progressively acquire their own characteristics and properties; other specific genes become activated after the initial sexual orientation.

(*c*) *No TDG expression outside the gonadal primordium*

The testis-determining gene(s) becomes activated only in the gonadal primordium. When germ cells, during their migration period, enter the adrenals rather than the gonadal primordium, they become oocytes and enter the meiotic prophase even in males (Upadhyay & Zamboni 1982; Zamboni & Upadhyay 1983). During the same time and in the same animal those germ cells that entered the testis become non-meiotic spermatogonia. In the adrenal gland neither follicular nor Sertoli cells differentiate, although adrenals and gonads are related structures developed from rather similar neighbouring tissues. The organ patterning, also reflected by the nature of the major steroid produced, is different in the two organs. TDG expression does not belong to the adrenal programme.

Sequences in the normal differentiation of a testis

One obvious way to contribute to the elucidation of the control mechanisms of testicular differentiation consists in carefully scrutinizing how a testis normally develops. An important part of this approach is the recognition of the chronological succession of the processes involved, because testicular differentiation is a stepwise process.

It has long been known (even if it is sometimes overlooked) that the foetal seminiferous cords (the core part of the future seminiferous tubules) differentiate much earlier than do the Leydig cells. In humans more than one week separates the two processes (Pelliniemi & Niemi 1969). As early as 1923, Kitahara drew attention to this point and suggested that the Leydig cells differentiate under the influence of the seminiferous cords. The idea that Sertoli cells might exert this influence has long appealed to the senior author of this paper.

The initial steps of testicular differentiation have rarely been scrutinized with enough precision. We tried to fill this gap by studying rat foetuses. Their age was reckoned from the assumed time of fertilization of the oocyte, which usually takes place at 01h00 or 02h00. Their sex was determined by the sex chromatin test in the cells of the amniotic membrane (Jost 1972).

Figure 1, plate 1, shows the appearance of the indifferent rat gonad. The first event we could recognize in rat foetuses aged 13 days 9 h was the emergence in the course of a few hours of a new cell type in the undifferentiated gonad: large clear cells, which aggregate and encompass the germ cells into the forming seminiferous cords (Jost 1972; Jost *et al.* 1973) (figure 2*a*, *b*, plate 2). Characteristic interdigitations between these cells are seen with the electron microscope (Magre & Jost 1980). This takes place first in the anterior part of the gonad and extends to the entire gonad during the next 24 h. During the same time a basal membrane progressively forms around these cords (Magre & Jost 1980) (figure 2*c*, plate 2.) By 15 days 13 h the Leydig cells have begun to differentiate (figure 3, plate 3). The myoid cells and the wall of the seminiferous tubules do not become conspicuous until after birth (22 days of pregnancy).

In contrast with the early organogenesis of the testis, ovarian follicles form postnatally. It is also noteworthy that the testicular seminiferous tubules, once established, become permanent even in case of disappearance of the germ cells, whereas persistence of ovarian follicles depends strictly on the presence of germ cells.

It is clear that the differentiation of a testis results from a cascade of processes and probably from the successive activation of many genes.

Interfering with testicular organogenesis *in vitro*

Morphological and endocrine testicular differentiation from undifferentiated primordia of rat foetuses can be obtained *in vitro*. Primordia taken from fetuses aged 12 days 16 h (before gonadal sex can be histologically recognized) or 13 days 9 h (at incipient differentiation), and explanted in a synthetic medium with the mesonephroi, complete their morphological and endocrine differentiation within 3 days. Though growth of these gonads is very limited *in vitro*, some seminiferous cords are formed (figure 4*a*, plate 4) and Leydig cells subsequently differentiate. Production of the Müllerian inhibitor was tested by the *in vitro* test devised by Picon (1969); testosterone and androstenedione were measured in the medium with a radioimmunoassay.

In the first series of experiments (Agelopoulou *et al.* 1984), it was observed that the addition of foetal calf serum, or other sera (Chartrain *et al.* 1984), to the synthetic medium prevented the differentiation of the seminiferous cords (figure 4*b*, plate 4). However, large clear cells, looking like foetal Sertoli cells, were scattered throughout the gonads; these were assumed to be true Sertoli cells because the cordless gonads produced the Müllerian inhibitor, a product of the Sertoli cells (Magre & Jost 1984). Moreover, these gonads contained cells showing 3β hydroxysteroid dehydrogenase (3β HSDH) activity and produced testosterone (Patsavoudi *et al.* 1985). These experiments suggested that testicular morphogenesis, i.e. formation of the seminiferous cords, could be dissociated from endocrine cytodifferentiation.

The histological structure of the gonads after 3 or 4 days *in vitro* suggested that serum prevented the aggregation of the Sertoli cells, and therefore morphogenesis of the seminiferous cords. Laminin and fibronectin, identified by immunohistochemical techniques, were expressed as small deposits interspersed between the Sertoli and the mesenchymal cells (Agelopoulou & Magre 1987).

The condition described after 4 days *in vitro* is transient. If the culture time in the presence of serum is prolonged for 9 days, or if at the end of the first 4 days the explants are grafted under the kidney capsule of castrated adult rats, the Sertoli cells aggregate and form seminiferous cords (A. Jost & S. Magre, unpublished results).

A second set of experiments was made with a competitor of proline, L-azetidine 2-carboxylic acid (LACA), a compound used in many embryological studies for studying the role of collagen in developing organs (lung, mammary gland, etc., references in Jost *et al.* (1985)).

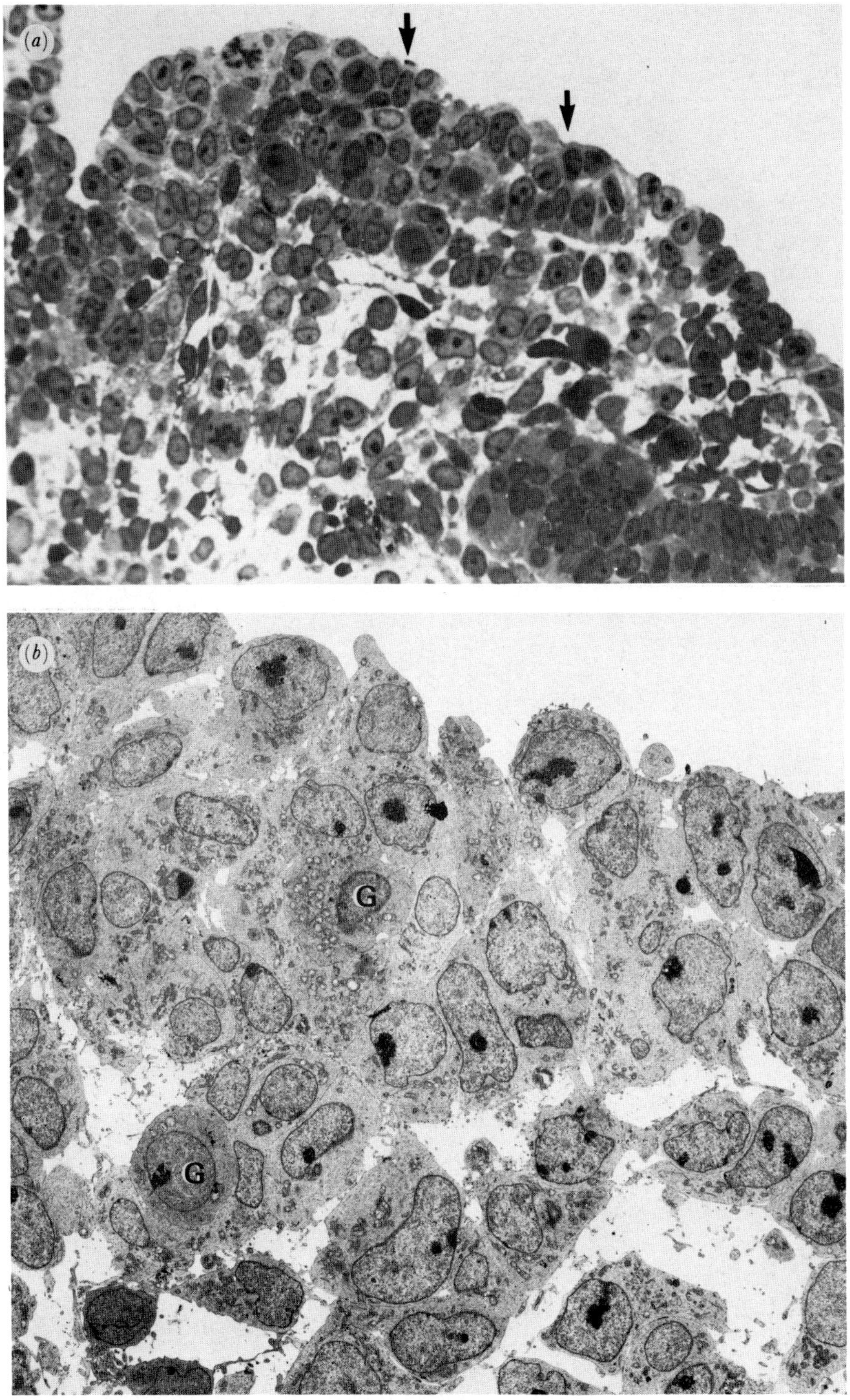

FIGURE 1. The indifferent stage of the rat gonad. Semi-thick (*a*) and thin (*b*) sections through the same gonad from a 12 day 15 h male rat foetus. The thin section illustrates the zone shown between the two arrows. The same germ cells (G) are seen in the two sections. Fixation in buffered glutaraldehyde (1 % by volume). (Magn. × 600 and × 2000 respectively) (From Magre 1983.)

(*Facing p.* 58)

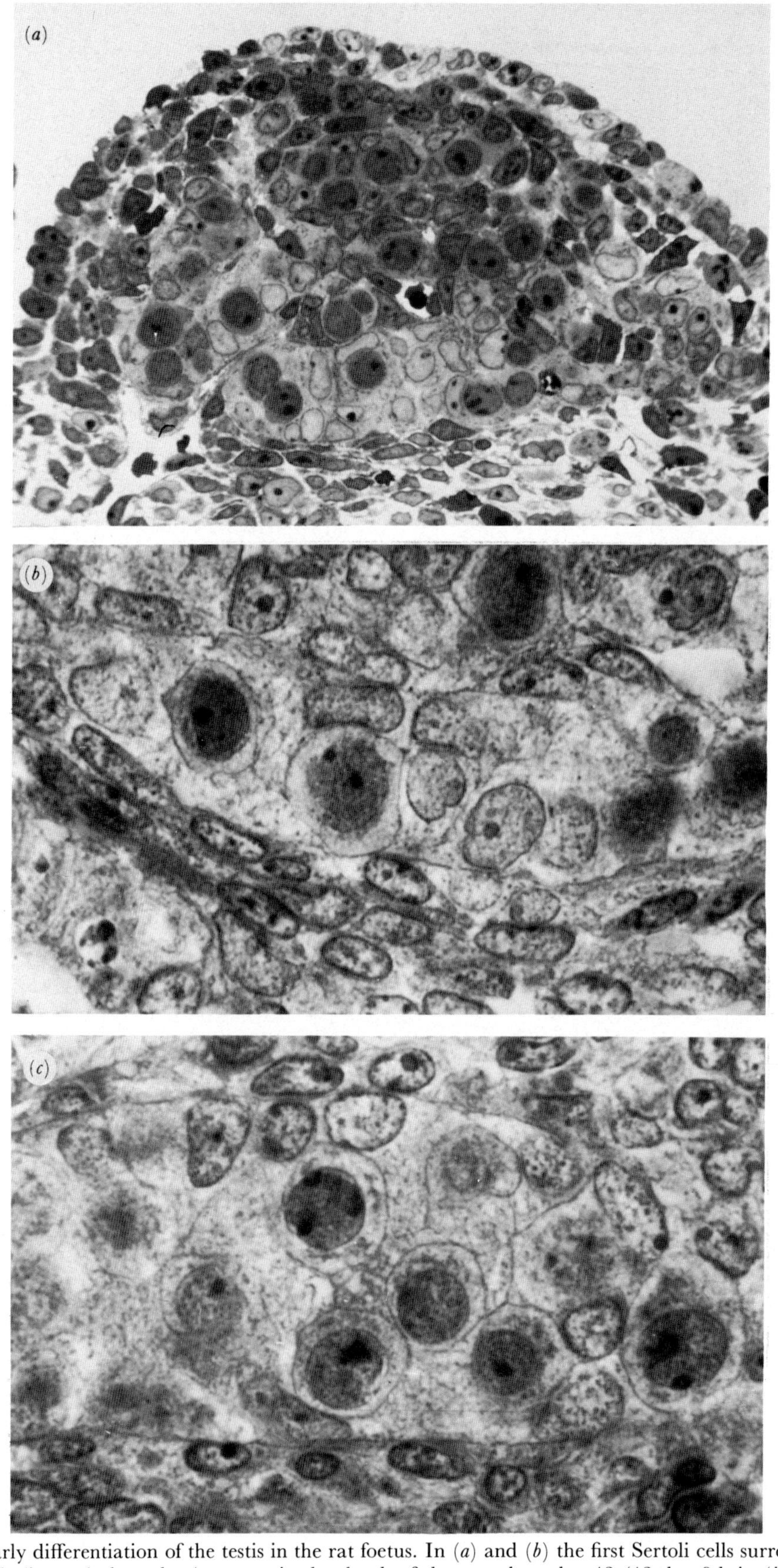

FIGURE 2. Early differentiation of the testis in the rat foetus. In (*a*) and (*b*) the first Sertoli cells surrounding some germ cells (large dark nucleus) appear in the depth of the gonad on day 13 (13 day 9 h in (*b*) and 13 day 15 h in (*a*)). (*c*) Differentiated seminiferous cord in the testis on day 14 (14 day 14 h foetus). (*a*) Semi-thick section, magn. ×600, from Magre & Jost (1980); (*b*, and *c*) Histological sections, magn. ×1400, fixed in glutaraldehyde plus picric acid, from Jost (1972).)

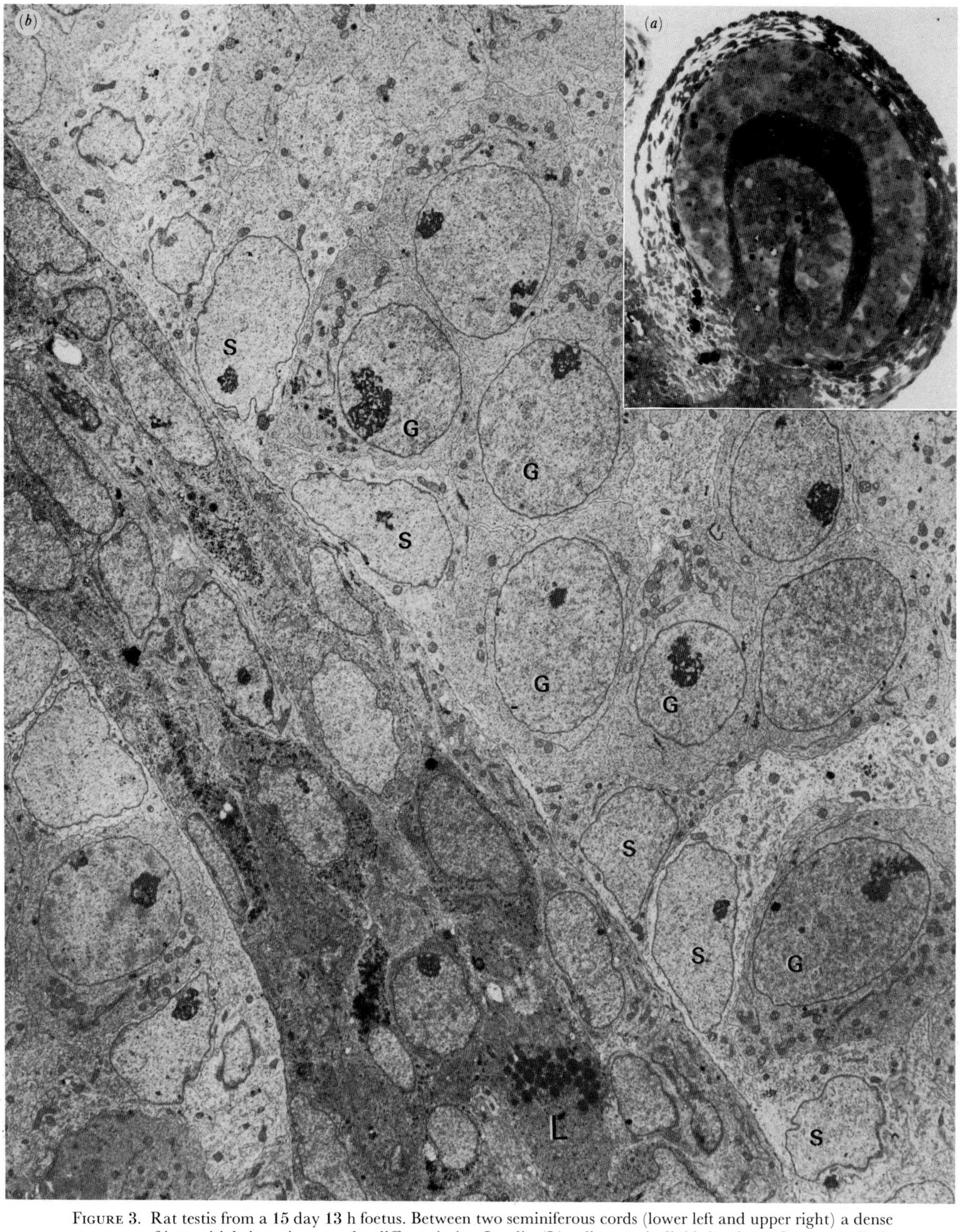

FIGURE 3. Rat testis from a 15 day 13 h foetus. Between two seminiferous cords (lower left and upper right) a dense zone of interstitial tissue is seen; the differentiating Leydig (L) cells contain lipid droplets. (G, germ cell; S, Sertoli cells; magn. × 3250). Inset: section through the same testis showing two seminiferous cords in a double arcade. The interstitial tissue is dense. (Magn. × 600.) (From Magre & Jost 1980.)

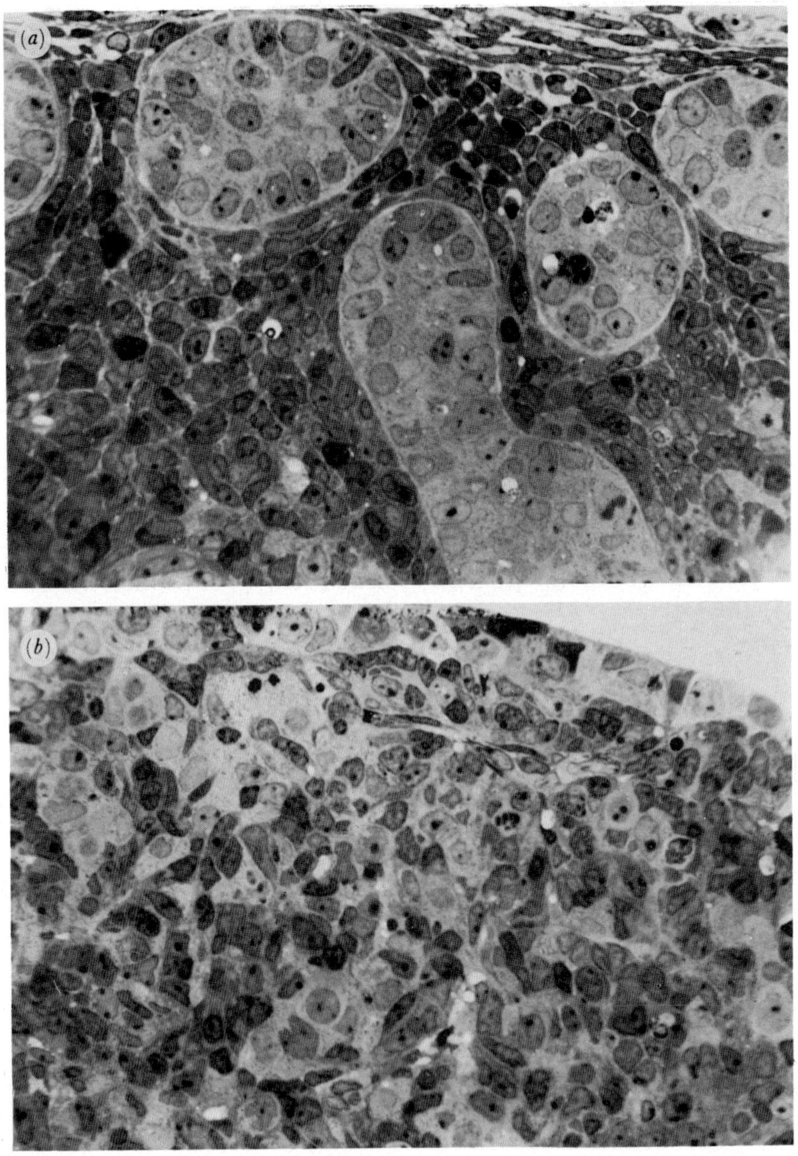

FIGURE 4. Semi-thick sections through male gonads taken from 13 day 9 h foetuses and cultured *in vitro* for 4 days. (*a*) Control gonad grown in synthetic medium (CMRL, 1066 medium). It contains well-differentiated seminiferous cords. (*b*) Gonad cultured in the same medium supplemented with foetal calf serum (15% by volume). The differentiation of seminiferous cords was prevented. (Fixation in buffered glutaraldehyde (0.5% by volume) and paraformaldehyde (20 g l^{-1}). (Magn. ×600.) (From Magre 1983.)

A complete report of the observations will be given elsewhere. To summarize the main findings, when LACA (100 μg ml^{-1}) is added to the culture medium, well-defined seminiferous cords fail to differentiate; however, the histological appearance of the gonad differs from that obtained after the addition of serum. Many large clear cells are present and grouped into large clusters rather than being scattered throughout the gonad. The mesenchymal cells situated adjacent to these clusters do not differ from the more distant ones; they display no tendency to flatten as they do in a normal testis. Unlike with the serum-treated gonads, no laminin or fibronectin expression could be detected by immunohistochemical techniques. The endocrine cytodifferentiation of the gonads was also different. The Müllerian inhibitory activity was present, in agreement with the histological aspect of the Sertoli cells. On the contrary, only a few exceptional cells gave a weak positive response to a histochemical test of 3β HSDH activity. At the same time, the test was highly positive in the adrenal cortex (when adrenals were included in the explant). Testosterone production, if any, was below or at the limit of sensitivity of the method. Dibutyryl cAMP (10^{-3} M) added to the medium only very slightly increased testosterone release, whereas in controls it multiplies it 8-fold. The addition of 250 μg ml^{-1} L-Proline to the medium in addition to LACA permitted the formation of seminiferous cords, the normal histochemical distribution of 3β HSDH activity and testosterone secretion, as well as the response to cAMP.

A third series of preliminary studies was done with gonads from mouse foetuses (OF_1, Iffa Credo) cultured in media with or without a high concentration of a commercial preparation of α-globulin (5 mg ml^{-1} human fraction IV_1, Sigma). Previously, the α globulin fraction of human serum was found to be responsible for the effect of serum in rats (Chartrain *et al.* 1984).

Seminiferous cord formation was prevented in undifferentiated gonad primordia from 11-day-old mice cultured for 4 or 8 days in the synthetic medium with added 'α globulin'. The cordless gonads produced the Müllerian inhibitor (Picon's test on rats) but they contained almost no cells positive for the β HSDH activity. Results obtained with rat primordia showed similar absence of cord organogenesis and of steroidogenesis; the production of Müllerian inhibitor has not yet been studied.

As in the rat gonads exposed to LACA, the mouse gonads cultured in the presence of the α-globulin fraction showed failure of seminiferous cords to form, and dissociation between Müllerian duct inhibiting activity which was expressed, and 3β HSDH activity which was virtually absent.

Conclusion

The differentiation of a testis results from a cascade of multifarious morphogenetic and cytophysiological processes staggered over a prolonged developmental period. Several of these processes can be experimentally dissociated from one another. The recognition of the successive processes of cell differentiation and morphogenesis gives clues suggesting separate control mechanisms.

In humans, some genes involved in gonadal endocrine activity can be assigned to definite chromosomes. The gene coding for the anti-Müllerian hormone resides on chromosome 19 (Cohen-Haguenauer *et al.* 1987), the gene for the cholesterol side-chain cleavage enzyme (P450scc) on chromosome 15 (Chung *et al.* 1986), and the gene for 17α hydroxylase/17,20 lyase (P450c17) on chromosome 10 (Matteson *et al.* 1986).

The same or similar genes probably also exist in the rat but their chromosomal localization is unknown. The situation created in male rat gonads cultured in the presence of serum would exemplify the expression of the three genes in the absence of seminiferous cord differentiation. Under the influence of LACA or α-globulin the formation of the cords is also prevented, and only the gene coding for the Müllerian inhibitor is expressed whereas steroidogenesis is silent.

The testis-determining gene(s) might well play no direct role in any of the cellular processes resulting in testicular differentiation, but rather 'turn on' other genes possibly residing on different chromosomes and expressed according to the particular testicular chronology.

References

Agelopoulou, R., Magre, S., Patsavoudi, E. & Jost, A. 1984 Initial phases of the rat testis differentiation *in vitro*. *J. Embryol. exp. Morph.* **83**, 15–31.

Agelopoulou, R. and Magre, S. 1987 Expression of fibronectin and laminin in fetal male gonads *in vivo* and *in vitro* with and without testicular morphogenesis. *Cell Differentiation* **21**, 31–36.

Chartrain, I., Magre, S., Maingourd, M. & Jost, A. 1984 Effect of serum on organogenesis of the rat testis *in vitro*. *In Vitro* **20**, 912–922.

Chung, B. C., Matteson, K. J., Voutilainen, R., Mohandas, T. K. & Miller, W. L. 1986 Human cholesterol side-chain cleavage enzyme, P450scc: cDNA cloning, assignment of the gene to chromosome 15, and expression in the placenta. *Proc. natn. Acad. Sci. U.S.A.* **83**, 8962–8966.

Cohen-Haguenauer, O., Picard, J. Y., Mattéi, M. G., Serero, S., Van Cong, N., de Tand, M. F., Guerrier, D., Hors-Cayla, M. C., Josso, N. & Frézal, J. 1987 Mapping of the gene for anti-Müllerian hormone to the short arm of human chromosome 19. *Cytogenet. Cell Genet.* **44**, 2–6.

Donahoe, P. K., Cate, R. L., McLaughlin, D. T., Epstein, J., Fuller, A. F., Takahashi, M., Coughlin, J. P., Ninfa, E. G. & Taylor, L. A. 1987 Müllerian inhibiting substance: gene structure and mechanism of action of a fetal regressor. *Recent Progr. Horm. Res.* **43**, 431–467.

Jost, A. 1965 Gonadal hormones in the sex differentiation of the mammalian fetus. In *Organogenesis* (ed. R. L. DeHaan & H. Ursprung), pp. 611–628. New York: Holt, Rinehart and Winston.

Jost, A. 1970 Hormonal factors in the sex differentiation of the mammalian foetus. *Phil. Trans. R. Soc. Lond.* B **259**, 119–130.

Jost, A. 1972 Données préliminaires sur les stades initiaux de la différenciation du testicule chez le rat. *Archs Anat. microsc. Morph. exp.* **61**, 415–438.

Jost, A., Valentino, O., Agelopoulou, R. & Magre, S. 1985 Action d'un analogue de la proline (acide L-azétidine-2-carboxylique) sur la différenciation *in vitro* du testicule foetal de rat. *C. r. Acad. Sci.*, Paris **301**, 225–232.

Jost, A., Vigier, B. & Prépin, J. 1972 Freemartins in cattle: the first steps of sexual organogenesis. *J. Reprod. Fert.* **29**, 349–379.

Jost, A., Vigier, B., Prépin, J. & Perchellet, J. P. 1973 Studies on sex differentiation in mammals. *Recent Progr. Horm. Res.* **29**, 1–41.

Kitahara, Y. 1923 Über die Entstehung der Zwischenzellen der Keimdrusen des Menschen und der Säugetiere und über deren physiologische Bedeutung. *Arch. EntwMech. Org.* **52**, 571–604.

Magre, S. 1983 Différenciation des cellules de Sertoli primordiales et organogenèse testiculaire chez le foetus de rat. Thesis, Université Pierre et Marie Curie, Paris.

Magre, S. & Jost, A. 1980 The initial phases of testicular organogenesis in the rat. An election microscopy study. *Archs Anat. microsc. Morph. exp.* **69**, 297–318.

Magre, S. & Jost, A. 1984 Dissociation between testicular organogenesis and endocrine cytodifferentiation of Sertoli cells. *Proc. natn. Acad. Sci. U.S.A.* **81**, 7831–7834.

Matteson, K. J., Picado-Leonard, J., Chung, B. C., Mohandas, T. K. & Miller, W. L. 1986 Assignment of the gene for adrenal P450c17 (steroid 17α-hydroxylase/17,20 lyase) to human chromosome 10. *J. clin. Endocr. Metab.* **63**, 789–791.

Patsavoudi, E., Magre, S., Castanier, M., Scholler, R. & Jost, A. 1985 Dissociation between testicular morphogenesis and functional differentiation of Leydig cells. *J. Endocr.* **105**, 235–238.

Pelliniemi, L. J. & Niemi, M. 1969 Fine structure of the human foetal testis. I. The interstitial tissue. *Z. Zellforsch. mikrosk. Anat.* **99**, 507–522.

Picon, R. 1969 Action du testicule foetal sur le développement *in vitro* des canaux de Müller chez le rat. *Archs Anat. microsc. Morph. exp.* **58**, 1–19.

Upadhyay, S. & Zamboni, L. 1982 Ectopic germ cells: Natural model for the study of germ cell sexual differentiation. *Proc. natn. Acad. Sci. U.S.A.* **79**, 6584–6588.

Vigier, B., Picard, J. Y., Tran, D., Legeai, L. & Josso, N. 1984 Production of anti-Müllerian hormone: another homology between Sertoli and granulosa cells. *Endocrinology* **114**, 1315–1320.

Voutilainen, R. & Miller, W. L. 1986 Developmental expression of genes for the stereoidogenic enzymes P450scc (20,22-desmolase), P450c17 (17α-hydroxylase/17,20-lyase), and P450c21 (21-hydroxylase) in the human fetus. *J. clin. Endocr. Metab.* **63**, 1145–1150.

Witschi, E. 1930 The geographical distribution of the sex races of European grass frog (Rana temporaria). A contribution to the problem of the evolution of sex. *J. exp. Zool.* **56**, 149.

Witschi, E. 1942 Temperature factors in the development and the evolution of sex. *Biol. Symp.* **6**, 57–70.

Witschi, E. 1951 Embryogenesis of the adrenal and the reproductive glands. *Recent Progr. Horm. Res.* **6**, 1–27.

Witschi, E. 1957 The inductor theory of sex differentiation. *J. Fac. Sci. Hokkaido Univ.* VI **13**, 428–439.

Zamboni, L. & Upadhyay, S. 1983 Germ cell differentiation in mouse adrenal glands. *J. exp. Zool.* **228**, 173–193.

Discussion

ANNE MCLAREN, F.R.S. (*MRC Mammalian Development Unit, University College London, U.K.*). Anti-Müllerian hormone (= Müllerian inhibitor) is reported to be produced not only by foetal Sertoli cells, but also by follicle cells in the adult ovary. Is it known whether all follicle cells, even those in primordial follicles, produce this hormone, or is it restricted to growing follicles?

A. JOST. AMH is not produced by follicle cells during the first few days after birth, which would suggest that it is restricted to growing follicles.

H. SHARMA (71 *Barrack Road, Hounslow, U.K.*). In the role of foetal calf serum inhibiting development *in vitro*, was foetal calf serum pooled from male and female foetuses?

A. JOST. It certainly was, because we used a commercial preparation. We did other assays using serum from either male or female rats, in which the sex of the serum donor did not influence the mode of differentiation of the gonads.

Phil. Trans. R. Soc. Lond. B **322**, 63–72 (1988) [63]
Printed in Great Britain

Role of mammalian Y chromosome in sex determination

By P. S. Burgoyne
MRC Mammalian Development Unit, Wolfson House, 4 Stephenson Way, London NW1 2HE, U.K.

It has long been assumed that the mammalian Y chromosome either encodes, or controls the production of, a diffusible testis-determining molecule, exposure of the embryonic gonad to this molecule being all that is required to divert it along the testicular pathway. My recent finding that Sertoli cells in XX↔XY chimeric mouse testes are exclusively XY has led me to propose a new model in which the Y acts cell-autonomously to bring about Sertoli-cell differentiation. I have suggested that all other aspects of foetal testicular development are triggered by the Sertoli cells without further Y-chromosome involvement. This model thus equates mammalian sex determination with Sertoli-cell determination. Examples of natural and experimentally induced sex reversal are discussed in the context of this model.

Introduction

More than four decades have passed since Jost (1947, 1953) did an elegant series of experiments on rabbit foetuses, from which he concluded that the development of male characteristics was brought about by two testicular secretions: testosterone and a Müllerian inhibitor. As a consequence of this work, the term 'sex determination', as applied to mammals, has come to be used interchangeably with 'testis determination'. Although there are certain male characteristics of the tammar wallaby (and presumably of marsupials in general) that are independent of testicular development (O *et al.* 1988; Renfree & Short, this symposium), in the eutherian mammals one can still equate 'sex determination' with 'testis determination'.

What then is meant by testis determination? In the absence of a Y chromosome the mammalian embryonic gonad develops as an ovary, whereas in the presence of the Y the embryonic gonad is diverted to form a testis. Testis determination is the process, initiated by the Y chromosome, by which the embryonic gonad becomes 'locked in' to the testicular pathway. It is inherent to the concept of testis determination that, if the process were to be interrupted, the gonad would develop as an ovary (as distinct from an abnormal testis, or ovotestis). A testis-determining gene can be defined as any gene that is involved in this 'locking in' process. Complete inactivation of such a gene would result in ovarian development, although partial activity could result in the development of ovotestes.

What distinguishes early testicular development from early ovarian development?

Before considering how the Y acts to bring about testis determination, it is necessary to have a basic understanding of the differences between early ovarian and testicular development. An important point, emphasized by Jost in this symposium, is that the differentiation of testicular cell types occurs earlier than the differentiation of ovarian cell types: during the initial stages of sex differentiation the female gonad is recognized solely by the absence of testicular cell types and organization. There are thought to be three gonad-specific cell lineages in the embryonic gonad, each of which has to be diverted to a new fate in the developing testis. Firstly, there is the germ-cell lineage, destined to form meiotic oocytes in the foetal ovary, but which is diverted in the developing testis to form prospermatogonia arrested in the G1 phase of the mitotic cycle. Secondly, there is a 'supporting-cell' lineage which forms the follicles enveloping the oocytes in the ovary, but which is diverted to form the Sertoli cells that surround the germ cells in the foetal testis and are the source of Jost's 'Müllerian inhibitor'. Thirdly, there is a 'steroid-cell' lineage which contributes to the interstitial tissue of the foetal ovary, and ultimately to the oestrogen-secreting theca cells of the mature ovary, but which is diverted to form testosterone-secreting Leydig cells in the foetal testis. In addition to these lineages that form sex-specific cell types, there are vascular and connective tissue contributions to the developing gonads which adopt a more complex architecture in the foetal testis than the foetal ovary. The vascular and connective tissue framework of the foetal testis, of which the tunica albuginea is an integral part, provides the pathways for testosterone export.

How does the Y act to bring about testis determination?

Because the testicular cell types appear earlier than the corresponding ovarian cell types, the Y is acting to pre-empt ovarian development. The most widely accepted view of how the Y achieves this has assumed that there is only one gene on the Y involved in testis determination. In the mouse, this gene has been given the label *Tdy*, and in man, the label *TDF*. For simplicity's sake, in what follows I shall refer to the gene as '*Tdy*', irrespective of species. *Tdy* has been assumed to either encode, or control the production of, a diffusible testis-determining molecule. Under this model, an embryonic XX gonad exposed to this molecule would be diverted along the testicular pathway. Wachtel *et al.* (1975) proposed that the minor histocompatibility antigen H-Y was the long-sought testis-determining molecule, but the discovery of H-Y-negative male mice (McLaren *et al.* 1984; Simpson *et al.* 1986) showed that this was incorrect. Burgoyne *et al.* (1986) questioned the view that there was a diffusible testis-determining molecule, suggesting that the Y was in fact acting at the level of single cells (cell autonomously) in diverting the supporting-cell lineage to form Sertoli cells. Subsequently Burgoyne *et al.* (1988) analysed the sex chromosomal constitution of the cell types in postnatal testes of XX$\leftrightarrow$XY mouse chimeras, and found that although the Leydig cells and connective tissue elements included both XX and XY cells, the Sertoli cells and germ cells were exclusively XY-derived. The failure of testicular XX germ cells was already known to be due to the presence of two X chromosomes, rather than to the absence of *Tdy*. Thus XX*Sxr* germ cells (*Sxr* includes *Tdy*) are also absent from adult testes of 'sex-reversed' mice although they do enter the testicular pathway as prospermatogonia (reviewed by Burgoyne 1987). However, the failure to find any XX Sertoli cells led the authors to conclude that *Tdy* did indeed act cell autonomously in bringing about Sertoli-cell differentiation. They went on to suggest that diversion of all the other components of the embryonic gonad to the testicular pathway was directed by the Sertoli cells, and did not involve further Y-chromosome activity. This model thus equates sex determination with Sertoli-cell determination. The essential feature of this model is that at no point in the testis-determination pathway is a diffusible testis-determining molecule produced which is capable of diverting an embryonic XX gonad to form a testis (figure 1).

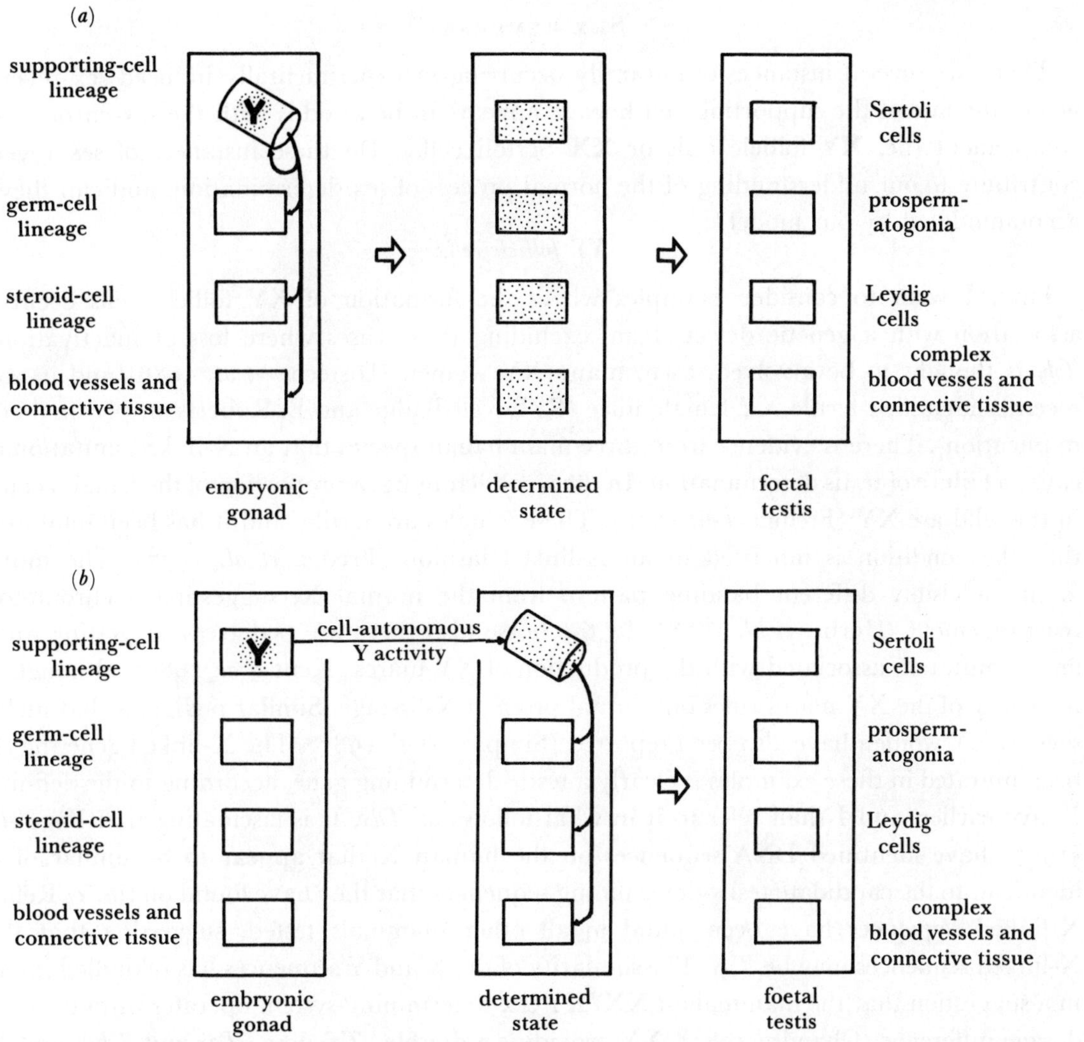

FIGURE 1. (*a*) Conventional model. In this model, Y-chromosome activity in the supporting cell lineage leads to the production of a diffusible testis-determining molecule which acts on all components of the embryonic gonad, including the supporting cells, and is responsible for 'locking' the embryonic gonad into the testicular pathway. Note that under this model an embryonic XX gonad exposed to the testis-determining molecule would develop as a testis. (*b*) Cell-autonomous Y-action model. In this model there is a Y-directed cell-autonomous step in the supporting cells which 'locks' them in to Sertoli-cell differentiation. Only after this cell-autonomous determination step does the supporting cell lineage interact with other components of the embryonic gonad to 'lock' them in to the testicular pathway. Note that there is no diffusible molecule produced that is capable of triggering the differentiation of Sertoli cells in an embryonic XX gonad.

Recently, a candidate testis-determining sequence has been cloned from the human Y chromosome (Page *et al.* 1987). The deduced protein sequence proved to be typical of a 'zinc finger' protein. This would be expected to bind to DNA or RNA, suggesting a cell-autonomous action for *Tdy*. Although this is consistent with the model we have proposed, it does not rule out the production of a diffusible testis-determining molecule in response to the zinc-finger protein 'trigger'. The findings of Page *et al.* (1987) are thus compatible with either of the models in figure 1.

Sex reversal

There are several instances of naturally occurring or experimentally induced sex reversal, where the fate of the supporting-cell lineage appears to be at odds with the sex-chromosome complement (i.e. XY follicle cells or XX Sertoli cells). Do these instances of sex reversal contribute to our understanding of the normal process of sex determination, and can they be accommodated by our model?

XY follicle cells

First, I want to consider examples where the formation of XY follicle cells occurs in association with a genetic defect. I am excluding those cases where loss or inactivation of *Tdy* is thought to be involved, as in many XY women (Disteche *et al.* 1986) and in some recently identified fertile XY female mice (R. Lovell-Badge and E. Robertson, personal communication). There is evidence from three mammalian species that an X-linked mutation can cause a failure of testis determination. In the wood lemming, a proportion of the females caught in the wild are XY (Fredga *et al.* 1976). These females are fertile, and it has been established that the condition is inherited in an X-linked fashion (Fredga *et al.* 1977). The mutant X has a visibly different banding pattern from the normal X, suggesting a chromosome rearrangement (Herbst *et al.* 1978). In the horse also there are pedigrees suggesting an X-linked mutation associated with the production of XY mares (Kent *et al.* 1986), although the infertility of the XY mares rules out formal proof of X-linkage. Similar pedigrees that include several XY women have also been reported (Simpson *et al.* 1981). The X-linked gene that has been mutated in these examples is clearly a testis-determining gene, according to the definition I gave earlier, and I shall refer to it in what follows as *Tdx*. It is fascinating that Page *et al.* (1987) have identified DNA sequences on the human X that appear to be similar, if not identical, to the candidate testis-determining sequences that they have found on the Y. Related X-linked sequences have been found in all other mammals tested, suggesting that these X-linked sequences may be *Tdx*. The similarity of the X and Y sequences has rekindled interest in a suggestion that the mammalian XX/XY sex-determining system operates through a gene dosage difference (Chandra 1985), XY providing a double '*Td*' dose (*Tdx* and *Tdy*), and XX providing a single '*Td*' dose, one of the two copies of *Tdx* being X-inactivated. Before leaving this topic, it is worth pointing out that a *Tdx* mutation has never been found in the mouse, despite extensive breeding tests with X-linked markers (Russell 1976). However, Page *et al.* (1987) have reported the mouse to be unusual in having two copies of the putative testis-determining sequence on the Y, raising the possibility that the mouse *Tdx* is redundant.

Autosomal genes have also been implicated in testis determination, both in man (de la Chapelle 1987) and mouse (reviewed by Eicher & Washburn 1986). The most interesting of these, T-associated sex reversal (*Tas*) in mice, is described in detail by Eicher elsewhere in this symposium, and appears to have the right credentials for a testis-determining gene. The other genes referred to by Eicher & Washburn are less well understood, and are not necessarily in the testis-determining pathway. *Tda-1*, for example, is defined by the finding that a *Mus domesticus* Y chromosome is inefficient in testis determination when on a C57BL/6 inbred background – adult XY individuals may be males, females or true hermaphrodites – although it functions normally on other inbred backgrounds. This could be because of the C57BL *Tda-1* allele responding poorly to the signal from the foreign Y. However, Eicher & Washburn (1987) have suggested that the *M. domesticus* Y is late-acting, so that *Tda-1* expression, rather than being reduced, may simply be too late in some cases to pre-empt ovarian development. In this latter scenario, *Tda-1* could instead be an ovary-determining gene, with C57BL/6 having an early acting *Tda-1* allele.

The preceding examples of XY follicle cells, although they point to there being several steps in the testis-determination process, do not pose any problems for the model we have proposed. However, Ford *et al.* (1974) reported obtaining XY mitotic cells (which they presumed to be follicle cells) from the ovaries of two XX↔XY female chimeras. Because of our finding that Sertoli cells in XX↔XY male chimeras are exclusively XY, we felt that the existence of XY follicle cells in XX↔XY female chimeras needed confirmation. Our first approach was to isolate follicles from an XX, CBA↔XY, BALB/c female chimera, separate the follicle cells from the oocytes, and then assay the follicle cells from single follicles for GPI-A (BALB/c) and GPI-B (CBA) activity. The results showed that approximately one third of the follicles included cells of both GPI types. To rule out the possibility that these GPI-A-positive cells were XO (the Y could be lost by nondisjunction) we did *in situ* hybridization to sections of XX↔XY chimeric ovaries by using a Bkm-related probe which hybridizes predominantly to the mouse Y (Singh *et al.* 1984). This confirmed the presence of XY cells in some follicles (P. S. Burgoyne, M. Buehr, P. Koopman and A. McLaren, unpublished data).

If follicle cells are derived from the supporting-cell lineage, and the Y acts in this lineage to bring about Sertoli-cell differentiation, how can one account for these XY follicle cells? McLaren (1987) suggested 'that the presence of *Tdy* sequences in the genome of a supporting cell is a necessary but not a sufficient condition to determine its development as a Sertoli cell. There needs also to be an inducing signal that has to reach a certain threshold intensity, reflecting perhaps a minimum ratio of XY to XX cells'. In terms of our model, it seems to me that this 'inducing signal' must come from the supporting-cell lineage because it is produced as a consequence of *Tdy* activity. Moreover, it cannot be sufficient by itself to bring about Sertoli-cell differentiation from the supporting-cell lineage, because it does not meet the criterion of cell-autonomous action. McLaren (1987) has envisaged this 'inducing signal' acting back on the supporting-cell lineage to close off the option for follicle-cell differentiation (a restriction of potency). An alternative explanation for the formation of XY follicle cells in XX↔XY females can be derived from Eicher & Washburn's (1986) hypothesis for explaining XY sex reversal. Briefly, if the XY component of the XX↔XY chimera has a late-acting *Tdy* allele, then *Tdy* action could be pre-empted by the ovary-determining programme of the XX component. The recruitment of XY cells to form follicle cells would require that a follicle cell 'inducing signal' was produced by the XX component. An attractive possibility is that this 'inducing signal' comes from early meiotic oocytes.

XX Sertoli cells

Let us now look at the other side of the coin and consider examples where XX supporting cells have formed Sertoli cells. First, I shall deal with examples where there is evidence for a genetic defect. I am excluding those cases where Y chromosomal material (presumed to include *Tdy*) has been shown to be present, such as in XX*Sxr* male mice (Singh & Jones 1982) and in most XX men (Affara *et al.* 1986; Vergnaud *et al.* 1986). There are human pedigrees that include several true hermaphrodites, sometimes also including XX males (de la Chapelle 1987). The pattern of inheritance suggests an autosomal recessive. The recessive nature of the defect certainly argues against the involvement of *Tdy*; indeed, all XX true hermaphrodites and some XX males appear to lack Y chromosomal sequences (Vergnaud *et al.* 1986; Waibel *et al.* 1987).

A second genetic defect leading to the formation of XX Sertoli cells is found in goats. Once again there is an autosomal recessive pattern of inheritance, and the sex reversal is intriguingly linked with a dominant polling effect (Soller & Angel 1964). Thus heterozygous polled XX goats lack horns and are female, whereas homozygous polled XX goats lack horns and are sex-reversed. The degree of sex reversal of the genital ducts and external genitalia is variable, with only a minority showing complete masculinization (Soller *et al.* 1969). Short (1972) has reported on the gonads of intersex XX goat foetuses, and it seems that the embryonic gonad may be diverted along the testicular pathway from the outset, although sufficient detail on early stages is not yet available.

How can we explain the diversion of the supporting-cell lineage to form Sertoli cells in the absence of a Y chromosome, and why is the degree of masculinization so variable? There are no satisfactory answers to these questions, and it is disappointing that intersex goats have received little attention for over a decade. It is perhaps worth commenting that under the '*Td*' gene dosage model for sex determination, expression of both copies of *Tdx* could lead to the development of testes in XX individuals.

I now want to consider examples where genetically normal XX cells have given rise to Sertoli cells. Into this category falls the classic case of the bovine freemartin, which is a genetically female calf masculinized as a consequence of placental anastomosis between its own placenta and that of a male twin. The solution to the bovine freemartin puzzle is particularly illuminating, because it illustrates how a seemingly watertight case for the involvement of a diffusible molecule in testis determination can prove to be unsound. The most pertinent observations came from Professor Jost's laboratory (Jost *et al.* 1972, 1973, 1975). They were able to show that during the period of testis differentiation in the male cotwin, the freemartin gonad shows no sign of masculinization. Subsequently, during the period when oogonial proliferation and gonadal growth occurs in normal females, the freemartin gonad is severely inhibited and a tunica albuginea develops. As a consequence of this inhibition the freemartin gonad becomes depleted of germ cells and very few enter meiosis. Only after this period of inhibition do cords of Sertoli-like cells develop adjacent to the intra-ovarian rete. These observations clearly demonstrate that the formation of XX Sertoli cells in freemartin gonads is not a case of primary sex reversal, but rather that the Sertoli cells are forming in an abnormal ovary. I shall refer to this as secondary sex reversal.

Parallels to the freemartin story are found in my second example of XX Sertoli cells. Macintyre *et al.* (1960) and Turner (1969) reported the development of 'testis cords' in foetal rat and mouse ovaries that had been cografted with developing testes to kidneys of castrated adult male hosts. Subsequent studies by Ozdzeński *et al.* (1976) and Burgoyne *et al.* (1986) showed that the initial effect of the developing testis on the ovarian cograft is to cause germinal failure and ovarian regression. If Sertoli cells are subsequently formed, then we are once again dealing with an example of secondary sex reversal.

Recently, Vigier *et al.* (1987) have reported that cultured foetal rat ovaries exposed to AMH (anti-Müllerian hormone: Jost's Müllerian inhibitor), show the ovarian inhibition, tunica albuginea formation and subsequent development of Sertoli-cell cords, which characterize the freemartin gonad. This strongly supports an earlier suggestion (Jost *et al.* 1975) that AMH from the male twin (see Vigier *et al.* 1984) is the mediator of the freemartin effect. It also seems reasonable to attribute the ovarian inhibition and subsequent development of Sertoli-cell cords in the ovaries cografted with developing testes, referred to above, to an effect of AMH originating from the testicular grafts. Similarly, a report of the appearance of 'testicular structures' (i.e. cords) in rotation cultures of newborn rat ovarian cells cultured in medium 'conditioned' by newborn rat testicular cells (Zenzes *et al.* 1978), could also be due to AMH secreted by the testicular (Sertoli) cells.

Foetal mouse ovaries grafted alone to adult male host kidneys may also develop Sertoli-cell cords after a period of ovarian regression (Taketo-Hosotani *et al.* 1985). Suspicions that AMH might again be responsible were allayed by the finding that it also occurred in castrated male hosts (Taketo & Merchant-Larios 1986), and in any case it now seems that adult mammalian testes do not produce detectable amounts of AMH (Tran *et al.* 1987). Although male hosts were at first thought to be necessary to obtain the masculinization of the foetal ovaries, it was later found to occur at a low frequency in female hosts. The frequency could be increased to that in male hosts if the mesonephros (usually present in the graft) was removed before grafting (Taketo-Hosotani & Sinclair-Thompson 1987). A notable feature of these studies was the convincing ultrastructural evidence that the Sertoli cells were derived from 'pre-granulosa cells', that is, cells that would have formed follicles if oocytes had been present. Also, it was shown that peritubular myoid cells and testosterone-secreting 'Leydig cells' differentiated in association with the Sertoli-cell cords.

Cords of Sertoli-like cells are also an occasional feature of ageing rat ovaries (Crumeyrolle-Arias *et al.* 1976, 1986), and here again there is evidence that they are derived from their ovarian counterparts, the follicle cells.

What can we learn from these examples of secondary sex reversal? First, because XX cells can form Sertoli cells, it is clear that the pattern of gene activity that defines the Sertoli cell phenotype does not involve genes on the Y chromosome. During normal testis development *Tdy* must act simply as a trigger for Sertoli cell differentiation, and continued expression of *Tdy* is presumably not required. Secondly, it does seem that supporting cells in the ovary in their various guises (pregranulosa cells, follicle cells) retain an ability to transdifferentiate into Sertoli cells. The fact that in all cases this 'transdifferentiation' is associated with germinal failure, makes one wonder whether oocytes have a positive role to play in maintaining ovarian supporting cells in their differentiated state. A third important point is that peritubular cells and Leydig cells form in the masculinized ovarian grafts described by Taketo-Hosotani *et al.* (1985). This implies that the differentiation of these cells is triggered by the Sertoli cells. Finally, the results of Vigier *et al.* (1987) focus attention on a possible autocrine role for AMH in testicular development, in addition to its known role in Müllerian duct regression.

Conclusion

The recent isolation of testis-determining sequences from the Y chromosome (Page *et al.* 1987), together with the earlier cloning of AMH (Cate *et al.* 1986; Picard *et al.* 1986), opens up new molecular approaches to the study of mammalian sex differentiation. We hope the model for testis determination presented here may prove useful in formulating hypotheses which can be tested in the years to come.

References

Affara, N. A., Ferguson-Smith, M. A., Tolmie, J., Kwok, K., Mitchell, M., Jamieson, D., Cooke, A. & Florentin, L. 1986 Variable transfer of Y-specific sequences in XX males. *Nucl. Acids Research* **14**, 5375–5387.

Burgoyne, P. S. 1987 The role of the mammalian Y chromosome in spermatogenesis. In *The mammalian Y chromosome: molecular search for the sex-determining factor* (*Development* **101** (suppl.)), pp. 133–141. Cambridge: Company of Biologists.

Burgoyne, P. S., Ansell, J. D. & Tournay, A. 1986 Can the indifferent mammalian XX gonad be sex-reversed by interaction with testicular tissue? In *Development and function of the reproductive organs* (ed. A. Eshkol, B. Eckstein, N. Dekel, H. Peters & A. Tsafriri), pp. 23–39. Rome: Ares-Serono Symposia.

Burgoyne, P. S., Buehr, M., Koopman, P., Rossant, J. & McLaren, A. 1988 Cell-autonomous action of the testis-determining gene: Sertoli cells are exclusively XY in XX↔XY chimaeric mouse testes. *Development* **102**, 443–450.

Cate, R. L., Mattaliano, R. J., Hession, C., Tizard, R., Farber, N. M., Cheung, A., Ninfa, E. G., Frey, A. Z., Gash, D. J., Chow, E. P., Fisher, R. A., Bertonis, J. M., Torres, G., Wallner, B. P., Ramachandran, K. L., Ragin, R. C., Manganaro, T. F., MacLaughlin, D. T. & Donahoe, P. K. 1986 Isolation of the bovine and human genes for Müllerian inhibiting substance and expression of the human gene in animal cells. *Cell* **45**, 685–698.

Chandra, H. S. 1985 Is human X chromosome inactivation a sex-determining device? *Proc. natn. Acad. Sci. U.S.A.* **82**, 6947–6949.

Crumeyrolle-Arias, M., Scheib, D. & Ascheim, P. 1976 Light and electron microscopy of the ovarian interstitial tissue in the senile rat: normal aspect and response to HCG of 'deficiency cells' and 'epithelial cords'. *Gerontology* **22**, 185–204.

Crumeyrolle-Arias, M., Zaborski, P., Scheib, D., Latouche, J. & Ascheim, P. 1986 Differentiation of Sertoli-like cells in senescent ovaries of both intact and hypophysectomized rats and its relation to ovarian H-Y antigen expression. In *Modern trends in ageing research* (ed. Y. Courtois, B. Faucheux, B. Forette, D. L. Knook & J. A. Tréton), vol. 147, pp. 117–120. John Libbey Eurotext Ltd.

de la Chapelle, A. 1987 The Y-chromosomal and autosomal testis-determining genes. In *The mammalian Y chromosome: molecular search for the sex-determining factor* (*Development* **101** (suppl.)), pp. 33–38. Cambridge: Company of Biologists.

Disteche, C. M., Casanova, M., Saal, H., Friedman, C., Sybert, V., Graham, J., Thuline, H., Page, D. C. & Fellous, M. 1986 Small deletions of the short arm of the Y chromosome in 46, XY females. *Proc. natn. Acad. Sci. U.S.A.* **83**, 7841–7844.

Eicher, E. M. & Washburn, L. L. 1986 Genetic control of primary sex determination in mice. *A. Rev. Genet.* **20**, 327–360.

Ford, C. E., Evans, E. P., Burtenshaw, M. D., Clegg, H., Barnes, R. D. & Tuffrey, M. 1974 Marker chromosome analysis of tetraparental AKR↔CBA – T6 mouse chimeras. *Differentiation* **2**, 321–333.

Fredga, K., Gropp, A., Winking, H. & Frank, F. 1976 Fertile XX- and XY-type females in the wood lemming *Myopus schisticolor*. *Nature, Lond.* **261**, 225–227.

Fredga, K., Gropp, A., Winking, H. & Frank, F. 1977 A hypothesis explaining the exceptional sex ratio in the wood lemming (*Myopus schisticolor*). *Hereditas* **85**, 101–104.

Herbst, E. W., Fredga, K., Frank, F., Winking, H. & Gropp, A. 1978 Cytological identification of two X-chromosome types in the wood lemming (*Myopus schisticolor*). *Chromosoma* **69**, 185–191.

Jost, A. 1947 Recherches sur la différenciation sexuelle de l'embryon de lapin. III. Rôle des gonades foetales dans la différenciation sexuelle somatique. *Archs Anat. microsc. Morphol. Exp.* **36**, 271–315.

Jost, A. 1953 Problems of fetal endrocrinology: the gonadal and hypophyseal hormones. *Recent Prog. Horm. Res.* **8**, 379–418.

Jost, A., Perchellet, J. P., Prépin, J. & Vigier, B. 1975 The prenatal development of bovine freemartins. In *Symposium on intersexuality* (ed. R. Reinboth), pp. 392–406. Berlin: Springer-Verlag.

Jost, A., Vigier, B. & Prépin, J. 1972 Freemartins in cattle: the first steps of sexual organogenesis. *J. Reprod. Fert.* **29**, 349–379.

Jost, A., Vigier, B., Prépin, J. & Perchellet, J. P. 1973 Studies on sex differentiation in mammals. *Recent Prog. Horm. Res.* **29**, 1–41.

Kent, M. G., Shoffner, R. N., Buoen, L. & Weber, A. F. 1986 XY sex-reversal syndrome in the domestic horse. *Cytogenet. Cell Genet.* **42**, 8–18.

Macintyre, M. N., Hunter, J. E. & Morgan, A. H. 1960 Spatial limits of activity of fetal gonadal inductors in the rat. *Anat. Rec.* **138**, 137–147.

McLaren, A. 1987 Sex determination and H-Y antigen in mice. In *Genetic markers of sex differentiation* (ed. F. P. Haseltine, M. E. McClure & E. H. Goldberg), pp. 87–97. New York: Plenum.

McLaren, A., Simpson, E., Tomonari, K., Chandler, P. & Hogg, H. 1984 Male sexual differentiation in mice lacking H-Y antigen. *Nature, Lond.* **312**, 552–555.

O, W.-S., Short, R. V., Renfree, M. B. & Shaw, G. 1988 Primary genetic control of somatic sexual differentiation in a mammal. *Nature, Lond.* **331**, 716–717.

Ozdzeński, W., Rogulska, T., Balakier, H., Brzozowska, A., Rembiszewska, A. & Stepińska, U. 1976 Influence of embryonic and adult testis on the differentiation of embryonic ovary in the mouse. *Archs Anat. microsc. Morph. exp.* **65**, 285–294.

Page, D. C., Mosher, R., Simpson, E. M., Fisher, E. M. C., Mardon, G., Pollack, J., McGillivray, B., de la Chapelle, A. & Brown, L. G. 1987 The sex-determining region of the human Y chromosome encodes a finger protein. *Cell* **51**, 1091–1104.

Picard, J.-Y., Benarous, R., Guerrier, D., Josso, N. & Kahn, A. 1986 Cloning and expression of cDNA for anti-Müllerian hormone. *Proc. natn. Acad. Sci. U.S.A.* **83**, 5464–5468.

Russell, L. B. 1976 Numerical sex-chromosome anomalies: their spontaneous occurrence and use in mutagenesis studies. In *Chemical mutagens* (ed. A. Hollaender), vol. 4, pp. 55–91. New York: Plenum.

Short, R. V. 1972 Germ cell sex. In *Edinburgh Symposium on the Genetics of the Spermatozoon* (ed. R. A. Beatty & S. Gluecksohn-Waelsch), pp. 325–345. Copenhagen: Bogtrykkeriet Forum.

Simpson, J. L., Blagowidow, N. & Martin, A. O. 1981 XY gonadal dysgenesis: genetic heterogeneity based upon clinical observations, H-Y antigen status and segregation analysis. *Hum. Genet.* **58**, 91–97.

Simpson, E., Chandler, P., Hunt, R., Hogg, H., Tomonari, K. & McLaren, A. 1986 H-Y status of X/XSxr′ male mice: in vivo tests. *Immunology* **57**, 345–349.

Singh, L. & Jones, K. W. 1982 Sex reversal in the mouse (*Mus musculus*) is caused by a recurrent nonreciprocal crossover involving the X and an aberrant Y chromosome. *Cell* **28**, 205–216.

Singh, L., Phillips, C. & Jones, K. W. 1984 The conserved nucleotide sequences of Bkm, which define *Sxr* in the mouse, are transcribed. *Cell* **36**, 111–120.

Soller, M. & Angel, H. 1964 Polledness and abnormal sex ratios in Saanen goats. *J. Hered.* **55**, 139–142.

Soller, M., Padeh, B., Wysoki, M. & Ayalon, N. 1969 Cytogenetics of Saanen goats showing abnormal development of the reproductive tract associated with the dominant gene for polledness. *Cytogenetics* **8**, 51–67.

Taketo, T. & Merchant-Larios, H. 1986 Gonadal sex reversal of fetal mouse ovaries following transplantation into adult mice. In *Progress in developmental biology* (ed. H. C. Slavkin) part A, pp. 171–174. New York: Alan R. Liss.

Taketo-Hosotani, T., Merchant-Larios, H., Thau, R. B. & Koide, S. S. 1985 Testicular cell differentiation in fetal mouse ovaries following transplantation into adult male mice. *J. exp. Zool.* **236**, 229–237.

Taketo-Hosotani, I. & Sinclair-Thompson, E. 1987 Influence of the mesonephros on the development of fetal mouse ovaries following transplantation into adult male and female mice. *Devl Biol.* **124**, 423–430.

Tran, D., Picard, J. Y., Campargue, J. & Josso, N. 1987 Immunocytochemical detection of anti-Müllerian hormone in Sertoli cells of various mammalian species including human. *J. Histochem. Cytochem.* **35**, 733–743.

Turner, C. D. 1969 Experimental reversal of germ cells. *Embryologia* **10**, 206–230.

Vergnaud, G., Page, D. C., Simmler, M.-C., Brown, L., Rouyer, F., Noel, B., Botstein, D., de la Chapelle, A. & Weissenbach, J. 1986 A deletion map of the human Y chromosome based on DNA hybridization. *Am. J. hum. Genet.* **38**, 109–124.

Vigier, B., Tran, D., Legeai, L., Bézard, J. & Josso, N. 1984 Origin of anti-Müllerian hormone in bovine freemartin fetuses. *J. Reprod. Fert.* **70**, 473–479.

Vigier, B., Watrin, F., Magre, S., Tran, D. & Josso, N. 1987 Purified bovine AMH induces a characteristic freemartin effect in fetal rat prospective ovaries exposed to it *in vitro*. *Development* **100**, 43–55.

Wachtel, S. S., Ohno, S., Koo, G. C. & Boyse, E. A. 1975 Possible role for H-Y antigen in the primary determination of sex. *Nature, Lond.* **257**, 235–236.

Waibel, F., Scherer, G., Fraccaro, M., Hustinx, T. W. J., Weissenbach, J., Wieland, J., Mayerová, A., Back, E. & Wolf, U. 1987 Absence of Y-specific DNA sequences in human 46, XX true hermaphrodites and in 45, X mixed gonadal dysgenesis. *Hum. Genet.* **76**, 332–336.

Zenzes, M. T., Wolf, U. & Engel, W. 1978 Organization in vitro of ovarian cells into testicular structures. *Hum. Genet.* **44**, 333–338.

Discussion

U. Wolf (*Institut für Humangenetik und Anthropologie der Universität Freiburg, F.R.G.*). Serological H-Y antigen has been shown to occur as a soluble factor, and to be present in the freemartin gonad (Wachtel *et al.* 1980). Is there evidence against the assumption that this factor is involved in the virilization of the freemartin gonad?

Reference

Wachtel, S. S., Hall, J. L., Müller, U. & Chaganti, R. S. K. 1980 Serum-borne H-Y antigen in the fetal bovine freemartin. *Cell* **21**, 917.

P. S. Burgoyne. Vigier *et al.* (1987) have demonstrated that the addition of purified bovine AMH to cultures of foetal rat ovaries *in vitro* causes the ovarian inhibition, tunica albuginea formation and development of Sertoli-cell cords which characterize the freemartin gonad. Jost had previously observed that the time of onset of the ovarian inhibition in the freemartin was correlated with the onset of AMH production of the cotwin. Vigier *et al.* (1987) therefore concluded that AMH is responsible for the virilization of the freemartin gonad. (It is of course possible that the 'H-Y' antiserum used by Wachtel *et al.* (1980) was cross reacting with AMH.)

M. W. J. Ferguson (*Department of Cellular and Structural Biology, University of Manchester, U.K.*). Dr Burgoyne's chimeric studies showed very nice exclusion of XX cells from the seminiferous tubules that were exclusively XY cells. This suggests differential cell sorting as a mechanism (as opposed to diffusible factors) and hence the expression of unique cell surface molecules such as cell-adhesion molecules, e.g. N-CAM, L-CAM, uvumorulin, or differential phosphorylation of such cell-adhesion molecules. Therefore has anyone studied the expression of cell-adhesion molecules in male and female gonads at different developmental times? This could be a possible mechanism for the organization of the medulla into a testis, which may in turn affect differentiation by altered cell–cell, cell–matrix interactions. Is the expression of the genes of cell-adhesion molecules regulated by sex genes or Y-specific genes or *TDF* even though the cell-adhesion genes may not themselves be on either an X or Y chromosome?

P. S. Burgoyne. As far as I am aware, there is no information on the expression of cell-adhesion molecules in the developing testis in response to Y-chromosome activity.

I believe the series of events leading to the absence of XX cells in the seminiferous tubules of adult XX↔XY chimeras to be as follows. (1) In the embryonic chimeric gonad, Y-chromosome expression in XY cells of the supporting cell lineage triggers their differentiation into Sertoli cells. (2) These XY Sertoli cells actively aggregate with each other and surround XX and XY germ cells to form testis cords. (The cell interactions presumably involve cell recognition and adhesion molecules.) (3) The Sertoli cells trigger the XX and XY germ cells to form prospermatogonia. (4) The XX prospermatogonia die perinatally because of the double X dosage.

Phil. Trans. R. Soc. Lond. B **322**, 73–81 (1988) [73]
Printed in Great Britain

H-Y antigen and sex determination

BY ELLEN H. GOLDBERG
Department of Microbiology, The University of New Mexico, School of Medicine, Albuquerque, New Mexico 87131, *U.S.A.*

The primary development of a male rather than a female gonad in mammals is determined by the presence of a Y chromosome. The other property unique to the Y chromosome is the occurrence of a cell-surface antigen (designated H-Y) which distinguishes male from female. Thus it was determined that male grafts were rejected by otherwise histocompatible females of the same inbred strain and later that H-Y-specific cytolytic T cells were produced by these grafted mice. When it was determined that females grafted with male skin produced antibody defining a serologically detectable male antigen (which may or may not be the same as H-Y), further immunogenetic analysis of this antigenic system became possible in terms of humoral and cellular factors. By using this assay it was demonstrated that the antigen was phylogenetically conserved and that it was expressed in the male mouse embryo as early as the 8-cell stage of development. The notion that H-Y was a single molecular species responsible for triggering the indifferent gonad to differentiate into the testis became a widely accepted hypothesis. In this report the H-Y antigenic system is traced historically from its original description to the role played in testis development. Data are presented which suggest that although H-Y is a male-specific factor and may play a role in male sex determination, it is unlikely that it is the primary inducer of testis differentiation.

1. HISTORY OF H-Y ANTIGEN

The H-Y antigen was originally defined by the ability of female mice to reject otherwise histocompatible male skin of the same inbred strain (Eichwald & Silmser 1955). In fact, the antigen was discovered by serendipity because the original design of Eichwald & Silmser's experiment was to look at the phenomenon of tolerance. C57BL/6(B6) mice were selected because of the inability to induce acquired immunological tolerance in this strain via the intra-uterine route of antigen administration. Without exception B6 male skin grafted to B6 female mice was rejected. Because the incompatibility between male and female was thought to be somehow linked to a gene or genes on the Y chromosome, the antigen responsible was designated H-Y (Billingham & Silvers 1960).

In the case of H-Y, in contrast to other alloantigenic systems, there was no conclusive serological demonstration of the antigen. Because this limited further genetic analysis and also restricted additional studies regarding the nature of the H-Y immune response in terms of cellular and humoral factors, we decided to determine whether or not the antigen could be detected serologically. Because of our interest in sperm-surface antigens and also because H-Y was male specific, the complement-mediated cytotoxic test was applied to mouse spermatozoa for the detection of a male-specific antigen, possibly the same as H-Y. Serum raised in B6 female mice that had rejected several male grafts was used with rabbit serum as a source of complement for the detection of male-specific antigen on B6 sperm. Results from this early work clearly showed that male-specific antigen was detectable serologically by the cytotoxicity test (hereafter denoted sperm cytotoxicity assay) *in vitro* (Goldberg *et al.* 1971), and secondly that it was present on sperm as was suggested earlier by indirect evidence (Katsh *et al.* 1964). This assay opened the floodgates to further analysis of this male-specific antigen. By using the sperm cytotoxicity assay it was demonstrated that the antigen was phylogenetically conserved, being expressed in cells from XY males of the guinea pig, human, rabbit and rat (Wachtel *et al.* 1975*a*; Wachtel 1983). For this reason it was proposed that H-Y antigen (whether the transplantation H-Y or the serologically detected male antigen was not discussed) played a critical role in male sex differentiation (Wachtel *et al.* 1975*b*; Ohno & Matsunaga 1981). This hypothesis was supported by the finding that serologically detected male antigen was expressed in the male embryo as early as the 8-cell stage of development in the mouse. By using the complement-dependent cytotoxicity assay and male-specific antiserum it was shown that 50% of 8-cell mouse embryos were lysed (Krco & Goldberg 1976). Affected embryos were male as demonstrated by chromosomal analysis in which more than 90% of the unaffected embryos were XX (Epstein *et al.* 1980), and also by embryo transfer techniques in which 82% of offspring resulting from transfer of unaffected embryos to surrogate mothers were female (Shelton & Goldberg 1984).

To provide an *in vitro* parallel to the rejection of male skin grafts, we modified the cell-mediated cytotoxicity (CMC) assay for the lysis of male target cells by H-Y specific cytolytic T lymphocytes (CTL) (Goldberg *et al.* 1973). Spleen cells from B6 female mice that were grafted with male skin served as a source of H-Y specific CTLs which were reacted with ^{51}Cr-labelled male lymph-node target cells; the results clearly indicated a specific lysis of male cells. This assay was further modified and extended by Gordon *et al.* (1975) to show that susceptibility of the male target cell to lysis was restricted by genes within the Major Histocompatibility Complex (Simpson & Gordon 1977; von Boehmer & Haas 1979). H-Y-specific T-cell clones were subsequently produced from immunized female mice (von Boehmer *et al.* 1979; Tomonari 1983; Simpson *et al.* 1984) and more recently human H-Y specific CTL clones have been described (Goulmy 1985). By using CTL clones in proliferation assays and cell-mediated cytotoxicity tests, it has been possible to H-Y type sex-reversed mice (McLaren *et al.* 1984) and humans (Simpson *et al.* 1987). The cell-mediated cytotoxicity assay has proved useful for providing an *in vitro* correlate to skin-graft rejection and has therefore permitted further analysis of H-Y, especially as it relates to sex determination.

(a) *Does H-Y represent a single molecular species?*

The male-specific antigen identified by serological assays and the H-Y antigen originally described by female rejection of male skin were thought to be the same (i.e. H-Y was a single molecular species). This assumption was questioned by Melvold *et al.* (1977) based on the finding of a single XO mutant male mouse. The mouse was H-Y negative by transplantation experiments and skin from this mouse was accepted by 13 females of the same strain. Moreover it rejected male skin much like females of that strain. On the other hand, it was positive for male-specific antigen when typed serologically. On the basis of this finding, it was concluded that two distinct male-specific antigenic systems existed, one recognized by transplantation assays and the other detectable serologically. In addition, it provided evidence that the structural gene for the serologically detected male-specific antigen was not on the Y chromosome.

Further support that there were two distinct male-specific antigens resulted from findings that XO female mice expressed the serologically detectable antigen (Koo *et al.* 1983; Engel *et al.* 1981) despite the fact that these females were able to reject male skin (Simpson *et al.* 1982). In addition, H-Y-specific CTLs were unable to lyse cells donated by XO mice, indicating the absence of H-Y (Simpson *et al.* 1982). These studies supported the concept that two distinct male-specific antigenic systems existed, one detectable by transplantation and cell-mediated immunological assays (designated H-Y) and the second recognized serologically (designated the serologically detectable male antigen (SDMA) (Silvers *et al.* 1982)). However, more recently a conflicting report appeared in which SDMA-negative XO female mice were described, suggesting again that H-Y and SDMA are the same (Wiberg & Mayerova 1985). Thus the question of multiplicity of the H-Y antigenic system is not yet resolved.

With the use of molecular probes and biochemical technology, the question of whether or not H-Y represents one or more antigens should be answered in the near future. Results recently reported by Lau *et al.* (1987) suggest that a gene encoding the serologically detected male antigen, designated 'male enhanced antigen (MEA)' gene, has been isolated from a mouse complementary DNA (cDNA) library. Interestingly, it was shown that the gene for MEA was conserved among the genome of several mammalian species including guinea pig, rabbit, bull, dog and human. However, additional technical controls and experiments designed to determine specificity need to be done before it can be concluded that this gene encodes SDMA.

It has been proposed recently that the abbreviation 'Sxs' (serological sex specific antigen) (Wiberg 1987) be used when referring to SDMA because the serological antigen is detectable in a variety of species in which the heterogametic sex is female. However, for this report, SDMA is used throughout to define the male-specific antigen detected by antibody-mediated reactions. (It should be noted that the above discussion does not preclude the possibility that there are more than two male-specific antigens.)

2. H-Y and SDM antigens: are they involved in testicular differentiation?

The presence of a Y chromosome is almost always associated with testicular differentiation in mammals: hence XY, XXY and XYY individuals develop as males, whereas XX and XO individuals develop as females. As pointed out by Eicher & Washburn (1986), there are clearly non-Y-chromosome genes involved in testicular differentiation, but the initial event is most likely encoded by a Y-linked gene designated testis-determining-Y (or *Tdy*). Using Y-chromosome-specific DNA probes, Page *et al.* (1987) recently found that human males with the incongruous XX karyotype bear a small part of the short arm of the Y chromosome and that females with the XY karyotype lack that part of the Y, indicating that this portion includes a gene or genes encoding the testis determining factor (TDF). A central question addressed here is whether the gene encoding TDF is the same as that which encodes the SDM or H-Y antigens. Evidence is given here in mouse and man that neither antigen is TDF, although indirect evidence may implicate these antigens in later events of testicular development.

(*a*) *Evidence supporting the hypothesis that H-Y or SDMA or both identify the testicular determining factor*

Phylogenetic conservation of the antigen and expression of SDMA on the early male mouse embryo (§1) has been used as indirect evidence that SDMA is involved in testis development (for additional reviews see Nakamura *et al.* (1987); Polani & Adinolfi (1983); Zenzes & Reed

(1984)). Direct evidence supporting the concept that SDMA served as a signal for testicular development came from experiments in which it was demonstrated that disaggregated newborn rodent testicular cells reassociated to form structures that were morphologically and histologically similar to seminiferous tubules, and that H-Y-specific antibody blocked the development of these structures (Ohno *et al.* 1978). Moreover, *in vitro* treatment of disaggregated newborn rat ovarian tissue with soluble SDMA induced the formation of testicular structures (Ohno *et al.* 1979; Muller & Urban 1981).

Sex-reversed mice that carry the sex-determining locus of the Y chromosome, designated Sxr, on the distal end of the paternal X chromosome have been described (Evans *et al.* 1982; Singh & Jones 1982). Although these mice are of the XX genotype, they are indisputably male. They typed positive for the H-Y and SDMAs by cell-mediated cytotoxicity and transplantation assays as well as by sperm cytotoxicity tests (Bennett *et al.* 1977; Simpson *et al.* 1981). These findings supported the proposition that H-Y or SDMA or both play a role in testis induction, perhaps as a product of the testis-determining Y gene.

However, reports of work using sex-reversed mice and humans demonstrated, in several situations, a lack of correlation between H-Y antigen expression and phenotypic sex, thereby challenging the original proposal that H-Y, but not SDMA, was the trigger for male testicular differentiation.

(*b*) *Evidence against H-Y being the testicular determining factor*

Eicher developed a strain of mouse that provided one of the earlier clues that H-Y as detected by cell-mediated assays and transplantation techniques was not the product of *Tdy*. She and colleagues (Eicher *et al.* 1982) were able to transfer the Y chromosome from *Mus poschiavinus* to the C57BL/6 background (denoted C57BL/6Y^{POS}), causing XY individuals to develop either as females with two ovaries or as hermaphrodites. None of the XY individuals developed normal testes. What is relevant to the argument presented here, is that C57BL/6-Y^{POS} XY females were H-Y positive as determined by transplantation assays (i.e. XY^{POS} female skin was rejected by XX female recipients as rapidly as skin donated by normal XY males; Silvers *et al.* 1986), indicating that H-Y was not acting as a signal for testicular differentiation. It was suggested that inappropriate interactions between the *M. poschiavinus* Y-linked *Tdy* gene and other non-Y-linked testis-determining genes on the B6 genomic background resulted in abnormal testis differentiation; thus the H-Y antigen might remain intact but be non-functional (Ohno 1985).

XXSxr mice in which the Sxr-bearing chromosome is partnered by an X-autosome translocated chromosome, abbreviated T16H/X^{Sxr}, can develop as males, females or hermaphrodites (McLaren & Monk 1982; Cattanach *et al.* 1982). Presumably this is due to preferential inactivation of the Sxr-bearing X chromosome in which there is variable inactivation of the Sxr segment. By using T-cell clones in proliferation assays and H-Y specific CTL-mediated reactions *in vitro*, T16H/X^{Sxr} females were shown to be H-Y antigen positive. However, one variant female derived from this stock was H-Y negative (Simpson *et al.* 1986; Wiberg & Lattermann 1987) and when mated to a normal male gave rise to XXSxr sons that lacked H-Y (McLaren *et al.* 1984). The authors conclude that this variant form of Sxr (designated Sxr′) retained the testis-inducing signal while losing the gene or genes encoding H-Y. In fact, these XXSxr′ males are able to reject male skin (Simpson *et al.* 1986), further supporting the finding that H-Y antigen is not expressed despite testicular differentiation in this experimental situation. Interestingly, Burgoyne *et al.* (1986) showed that in contrast to

XOSxr males, the testes of XOSxr′ males lack spermatocytes and spermatids, indicating an almost total block of spermatogenesis. These authors suggest that the segment of Sxr either mutated or lost in the Sxr′ DNA may contain the gene or genes responsible for spermatogenesis and that this gene may be the same as, or closely linked to, that encoding H-Y.

The finding that the genes encoding H-Y antigen and TDF were separable was confirmed in humans by Simpson *et al.* (1987), using human H-Y-specific CTL clones and sex-reversed individuals. Six XX males who carried part of the distal short arm of the Y chromosome necessary for testicular differentiation as described above (Page *et al.* 1987) were H-Y negative, whereas two XY females lacking this portion of the Y short arm were indisputably H-Y positive.

Although the findings described here indicate that H-Y, at least as detected by skin-graft rejection and cell-mediated assays, is not the primary sex determinant in mouse and humans, a central question is whether SDMA is the factor responsible for testicular development.

(*c*) *Evidence against SDMA being the testicular determining factor*

To determine the SDMA phenotype of XXSxr′ males, three coded groups of XX female mice were grafted respectively with skin from XXSxr males, XXSxr′ males or XX females; their serum was then tested for the presence of sperm cytotoxic antibody. The results summarized in table 1 show that a significant number of females immunized with XXSxr, but not with

TABLE 1. DETECTION OF ANTIBODY PRODUCED AGAINST SDMA BY USING SERUM FROM B6 FEMALE MICE IMMUNIZED WITH TISSUE FROM XX FEMALES, XXSXR MALES OR XXSXR′ MALES

(Absorption of serum with male and female tissue demonstrated specificity of the reaction for SDMA. Clearly then, neither H-Y nor SDM antigens identify a determinant involved in testicular differentiation (summarized in table 2), but may well be involved in later events of testis development.)

B6 female mice immunized with tissue from[a]	presence of SDMA antibody[b]
XX females	−
XXSxr males	+
XXSxr′ males	−

[a] All mice were initially inoculated with spleen cells from either XX females, XXSxr males or XXSxr′ males, followed by a skin graft from a donor of the same genotype 13 days later. All mice received a subsequent intraperitoneal injection of donor spleen cells 14–25 days before serum collection.

[b] As determined by sperm cytotoxicity assay against BALB/c epididymal sperm.

TABLE 2. SUMMARY OF H-Y AND SDM ANTIGEN EXPRESSION IN MICE OF VARIOUS KARYOTYPES AND PHENOTYPIC SEX

karyotype	phenotypic sex	H-Y *phenotype*[a]	SDMA *phenotype*
XX	female	−	−
XY	male	+	+
XXSxr	male	+	+
XXSxr′	male	−	−
XY^{POS}	female	+	not determined
XO	female	−	±[b]

[a] +, Presence; −, absence.

[b] XO females have been typed SDMA-positive and SDMA-negative in different studies (see § 1*a*).

XXSxr′, male tissue produced antibody that was cytotoxic to sperm (Ellen Goldberg, Anne McLaren and Brian Reilly, unpublished results). H-Y and SDMA phenotypes in mice of various phenotypes and karyotypic sex are shown in table 2.

Conclusion

The original description of H-Y by skin grafting experiments and the serological identification of H-Y opened an exciting and important field of study related to male sexual development. Controversies currently exist because of lack of identification of molecular factors involved in the events associated with testicular development. Now, with the application of molecular probes and biochemical technology, together with the availability of sex-reversed mice and humans, much of the controversy will be resolved and the role of H-Y in sexual differentiation will be determined.

References

Bennett, D., Mathieson, B. J., Scheid, M., Yanagisawa, K., Boyse, E. A., Wachtel, S. S. & Cattanach, B. M. 1977 Serological evidence for H-Y antigen in Sxr, XX sex-reversed phenotypic males. *Nature, Lond.* **265**, 255–257.

Billingham, R. E. & Silvers, W. K. 1960 Studies on tolerance of the Y chromosome antigen in mice. *J. Immun.* **85**, 14–26.

Boehmer, H. von & Haas, W. 1979 Distinct Ir genes for helper and killer cells in the cytotoxic response to H-Y antigen. *J. exp. Med.* **150**, 1134–1142.

Boehmer, H. von, Hengartner, H., Nabholz, M., Lernhardt, W., Schreier, M. H. & Haas, W. 1979 Fine specificity of a continuously growing killer cell clone specific for H-Y antigen. *Eur. J. Immun.* **9**, 592–597.

Burgoyne, P. S., Levy, E. R. & McLaren, A. 1986 Spermatogenic failure in male mice lacking H-Y antigen. *Nature, Lond.* **320**, 170–172.

Cattanach, B. M., Evans, E. P., Burtenshaw, M. D. & Barlow, J. 1982 Male, female and intersex development in mice of identical chromosome constitution. *Nature, Lond.* **300**, 445–446.

Eicher, E. M. & Washburn, L. L. 1986 Genetic control of primary sex determination in mice. *A. Rev. Genet.* **20**, 327–360.

Eicher, E. M., Washburn, L. L., Whitney, J. B. III & Morrow, K. E. 1982 *Mus poschiavinus* Y chromosome in the C57BL/6J murine genome causes sex reversal. *Science, Wash.* **217**, 535–537.

Eichwald, E. J. & Silmser, C. R. 1955 Communication. *Transplantn Bull.* **2**, 148–149.

Engel, W., Klemme, B. & Ebrecht, A. 1981 Serological evidence for H-Y antigen in XO-female mice. *Hum. Genet.* **57**, 68–70.

Epstein, C. J., Smith, S. & Travis, B. 1980 Expression of H-Y antigen on preimplantation mouse embryos. *Tissue Antigens* **15**, 63–67.

Evans, E. P., Burtenshaw, M. P. & Cattanach, B. M. 1982 Cytological evidence of meiotic crossing over between the X and Y chromosome of male mice carrying the sex-reversing (Sxr factor). *Nature, Lond.* **300**, 443–445.

Goldberg, E. H., Boyse, E. A., Bennett, D., Scheid, M. & Carswell, E. A. 1971 Serological demonstration of H-Y (male) antigen on mouse sperm. *Nature, Lond.* **232**, 478–480.

Goldberg, E. H., Shen, F.-W. & Tokuda, S. 1973 Detection of H-Y (male) antigen on mouse lymph node cells by the cell to cell cytotoxicity test. *Transplantation* **15**, 334–336.

Gordon, R. D., Simpson, E. & Samelson, L. E. 1975 In vitro cell-mediated immune responses to the male specific (H-Y) antigen in mice. *J. exp. Med.* **142**, 1108–1120.

Goulmy, E. 1985 Class-I-restricted human cytotoxic T lymphocytes directed against minor transplantation antigens and their possible role in organ transplantation. *Prog. Allergy* **36**, 44–72.

Katsh, G. F., Talmage, D. W. & Katsh, S. 1964 Acceptance or rejection of male skin by isologous female mice: effect of injection of sperm. *Science, Wash.* **143**, 41–42.

Koo, G. C., Reidy, J. A. & Nagamine, C. M. 1983 H-Y antigen in X0 mice. *Immunogenetics* **18**, 37–44.

Krco, C. J. & Goldberg, E. H. 1976 H-Y (male) antigen: detection on eight-cell mouse embryos. *Science, Wash.* **193**, 1134–1135.

Lau, Y.-F, Chan, K., Kan, Y. W. & Goldberg, E. 1987 Male-enhanced expression and genetic conservation of a gene isolated with an anti-H-Y antibody. *Trans. Ass. Am. Physns* **100**, 45–53.

McLaren, A. & Monk, M. 1982 Fertile females produced by inactivation of an X chromosome of 'sex-reversed' mice. *Nature, Lond.* **300**, 446–448.

McLaren, A., Simpson, E., Tomonari, K., Chandler, P. & Hogg, H. 1984 Male sexual differentiation in mice lacking H-Y antigen. *Nature, Lond.* **312**, 552–555.

Melvold, R. W., Kohn, H. I., Yergenian, G. & Fawcett, D. W. 1977 Evidence suggesting the existence of two H-Y antigens in the mouse. *Immunogenetics* **5**, 33–41.

Muller, U. & Urban, E. 1981 Reaggregation of rat gonadal cells in vitro: experiments on the function of H-Y antigen. *Cytogenet. Cell Genet.* **31**, 104–107.

Nakamura, D., Wachtel, S. S., Lance, U. & Beçak, W. 1987 On the evolution of sex determination. *Proc. R. Soc. Lond.* B**232**, 159–180.

Ohno, S. 1985 The Y-linked testis determining gene and H-Y plasma membrane antigen gene: are they one and the same? *Endocr. Rev.* **6**, 421–431.

Ohno, S. & Matsunaga, T. 1981 The role of H-Y plasma membrane antigen in the evolution of the chromosomal sex determining mechanism. In *Levels of genetic control* (ed. S. Subtelny & U.K. Abbott) pp. 235–246. New York: Alan R. Liss.

Ohno, S., Nagai, Y. & Ciccarese, S. 1978 Testicular cells lysostripped of H-Y antigen organize ovarian follicle-like aggregates. *Cytogenet. Cell Genet.* **20**, 351–364.

Ohno, S., Nagai, Y., Ciccarese, S. & Iwata, H. 1979 Testis-organizing H-Y antigen and the primary sex-determining mechanism of mammals. *Recent Prog. Horm. Res.* **35**, 449–476.

Page, D. C., Mosher, R., Simpson, E. M., Fisher, E. M. E., Mardon, G., Pollack, J., McGillivray, B., de la Chapelle, A. & Brown, L. G. 1987 The sex-determining region of the human Y chromosome encodes a finger protein. *Cell* **51**, 1091–1104.

Polani, P. E. & Adinolfi, M. 1983 The H-Y antigen and its functions: a review and a hypothesis. *J. Immunogenet.* **10**, 85–102.

Shelton, J. A. & Goldberg, E. H. 1984 Male-restricted expression of H-Y antigen on preimplantation mouse embryos. *Transplantation* **37**, 7–8.

Silvers, W. K., Gasser, D. L. & Eicher, E. M. 1982 H-Y antigen, serologically detectable male antigen and sex determination. *Cell* **28**, 439–440.

Silvers, W. K., Raab, S., Washburn, L. L. & Eicher, E. M. 1986 Expression of H-Y antigen unaltered in XY female mice. *Immunogenetics* **23**, 67–68.

Simpson, E. & Gordon, R. D. 1977 Responsiveness to H-Y antigen, Ir gene complementation and target cell specificity. *Immun. Rev.* **35**, 59–75.

Simpson, E., Chandler, P., Goulmy, E., Disteche, C. M., Ferguson-Smith, M. A. & Page, D. C. 1987 Separation of the genetic loci for the H-Y antigen and for testis determination on the human Y chromosome. *Nature, Lond.* **326**, 876–878.

Simpson, E., Chandler, P., Hunt, R., Hogg, H., Tomonari, K. & McLaren, A. 1986 H-Y status of X/XSxr′ male mice: in vivo tests. *Immunology* **57**, 345–349.

Simpson, E., Edwards, P., Wachtel, S. S., McLaren, A. & Chandler, P. 1981 H-Y antigen in Sxr mice detected by H-2-restricted cytotoxic T cells. *Immunogenetics* **13**, 355–358.

Simpson, E., McLaren, A. & Chandler, P. 1982 Evidence for two male antigens in mice. *Immunogenetics* **15**, 609–614.

Simpson, E., McLaren, A., Chandler, P. & Tomonari, K. 1984 Expression of H-Y antigen by female mice carrying Sxr. *Transplantation* **37**, 17–21.

Singh, L. & Jones, K. W. 1982 Sex reversal in the mouse (*Mus musculus*) is caused by a recurrent nonreciprocal crossover involving the X and an aberrant Y chromosome. *Cell* **28**, 205–216.

Tomonari, K. 1983 Antigen & MHC restriction specificity of two types of cloned male-specific T cell lines. *J. Immun.* **131**, 1641–1645.

Wachtel, S. S. 1983 Phylogenetic conservation of H-Y antigen: H-Y as inducer. In *H-Y antigen and the biology of sex determination* (ed. S. S. Wachtel), p. 55. New York: Grune & Stratton.

Wachtel, S. S., Koo, G. C. & Boyse, E. A. 1975*a* Evolutionary conservation of H-Y ('male') antigen. *Nature, Lond.* **254**, 270–272.

Wachtel, S. S., Ohno, S., Koo, G. C. & Boyse, E. A. 1975*b* Possible role for H-Y antigen in the primary determination of sex. *Nature, Lond.* **257**, 235–236.

Wiberg, U. H. 1987 Facts and consideration about sex-specific antigens. *Hum. Genet.* **76**, 207–219.

Wiberg, U. H. & Lattermann, U. 1987 Syngeneic male graft rejection by B6 female mice primed with spleen and testes of Sxr and Sxr′ mice. *Expl clin. Immunongenet.* **4**, 167–173.

Wiberg, U. H. & Mayerova, A. 1985 Serologically H-Y antigen-negative X0 mice. *J. Immunogenet.* **12**, 55–63.

Zenzes, M. T. & Reed, T. E. 1984 Variability of serologically detected male antigen titer and some resulting problems: a critical review. *Hum. Genet.* **66**, 103–109.

Discussion

M. Adinolfi (*Paediatric Research Unit, Guy's Hospital, London, U.K.*). I understand that Dr Goldberg has not been able to detect H-Y antigen on fresh sperms by immunofluorescence; however, she has detected H-Y molecules by immunofluorescent technique on mouse blastocyst at 8- to 15-cell stage. Does she think that the H-Y antigen is synthesized by these cells and, if so, what can be the biological function of these molecules at such an early stage of development?

Ellen H. Goldberg. H-Y antigen was detected serologically on the 8-cell mouse embryo by the complement-mediated cytotoxicity assay (Krco & Goldberg 1976). We did not use immunofluorescent labelling techniques for the detection of the antigen. When the 4-cell embryo was examined for the presence of H-Y it was not detectable. For this reason, we feel that the antigen is synthesized by the embryo and is not an adsorbed product of the sperm tail. In addition, further work demonstrated that H-Y, as detected serologically, is expressed by the male embryo.

Reference

Krco, C. J. & Goldberg, E. H. 1976 H-Y (male) antigen: detection on eight-cell mouse embryos. *Science, Wash.* **193**, 1134–1135.

U. Wiberg (*Institut für Humangenetik, Freiburg, F.R.G.*). Referring to Dr Goldberg's transplantation experiments with Sxr and Sxr′ males, to try to raise anti-Sxr antisera did she absorb such antisera with testis of Sxr and Sxr′?

Ellen H. Goldberg. To test for specificity for SDMA, antisera raised in B6 females against tissue from Sxr and Sxr′ males were absorbed with B6 male and female spleen cells before being tested for the presence of antibody to SDMA. The antisera were not absorbed with testes from Sxr and Sxr′ mice.

M. Bradley (*Medical School, University of Otago, New Zealand*). Firstly, does Dr Goldberg see killing of more than 50% of sperm in cytotoxic assay?

Has she tried using fluorescent-labelled antibodies to map distribution of H-Y on sperm?

Ellen H. Goldberg. Firstly, yes, we routinely see killing of more than 50% of sperm in the cytotoxic assay using H-Y specific antiserum and rabbit serum as a source of complement. However, there is variability from test to test and also among sperm from different mouse strains.

No, we have not tried using fluorescent-labelled antibodies to map the distribution of H-Y on sperm. However, Koo (1973), by using tobacco mosaic virus as a marker, was able to visualize a reaction on the acrosomal cap of mouse sperm by using immunoelectronmicroscopy and H-Y-specific antiserum.

Reference

Koo, G. C., Stackpole, C. W., Boyse, E. A., Hammerling, U. & Lardis, M. 1973 Topographical location of H-Y antigen on mouse spermatozoa by immuno-electron microscopy. *Proc. natn. Acad. Sci. U.S.A.* **70**, 1502–1505.

H. Sharma (71 *Barrack Road, Hounslow, U.K.*). Have cell lines been tested for H-Y positivity? Do any cancers produce 'aberrant' H-Y expression? Can Y-chromosomes or other chromosomes be introduced in H-Y negative cells to study H-Y expression?

Ellen H. Goldberg. Yes, cell lines have been tested for H-Y antigen expression and in some laboratories have been found to be positive. We have tested several murine tumour cell lines for the expression of SDMA and have found variable expression of the antigen depending on the line tested. We cannot determine with the serological assay 'aberrant' expression of the antigen. We have no experience in determining whether or not cells in which the Y-chromosome was introduced will express the H-Y antigen. To study H-Y further in terms of gene expression, it would be useful to be able to transfect H-Y negative cell lines and look for the expression of H-Y.

Phil. Trans. R. Soc. Lond. B **322**, 83–95 (1988) [83]
Printed in Great Britain

Aberrant chromosomal sex-determining mechanisms in mammals, with special reference to species with XY females

By K. Fredga

Department of Genetics, Uppsala University, Box 7003, S-750 07 Uppsala, Sweden

Both mouse and man have the common XX/XY sex chromosome mechanism. The X chromosome is of original size (5–6 % of female haploid set) and the Y is one of the smallest chromosomes of the complement. But there are species, belonging to a variety of orders, with composite sex chromosomes and multiple sex chromosome systems: XX/XY_1Y_2 and $X_1X_1X_2X_2/X_1X_2Y$. The original X or the Y, respectively, have been translocated on to an autosome. The sex chromosomes of these species segregate regularly at meiosis; two kinds of sperm and one kind of egg are produced and the sex ratio is the normal 1:1. Individuals with deviating sex chromosome constitutions (XXY, XYY, XO or XXX) have been found in at least 16 mammalian species other than man. The phenotypic manifestations of these deviating constitutions are briefly discussed. In the dog, pig, goat and mouse exceptional XX males and in the horse XY females attract attention. Certain rodents have complicated mechanisms for sex determination: *Ellobius lutescens* and *Tokudaia osimensis* have XO males and females. Both sexes of *Microtus oregoni* are gonosomic mosaics (male OY/XY, female XX/XO). The wood lemming, *Myopus schisticolor*, the collared lemming, *Dicrostonyx torquatus*, and perhaps also one or two species of the genus *Akodon* have XX and XY females and XY males. The XX, X*X and X*Y females of *Myopus* and *Dicrostonyx* are discussed in some detail. The wood lemming has proved to be a favourable natural model for studies in sex determination, because a large variety of sex chromosome aneuploids are born relatively frequently. The dosage model for sex determination is not supported by the wood lemming data. For male development, genes on both the X and the Y chromosomes are necessary.

Introduction

There are more than 4000 living species of mammal in the world. Like man and the mouse, the great majority have XX and XY sex chromosomes, but there are exceptions to the rule. In this paper I briefly discuss those exceptions, and also point out how exceptional individuals, and species with aberrant sex chromosome mechanisms, may contribute to our understanding of sex determination.

Multiple sex chromosome systems

Apparently complex sex chromosome systems can occur by translocations between one of the sex chromosomes and an autosome (Fredga 1970). When the original X has been translocated on to an autosome the sex chromosome mechanism is designated $XX(♀)/XY_1Y_2(♂)$ (or A^XA^X/A^XYA). The Y_1 is the original Y chromosome and Y_2 is the homologous autosome to which X was translocated. Thus Y_2 has nothing to do with sex determination. In species of this group the male has one chromosome more than the female. The long-nosed rat-kangaroo (*Potorous tridactylus*), the common shrew (*Sorex araneus*) and the Indian muntjac (*Muntiacus muntjak*) are the best-known examples of this group.

When the Y has been translocated on to an autosome the sex chromosome mechanism is designated $X_1X_1X_2X_2$(♀)/X_1X_2Y(♂) (or XXAA/XAA^Y). The X_1 is the original X chromosome and X_2 is the homologous autosome to which the Y was translocated. In species of this group the female has one chromosome more than the male. Mongooses of the genus *Herpestes* and spiral-horned antelopes of the genus *Tragelaphus* belong to this group.

Sometimes both the X and the Y fuse with the homologues of an autosome pair. Then large sex chromosomes occur which form a distinct chiasma (or chiasmata) at male meiosis. Male and female have the same chromosome number. The Chinese hamster (*Cricetulus griseus*) is a well-known example of this group.

However, all these species with composite sex chromosomes are from the point of view of sex determination rather unexciting. The sex chromosomes are distributed regularly at male meiosis and two kinds of sperm and one kind of egg are produced.

Individuals with deviating sex chromosome constitutions in species with normal sex chromosomes

There are individuals with deviating sex chromosome constitutions in several mammalian species as well as in man. Table 1 lists these species, both wild and domesticated. Only the commonest types of deviation are included, and mosaics are excluded unless no other example of that particular type of sex chromosome aberration has been reported. This applies particularly to the XYY group. Occasional mosaic specimens have been reported in the common shrew (XY/XYY), the cat (XY/XXY/XXYY; XX/XY/XXY/XXYY), the horse (XO/XYY), and cattle (XY/XYY). (References are given in table 1; in each row with more than one sex chromosome type, the references are given from left to right.) I shall not describe in detail the individual chromosome deviations and their phenotypic manifestations in the various species and specimens listed, but only give some general comments. Reviews of this field are given by Gustavsson (1980), Benirschke (1981) and Rieck & Herzog (1984).

The sex chromosome aneuploids considered here are those most commonly found in man. The incidence of XXY and XYY is approximately 1 per 1000 among newborn males, as is the incidence of XXX among females, but XO individuals make up only 2 per 10000 newborn females (Bond & Chandley 1983).

Thus it is not surprising that XXY individuals have been reported in several (10) of the 16 species listed in table 1. In addition, XXY wood lemmings have been found (table 3). It is remarkable that 'pure' XYY and XXX are so rare, only found in two species each: for example, no XXX mouse has been reported so far. The XO constitution, on the other hand, is relatively common and has been found in 11 of the species listed. It is also found in the wood lemming where it is the commonest sex chromosome deviation; among 220 wild-captured wood lemmings 6 were XO (Fredga *et al.* 1989).

The XXY constitution gives the same phenotypic manifestation in all species: they have a male phenotype in terms of external appearance and accessory reproductive structures, but are infertile due to testicular hypoplasia.

The XO constitution always gives a female phenotype, but there is a remarkable difference between large and small species with regard to fertility. Large mammals (with a long generation time) are infertile, small mammals are fertile. The rhesus monkey, the horse and the sheep have gonadal dysgenesis as in man. The XO tammar wallaby and XO pigs are infertile intersexes. In cattle only one single XO heifer has been reported; it had low-grade ovarian hypoplasia with follicles. The fertility of the few XO cats reported is as yet unknown.

In small rodents like the black rat, the mouse and the wood lemming, XO females are fertile, but at least in the mouse the reproductive lifespan is reduced owing to premature exhaustion of the supply of oocytes. The important difference between XO mice and XO women may simply be one of timescale, XO mice reaching puberty before X-deficiency effects in the oocyte become severe, XO women reaching puberty after all oocytes have degenerated (Lyon & Hawker 1973; Burgoyne & Biggers 1976).

In table 1 several species are also listed as having individuals with the 'wrong' chromosome constitution in relation to phenotypic sex. XX male individuals have been reported in the dog, pig, goat and mouse: they all have different genetic causes for the discrepancies between sex chromosome constitution and phenotypic sex.

TABLE 1. EXCEPTIONAL INDIVIDUALS IN NORMAL XX/XY MAMMAL SPECIES (MOSAICS IN BRACKETS)

	phenotype						
	male			female			
species	XXY	XYY	XX	XO	XXX	XY	references[a]
tammar wallaby, *Macropus eugenii*	x	·	·	x	·	·	1
common shrew, *Sorex araneus*	x	(x)	·	·	·	·	2–3
rhesus monkey, *Macaca mulatta*	·	·	·	x	·	·	4
dog, *Canis familiaris*	x	·	x	·	·	·	5–6
cat, *Felis catus*	x	(x)	·	x	·	·	7–9
horse, *Equus caballus*	(x)	(x)	·	x	x	x	10–14
pig, *Sus scrofa*	x	·	x	x	·	·	15–17
cattle, *Bos taurus*	x	(x)	x	x	x	·	18–25
goat, *Capra hircus*	·	·	x	·	·	·	26–27
sheep, *Ovis aries*	x	·	·	x	·	·	28–29
South American field mouse, *Akodon azarae*	·	·	·	x	·	·	30
Chinese hamster, *Cricetulus griseus*	x	·	·	·	·	·	31
mole rat, *Bandicota bengalensis*	·	·	·	x	·	·	32
black rat, *Rattus rattus*	x	·	·	x	·	·	33–35
brown rat, *Rattus norvegicus*	·	x	·	·	·	·	36
mouse, *Mus musculus*	x	x	x	x	·	x	37–45

[a] 1, Sharman *et al.* (1970); 2, Searle (1984); 3, Searle & Wilkinson (1986); 4, Weiss *et al.* (1973); 5, Clough *et al.* (1970); 6, Selden *et al.* (1978); 7, Centerwall & Benirschke (1973); 8, Loughman & Frye (1974); 9, Norby *et al.* (1974); 10, Chandley *et al.* (1975); 11, Höhn *et al.* (1980); 12, Kent *et al.* (1986); 13, Kent *et al.* (1988); 14, Trommershausen Bowling *et al.* (1987); 15, Breeuwsma (1968); 16, Breeuwsma (1970); 17, Nes (1968); 18, Scott & Gregory (1965); 19, Rieck (1970); 20, Dobryanov & Konstantinov (1970); 21, Handa & Muramatsu (1981); 22, Miyake *et al.* (1984); 23, Refsdal (1979); 24, Rieck *et al.* (1970); 25, Norberg *et al.* (1976); 26, Hamerton *et al.* (1969); 27, Soller *et al.* (1969); 28, Bruère *et al.* (1969); 29, Zartman *et al.* (1981); 30, Bianchi & Contreras (1967); 31, Ivett *et al.* (1978); 32, Sharma & Raman (1971); 33, Yong (1971); 34, Yosida *et al.* (1974); 35, Satya Prakash & Aswathanarayana (1977); 36, Yosida (1984); 37, Russell & Chu (1961); 38, Cattanach (1961); 39, Cattanach & Pollard (1969); 40, Rathenberg & Müller (1973); 41, Evans *et al.* (1978); 42, Das & Kar (1981); 43, Lyon *et al.* (1981); 44, Welshons & Russell (1959); 45, Eicher (1982).

In the dog intersexes are relatively common in cocker spaniels (Hare 1976). Selden *et al.* (1978) have described in some detail a family of cockers including an XX male with unilateral cryptorchidism (right inguinal testicle), hypoplastic penis, hypospadias and a uterus. The mother of this dog was an XX phenotypic female, but in fact she was a true hermaphrodite with bilateral ovotestes containing prominent testicular tubules as well as mature ovarian follicles. One possibility is that part of the Y (*Tdy*) had translocated on to one of the X chromosomes, and that the variable expression in mother and son was due to non-random inactivation of one or the other X chromosome (X or X^y).

The XX pigs included in table 1 are male pseudohermaphrodites, and so are the XX goats.

In the goat, sex reversal is closely associated with a dominant autosomal gene for hornlessness (Polled). All genetic females that are homozygous for Polled develop as phenotypic intersexes with testes and ovotestes.

The mouse XX males are the well-known XX^{Sxr} individuals. Sex reversal is explained by the translocation of a male-determining gene (*Tdy*) from the Y to one of the X chromosomes. XX^{Sxr} mice are phenotypically normal but sterile males.

The XY females in horses are of particular interest, because the XY sex-reversal syndrome is characterized by both genotypic and phenotypic heterogeneity. The gene(s) responsible for the syndrome can be transmitted through a carrier female or male. Pedigree analyses suggest two modes of inheritance: (i) an autosomal sex-limited dominant or an X-linked recessive transmitted though the female, and (ii) an autosomal sex-limited dominant or a Y-chromosomal mutation with variable expression transmitted though the male (Kent *et al.* 1986). The carrier stallion produced both XY daughters and normal XY sons, but no XX sons were found, as would be expected if this stallion had an increased probability of transferring a male-determining gene from his Y to his X at meiosis.

The phenotypic spectrum of the XY females ranges from nearly normal females to greatly masculinized mares. Kent *et al.* (1988) identified four phenotypic classes in 38 XY mares: (1) nearly normal female, of which two were fertile (5 mares); (2) female with gonadal dysgenesis, normal mullerian development (14 mares); (3) intersex mare with gonadal dysgenesis, abnormal mullerian development, enlarged clitoris (15 mares); and (4) virilized intersex characterized by high levels of testosterone (4 mares). The transmission of the XY sex-reversal syndrome probably involves at least two genes: a primary sex-reversing gene, and a modifier gene or group of genes (Kent *et al.* 1988).

Species with aberrant sex-chromosome mechanisms

Several species, all rodents, have aberrant sex-chromosome mechanisms (table 2). Two species, the collared lemming (*Dicrostonyx torquatus*) and the wood lemming (*Myopus schisticolor*) are well known because they have XY females. They will be dealt with in some detail below.

The next species in this group is the creeping vole (*Microtus oregoni*), famous for being a gonosomic mosaic in both the male (YO/XY) and the female (XX/XO) (table 2).

Table 2. Species with aberrant sex-chromosome mechanisms

	sex chromosomes				
	female		male		
	soma	germ	soma	germ	references[a]
Dicrostonyx torquatus	XX, X*X, X*Y	XX, X*X, X*Y	XY	XY	1–4
Myopus schisticolor	XX, X*X, X*Y	XX, X*X, X*X*	XY	XY	5–9
Microtus oregoni	XO	XX	XY	YO	10–12
Ellobius lutescens	XO	XO(?)	XO	XO	13–23
Tokudaia osimensis	XO	?	XO	XO	24–25

[a] 1, Gileva & Chebotar (1979); 2, Gileva (1980); 3, Gileva *et al.* (1982); 4, Gileva (1983); 5, Fredga *et al.* (1976); 6, Gropp *et al.* (1976); 7, Fredga *et al.* (1977); 8, Herbst *et al.* (1978); 9, Schempp *et al.* (1985); 10, Matthey (1958); 11, Ohno *et al.* (1963); 12, Ohno *et al.* (1966); 13, Matthey (1953); 14, Matthey (1964); 15, Castro-Sierra & Wolf (1967); 16, Schmid (1967); 17, Castro-Sierra & Wolf (1968); 18, Maza & Sawyer (1976); 19, Nagai & Ohno (1977); 20, Wolf *et al.* (1979); 21, Vorontsov *et al.* (1980); 22, Djalali *et al.* (1986); 23, Vogel *et al.* (1988); 24, Honda *et al.* (1977); 25, Honda *et al.* (1978).

Two species, the mole-vole (*Ellobius lutescens*) and the Amami spinous country rat (*Tokudaia osimensis osimensis*), have XO males and females without any visible difference in the karyotype of the two sexes. The smallest chromosome, no. 9, in *Ellobius lutescens* has long been presumed to be the X. This has recently been proved by Vogel *et al.* (1988). Still to be proven is whether or not a Y-chromosome-specific DNA sequence (*Tdy*) has been translocated to the X of males. Males express serological H-Y antigen; females do not (Nagai & Ohno 1977). It has been suggested that heteromorphism of autosome pair no. 1 might be associated with sex determination (Maza & Sawyer 1976; Wolf *et al.* 1979), but this does not seem to be so (Djalali *et al.* 1986).

The sex chromosomes of these species have puzzled scientists for a long time and their mode of sex determination is still a matter of debate. A critical review, with special emphasis on evolutionary aspects, was given by Fredga (1983).

Species with suspected XY females

In addition to *Dicrostonyx* and *Myopus* a few other rodent species may have XY females. Five species of South American field mice of the genus *Akodon* are characterized by variation in the size and shape of the X chromosome, and by the fact that some females have sex chromosomes indistinguishable from those of the male. *A. mollis* is perhaps the strongest candidate among the field mice to have XY females. In this species the Y chromosome has a morphology and G-band pattern similar to that shown by the short arm of the X, though the latter exhibits a pericentromeric C-band that is missing in the Y chromosome. Because the Y-like chromosome in heteromorphic females also lacks a C-band, these females were assumed to be XY (Lobato *et al.* 1982).

In the four other *Akodon* species, *A. azarae* (Bianchi & Contreras 1967; Bianchi *et al.* 1976), *A. varius* and *A. boliviensis* (Bianchi *et al.* 1971) and *A. puer* (= *A. coenosus*) (Vitullo *et al.* 1986), the Y chromosome of the male and the Y-like chromosome of some females are also morphologically indistinguishable. However, the very small size of these C-band-positive sex chromosomes makes a detailed comparison impossible. The Y-like chromosome of the females has usually been interpreted as an X with an extensive deletion of the long arm. Breeding experiments with females of the two main chromosome types, XX and Xx(XY?) in *Akodon azarae* did not conclusively solve the problem (Lizzarralde *et al.* 1982), but in my opinion the data presented may well be interpreted in favour of the XY hypothesis; *Akodon* would then be comparable to *Dicrostonyx*. However, in contrast to the situation in *Dicrostonyx* and *Myopus* there are no reports of a skewed sex ratio in favour of females in natural populations of any of the *Akodon* species.

In *Nesokia indica* the X and the Y chromosomes show a great variation in size and morphology (Jhanwar & Rao 1973; Kamali 1975; Rao *et al.* 1983). Because the karyotypes of some females are indistinguishable, in unbanded preparations, from those of the predominating type of male (Kamali 1975), the possibility that XY females might exist in this species was put forward (Fredga 1983). However, C-staining of the chromosomes of *Nesokia indica* from Delhi, India, showed that the variation in size and morphology of the sex chromosomes was due to differences in the amount and distribution of constitutive heterochromatin (Rao *et al.* 1983; I. Nanda 1987, personal communication). Thus 'true' XY females probably do not exist in *Nesokia*.

A situation similar to that of *Nesokia indica* has also been reported for *Bandicota bengalensis*

bengalensis (Sharma & Raman 1973), namely variation in size of the sex chromosomes due to addition or deletion of constitutive heterochromatin.

A comparison of the sex chromosomes in two lemming species with XY females

In the collared lemming (*Dicrostonyx torquatus*) and in the wood lemming (*Myopus schisticolor*) the mechanisms of sex determination are similar. Three sex-chromosome types of female exist, namely XX, X* X and X* Y. Males are XY. The asterisk designates an X-linked mutation that affects the interaction of sex-determining genes, thus converting X* Y individuals into females. The two types of X chromosome, X and X*, in *Myopus* are distinguishable by the G-band patterns of their short arms (Herbst *et al.* 1978). The short arm of the X* is about 7% shorter than that of the X, and this size difference corresponds to approximately 1000 kilobases of DNA. The presumed origin of the variant X* chromosome is demonstrated in figure 1.

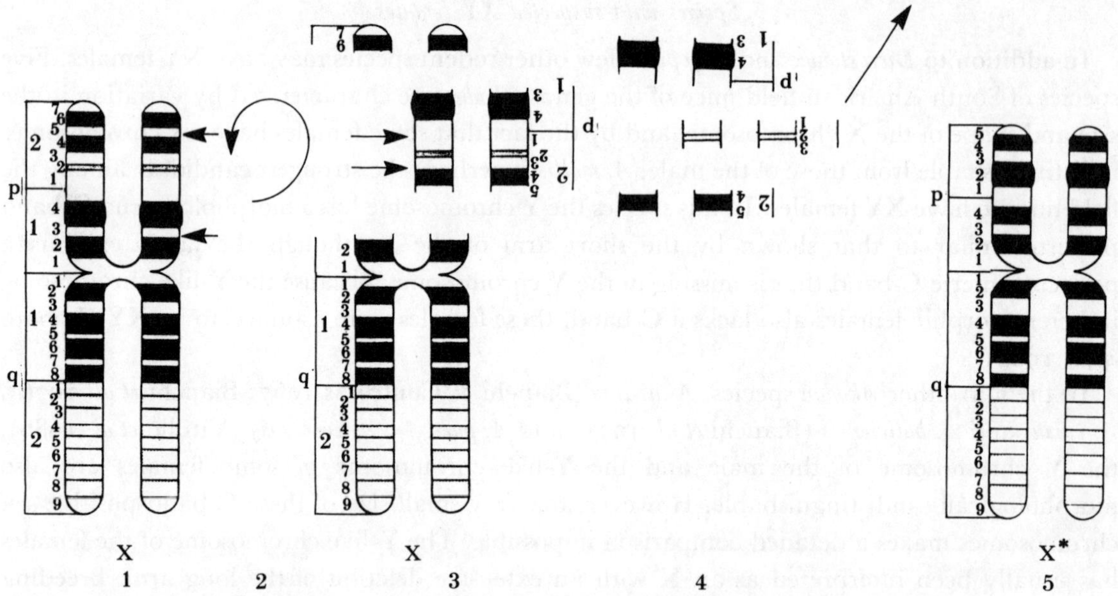

FIGURE 1. Presumed origin of the variant X chromosome (X*) in the wood lemming. 1. Two breaks in positions p13 and p25. 2. Inversion of this segment. 3. Two breaks in position p21 and p23. 4. Loss of this segment, including the tiny band p22. 5. Reunion of broken ends.

The Y chromosome of wood lemmings in Scandinavia is of intermediate size (relative length 5.7 of female haploid set) and is metacentric (centromeric index 41.2). It is a heterochromatic chromosome, easily recognized after C- or G-banding. There is no difference between the Y of XY males and X* Y females (Fredga *et al.* 1976). In geographically more eastern areas the centromere of the Y is more terminally located (Finland: K. Fredga, unpublished observation; U.S.S.R.: Gileva *et al.* (1983); Kozlovsky (1985)). All populations of *Myopus* studied have X* Y females and apparently the same kind of sex-determining mechanism.

In contrast to *Myopus*, the two types of X in *Dicrostonyx torquatus* cannot be distinguished cytologically. In addition, no easily distinguishable Y chromosome is present. The chromosome constitution in the various races and subspecies of the collared lemming is complex but may be explained by a series of translocations between the original sex chromosomes and certain autosomes (figure 2). Thus *D.t.chionopaes* from Chukotka and *D.t.torquatus* from the Polar

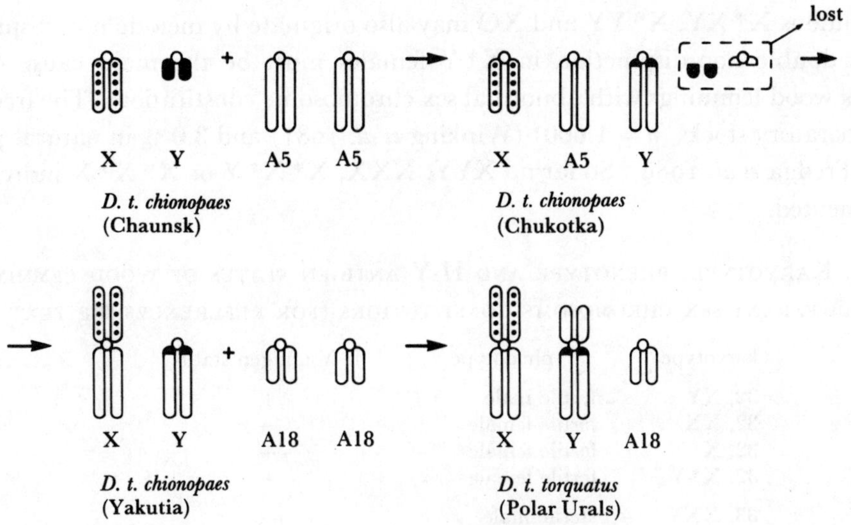

FIGURE 2. Sex chromosome evolution in *Dicrostonyx torquatus* from Siberia.

Urals have one chromosome less in XY males and X* Y females than in XX and X* X females, whereas all four sex-chromosome types of *D.t.chionopaes* from Chaunsk and from Yakutia have the same chromosome numbers. The elucidation of the sex-chromosome constitution in *Dicrostonyx* was further complicated by the presence of a varying number (0–15) of small B chromosomes (Gileva 1983).

It is remarkable that *Dicrostonyx* and *Myopus* have the same kind of X-linked mutations. This is in contrast to lemming species of the genera *Lemmus* and *Synaptomys*, which have ordinary XX/XY sex chromosomes. *Myopus* is phylogenetically much more closely related to *Lemmus* and *Synaptomys* than to *Dicrostonyx*. (*Synaptomys* is the ecological counterpart to *Myopus* in North America.) It therefore seems probable that mutations with similar effects have occurred on two separate occasions, and for unknown reasons have become established in populations all over the vast distribution range of *Myopus* and *Dicrostonyx*.

The X* chromosome leads to a skewed sex ratio in populations of these species. This is particularly evident in *Myopus* because their X* Y females almost always produce daughters only. Owing to a mechanism of double non-disjunction at mitotic anaphase in the foetal ovary of X* Y females, only X* eggs are formed. The X* Y females of *Dicrostonyx* produce both X*- and Y-carrying eggs, and consequently because of the early death of YY zygotes their litter size should be smaller than that of XX and X* X females. Theoretically the litter size of X* Y females should be reduced by one quarter compared with XX and X* X females, but thanks to a higher ovulation rate in X* Y females their reproductive output is not significantly lower than that of females with two X chromosomes (Gileva *et al.* 1982).

Why is the wood lemming such a good model for studies in sex determination?

The double non-disjunction mechanism in X* Y females of *Myopus* must be regarded as an evolutionarily advanced way to avoid reduced fertility in the X* Y females. However, the non-disjunction mechanism sometimes fails, and so Y-, X* Y- and O-carrying eggs are produced exceptionally, giving rise to XY males and X* XY, X* YY and XO individuals (Winking *et al.* 1981). Less common non-disjunction events at first or second meiotic division in males or females have also been documented by the occurrence of X* XX, XXY and X* O specimens.

The constitutions X* XY, X* YY and XO may also originate by meiotic non-disjunction, but the mitotic double non-disjunction in X* Y females must be the main cause of the high frequency of wood lemmings with abnormal sex chromosome constitutions. The frequency was 2.3 % in laboratory stocks ($n = 1.600$) (Winking *et al.* 1981) and 3.0 % in natural populations ($n = 270$) (Fredga *et al.* 1989). So far no XYY, XXX, X* X* Y or X* X* X individuals have been documented.

TABLE 3. KARYOTYPE, PHENOTYPE AND H-Y ANTIGEN STATUS OF WOOD LEMMINGS WITH DIFFERENT SEX CHROMOSOME CONSTITUTIONS (FOR REFERENCES SEE TEXT)

karyotype	phenotype	H-Y antigen status
32, XY	fertile male	+
32, XX	fertile female	–
32, X* X	fertile female	+
32, X* Y	fertile female	+
33, XXY	sterile male	n.t.
33, X* XY	sterile male	n.t.
33, X* XY	fertile female	n.t.
33, X* XY	true hermaphrodite	n.t.
33, X* YY	fertile female	n.t.
33, X* XX	(fertile) female	n.t.
31, XO	fertile female	+
31, X* O	fertile female	+

+, positive. –, negative. n.t., Not tested.

The various sex-chromosome types of normal and abnormal wood lemmings, their phenotypes and H-Y antigen status are listed in table 3. H-Y antigen typing has been done by serological and transplantation methods with concordant results (Wiberg *et al.* 1982; Wiberg & Günther 1985; Wiberg & Fredga 1985).

From a chromosomal point of view the following facts are of particular interest in connection with sex determination:

(i) The 33, X* XY individuals may be sterile males, fertile females or hermaphrodites (Winking *et al.* 1981), which demonstrates that this genotype is heterogeneously expressed. One true lateral hermaphrodite was found with a small undescended testis on the right side and an ovary on the left. Spermatogenic activity was completely lacking in the testis, whereas the ovary appeared normal. Winking *et al.* (1981) suggested that the variable phenotypic expression was a consequence of non-random inactivation of X and X*, with the two types either in unequal proportion or unequally distributed. Support for the non-random inactivation hypothesis was received from studies of the replication patterns of the X chromosomes in fibroblast cultures initiated from one X* XY male and one X* XY female (Schempp *et al.* 1985). The normal X was late-replicating (i.e. inactivated) in all cells of the female, whereas the mutated X* was late-replicating in all cells of the male. Thus it is likely that the actual gene (or genes) involved in sex determination does not escape inactivation.

(ii) The 33, X* YY individuals are normal fertile females. Thus two Y chromosomes cannot override the female-determining effect of X*.

(iii) The 31, X* O individuals are fertile females. This means that even in the absence of any sex-chromosomally located sex-determining genes, a fully fertile female can develop.

In the light of recent findings by Page *et al.* (1987), the two last-mentioned types of wood lemming are of particular interest.

Page *et al.* (1987) identified a 140 kilobase DNA sequence on the human Y chromosome, which they considered to be the long-sought testis determining factor (*TDF*) gene. They also demonstrated the presence of a similar sequence on the human X chromosome. The sequences are not identical but could be functionally equivalent, possibly encoding similar finger proteins. They discuss four models for sex determination, of which Page is said to favour the dosage model (Roberts 1988). This model postulates that 'the X and Y loci are functionally interchangeable, both are testis determining and the X locus is subject to X-chromosome inactivation. According to this model sex is determined by the total number of expressed X and Y loci: a single dose is female determining while a double (or greater) dose is male determining' (Page *et al.* 1987). Our data in the wood lemming are not compatible with all aspects of this dosage model, provided that our prediction is correct, namely that it is the *Tdx* gene (= *TDFX* in man) that has been lost from the X* chromosome. Our findings may be summarized as follows.

1. The gene *Tdx* does not escape X-inactivation (X* XY, fertile females, sterile males or hermaphrodites, may be explained by non-random inactivation of X or X*).
2. One dose of *Tdx* gives rise to females (XO, fertile).
3. One dose of *Tdy* gives rise to females (X* Y, fertile).
4. No dose at all, neither *Tdx* nor *Tdy*, gives rise to females (X* O, fertile).
5. Two doses of *Tdy* and none of *Tdx* give rise to females (X*YY, fertile). I postulate that Y-chromosome inactivation does not occur in individuals with more than one Y chromosome.
6. Two doses give rise to males (XY, fertile; X* XY, sterile). The crucial point is that both alleles(?), *Tdx* and *Tdy*, must be present for normal male development.

It is possible to construct different models to explain the interaction between genes on the X and Y chromosome for male determination, for example *Tdy* and *Tdx* may encode similar but not identical proteins which together form a specific finger protein necessary for male development. Or finger proteins, encoded by *Tdy* and *Tdx*, may 'remove' different inhibitors along the route of male development, and not until both are 'removed' is a substance formed that switches off female development. However, as long as we do not know the molecular difference between X and X* of the wood lemming, it is too early to speculate in great detail. Research is in progress to find out whether or not *Tdx* is missing from X*.

Interaction between sex chromosomal and autosomal genes must of course also be considered. Polani (1981) concludes that in man more than two dozen major genes concerned with sex development, both 'determination' and 'differentiation', have been identified. Nevertheless, I think that there must be one simple and universal mechanism for normal sex determination in mammals. A Y chromosome, or at least a small part of it, is necessary for male development, but a normal X is equally important.

References

Benirschke, K. 1981 Hermaphrodites, freemartins, mosaics and chimaeras in animals. In *Mechanisms of sex differentiation in animals and man* (ed. C. R. Austin & R. G. Edwards), pp. 421–463. London: Academic Press.

Bianchi, N. O. & Contreras, J. 1967 The chromosomes of the field mouse *Akodon azarae* (Cricetidae Rodentia) with special reference to sex chromosome anomalies. *Cytogenetics* **6**, 306–313.

Bianchi, N. O., Reig, O. A., Molina, O. J. & Dulout, F. N. 1971 Cytogenetics of the South American akodont rodents (Cricetidae). I. A progress report of Argentinian and Venezuelan forms. *Evolution* **25**, 724–736.

Bianchi, N. O., Vidal-Rioja, L. & Bianchi, M. S. 1976 Cytogenetics of the South American akodont rodents (Cricetidae). II. Interspecific homology of G-banding patterns. *Cytologia* **41**, 139–144.

Bond, D. J. & Chandley, A. C. 1983 *Aneuploidy*. Oxford University Press.
Breeuwsma, A. J. 1968 A case of XXY sex chromosome constitution in an intersex pig. *J. Reprod. Fert.* **16**, 119–120.
Breeuwsma, A. J. 1970 *Studies on intersexuality in pigs*. Rotterdam: Drukkerij Bronder, Offset.
Bruère, A. N., Marshall, R. B. & Ward, D. P. J. 1969 Testicular hypoplasia and XXY sex chromosome complement in two rams; the ovine counterpart of Klinefelter's syndrome in man. *J. Reprod. Fert.* **19**, 103–108.
Burgoyne, P. S. & Biggers, J. D. 1976 The consequences of X-dosage deficiency in the germ line: impaired development *in vitro* of preimplantation embryos from XO mice. *Devl Biol.* **51**, 109–117.
Castro-Sierra, E. & Wolf, U. 1967 Replication patterns of the unpaired chromosome no 9 of the rodent *Ellobius lutescens* Th. *Cytogenetics* **6**, 268–275.
Castro-Sierra, E. & Wolf, U. 1968 Studies on the male meiosis of *Ellobius lutescens* Th. *Cytogenetics* **7**, 241–248.
Cattanach, B. M. 1961 XXY mice. *Genet. Res.* **2**, 156–158.
Cattanach, B. M. & Pollard, C. E. 1969 An XYY sex chromosome constitution in the mouse. *Cytogenetics* **8**, 80–86.
Centerwall, W. R. & Benirschke, K. 1973 Male tortoiseshell and calico (T–C) cats: animal models of sex chromosome mosaics, aneuploids, polyploids and chimaeras. *J. Hered.* **64**, 272–278.
Chandley, A. C., Fletcher, J., Rossdale, P. D., Peace, C. K., Ricketts, S. W., McEnery, R. J., Thorn, J. P., Short, R. V. & Allen, W. R. 1975 Chromosome abnormalities as a cause of infertility in mares. *J. Reprod. Fert.* **23** (suppl.), 377–383.
Clough, E., Pyle, R. L., Hare, W. C., Kelly, D. F. & Pattersson, D. F. 1970 An XXY sex chromosome constitution in a dog with testicular hypoplasia and congenital heart disease. *Cytogenetics* **9**, 71–77.
Das, R. K. & Kar, R. N. 1981 A 41, XYY mouse. *Experientia* **37**, 821–822.
Djalali, M., Hameister, H. & Vogel, W. 1986 Further chromosomal studies on *Ellobius lutescens*: heteromorphism of chromosome no. 1 is not associated with sex determination. *Experientia* **42**, 1281–1282.
Dobryanov, D. & Konstantinov, G. 1970 A case of mosaicism of the 58 A XY, 58 A XYY type in a male calf of the Bulgarian brown cattle breed. *C.R. Akad. Sci. agric., Bulg.* **3**, 271–276.
Eicher, E. M. 1982 Primary sex determining genes in mice. In *Prospects for sexing mammalian sperm* (ed. R. P. Amann & G. E. Seidel, Jr), pp. 121–135. Boulder: Colorado Associated University Press.
Evans, E. P., Beechey, C. V. & Burtenshaw, M. D. 1978 Meiosis and fertility in XYY mice. *Cytogenet. Cell Genet.* **20**, 249–263.
Fredga, K. 1970 Unusual sex chromosome inheritance in mammals. *Phil. Trans. R. Soc. Lond.* B **259**, 15–36.
Fredga, K. 1983 Aberrant sex chromosome mechanisms in mammals. Evolutionary aspects. *Differentiation* **23** (suppl.), 23–30.
Fredga, K., Gropp, A., Winking, H. & Frank, F. 1976 Fertile XX- and XY-type females in the wood lemming *Myopus schisticolor. Nature, Lond.* **261**, 225–227.
Fredga, K., Gropp, A., Winking, H. & Frank, F. 1977 A hypothesis explaining the exceptional sex ratio in the wood lemming (*Myopus schisticolor*). *Hereditas* **85**, 101–104.
Fredga, K., Fredriksson, R., Bondrup-Nielsen, S. & Ims, R. A. 1989 Sex ratio, chromosomes and isozymes in natural populations of the wood lemming, *Myopus schisticolor. Biol. J. Linn. Soc.* (In the press.)
Gileva, E. A. 1980 Chromosomal diversity and an aberrant genetic system of sex determination in the arctic lemming, *Dicrostonyx torquatus* Pallas (1779). *Genetica* **52–53**, 99–103.
Gileva, E. A. 1983 A contrasted pattern of chromosome evolution in two genera of lemmings, *Lemmus* and *Dicrostonyx*. *Genetica* **60**, 173–179.
Gileva, E. A. & Chebotar, N. A. 1979 Fertile XO males and females in the varying lemming *Dicrostonyx torquatus* Pall. (1779). *Heredity* **42**, 67–77.
Gileva, E. A., Benenson, I. E., Konopisteva, L. A., Puchkov, V. F. & Makaranets, I. A. 1982 X0 females in varying lemming *Dicrostonyx torquatus*: reproductive performance and its evolutionary significance. *Evolution* **36**, 601–609.
Gileva, E. A., Bolshakov, V. N., Sadykov, O. F. & Omariev, T. J. 1983 Chromosome variability and deviating sex ratio in two Ural populations of the wood lemming *Myopus schisticolor* Lilljeborg 1844. (In Russian.) *Proc. Acad. Sci. U.S.S.R.* **270**, 453–456.
Gropp, A., Winking, H., Frank, F., Noack, G. & Fredga, K. 1976 Sex-chromosome aberrations in wood lemmings (*Myopus schisticolor*). *Cytogenet. Cell Genet.* **17**, 343–358.
Gustavsson, I. 1980 Chromosome aberrations and their influence on the reproductive performance of domestic animals – a review. *Z. Tierzücht. ZüchtBiol.* **97**, 176–195.
Hamerton, J. L., Dickson, J. M., Pollard, C. E., Grieves, S. A. & Short, R. V. 1969 Genetic intersexuality in goats. *J. Reprod. Fert.* **7** (suppl.), 25–51.
Handa, H. & Muramatsu, S. 1981 A phenotypically normal cattle with 60, XY/61, XYY karyotype. *Jap. J. Genet.* **56**, 519–522.
Hare, W. C. D. 1976 Intersexuality in the dog. *Can. vet. J.* **17**, 7–15.
Herbst, E. W., Fredga, K., Frank, F., Winking, H. & Gropp, A. 1978 Cytological identification of two X-chromosome types in the wood lemming (*Myopus schisticolor*). *Chromosoma* **69**, 185–191.

Honda, T., Suzuki, H. & Itoh, M. 1977 An unusual sex chromosome constitution found in the Amami spinous country-rat, *Tokudaia osimensis osimensis*. *Jap. J. Genet.* **52**, 247–249.

Honda, T., Suzuki, H., Itoh, M. & Hayashi, K. 1978 Karyotypical differences of the Amami spinous country-rat, *Tokudaia osimensis osimensis* obtained from two neighbouring islands. *Jap. J. Genet.* **53**, 297–299.

Höhn, H., Klug, E. & Rieck, G. W. 1980 A 63, XO/65, XYY mosaic in a case of questionable equine male pseudohermaphroditism. In *4th European Colloquium on Cytogenetics of Domestic Animals, Uppsala*, pp. 82–92.

Ivett, J. L., Tice, R. R. & Bender, M. 1978 Y two X's? An XXY genotype in Chinese hamster, *C. griseus*. *J. Hered.* **69**, 128–129.

Jhanwar, S. C. & Rao, S. R. V. 1973 Polymorphism in the Y chromosome of the short-tailed bandicoot rat, *Nesokia indica*. In *Chromosomes today* (ed. J. Wahrman & K. R. Lewis), vol. 4, pp. 379–382. Israel Universities Press.

Kamali, M. 1975 Karyotype and sex-chromosome polymorphism in *Nesokia indica* from Iran. *Mammal. Chromos. Newslett.* **16**, 165–167.

Kent, M. G., Shoffner, R. N., Buoen, L. & Weber, A. F. 1986 XY sex-reversal syndrome in the domestic horse. *Cytogenet. Cell Genet.* **42**, 8–18.

Kent, M. G., Schoffner, R. N., Hunter, A., Elliston, K. O., Schroder, W., Tolley, E. & Wachtel, S. S. 1988 XY sex reversal syndrome in the mare: clinical and behavioral studies, H-Y phenotype. *Hum. Genet.* **79**, 321–328.

Kozlovsky, A. I. 1985 Chromosome polymorphism and cytogenetic mechanism of sex ratio regulation in the wood lemming (*Myopus schisticolor* Lill.). (In Russian.) *Genetika* **21**, 60–68.

Lizzarralde, M. S., Bianchi, N. O. & Merani, M. S. 1982 Cytogenetics of South American akodont rodents (Cricetidae). VII. Origin of sex chromosome polymorphism in *Akodon azarae*. *Cytologia* **47**, 183–193.

Lobato, L., Cantes, G., Aranjo, B., Bianchi, N. O. & Merani, S. 1982 Cytogenetics of the South American akodont rodent (Cricetidae). X. *Akodon mollis*: a species with XY females and B chromosomes. *Genetica* **57**, 199–205.

Loughman, W. D. & Frye, F. L. 1974 XY/XYY bone marrow karyotype in a male Siamese-crossbred cat. *Vet. Med. small Anim. Clin.* **69**, 1007–1011.

Lyon, M. F., Cattanach, B. M. & Charlton, H. M. 1981 Genes affecting sex differentiation in mammals. In *Mechanisms of sex differentiation in animals and man* (ed. C. R. Austin & R. G. Edwards), pp. 329–386. London: Academic Press.

Lyon, M. F. & Hawker, S. G. 1973 Reproductive lifespan in irradiated and unirradiated chromosomally XO mice. *Genet. Res.* **21**, 185–194.

Matthey, R. 1953 La formule chromosomique et le problème de la détermination sexuelle chez *Ellobius lutescens* (Thomas) (Rodentia–Muridae–Microtinae). *Arch. Julius Klaus-Stift. VererbForsch.* **28**, 65–73.

Matthey, R. 1958 Un nouveau type de détermination chromosomique du sexe chez les mammifères *Ellobius lutescens* Th. et *Microtus* (*Chilotus*) *oregoni* Bachm. (Muridés–Microtinés). Experientia **14**, 240–241.

Matthey, R. 1964 Etudes sur les chromosomes d'*Ellobius lutescens* (Mammalia.Muridae–Microtinae). II. Informations complémentaires sur les divisions méiotiques. *Rev. Suisse Zool.* **71**, 401–410.

Maza, L. M. de la & Sawyer, J. R. 1976 The G and Q banding pattern of *Ellobius lutescens*. A unique case of sex determination in mammals. *Can. J. Genet. Cytol.* **18**, 497–502.

Miyake, Y.-J., Kanagawa, H. & Ishikawa, T. 1984 Further chromosomal and clinical studies on the XY/XYY mosaic bull. *Jap. J. vet. Res.* **32**, 9–21.

Nagai, Y. & Ohno, S. 1977 Testis-determining H-Y antigen in XO males of the mole vole (*Ellobius lutescens*). *Cell* **10**, 729–732.

Nes, N. 1968 Betydningen av kromosomaberrationer hos dyr. *Forsk. Fors. Landbr.* **19**, 393–410.

Norberg, H. S., Refsdal, A. O., Garm, O. N. & Nes, N. 1976 A case report on X-trisomy in cattle. *Hereditas* **82**, 69–72.

Norby, D. E., Hegreberg, G. A., Thuline, H. C. & Findley, D. 1974 An XO cat. *Cytogenet. Cell Genet.* **13**, 448–453.

Ohno, S., Jainchill, J. & Stenius, C. 1963 The creeping vole (*Microtus oregoni*) as a gonosomic mosaic. I. The OY/XY constitution of the male. *Cytogenetics* **2**, 232–239.

Ohno, S., Stenius, C. & Christian, L. 1966 The XO as the normal female of the creeping vole (*Microtus oregoni*). In *Chromosomes today* (ed. C. D. Darlington & K. R. Lewis), vol. 1, pp. 182–187. Edinburgh and London: Oliver and Boyd.

Page, D. C., Mosher, R., Simpson, E. M., Fisher, E. M. C., Mardon, G., Pollack, J., McGillivray, B., de la Chapelle, A. & Brown, L. 1987 The sex-determining region of the human Y chromosome encodes a finger protein. *Cell* **51**, 1091–1104.

Polani, P. E. 1981 Abnormal sex development in man. II. Anomalies of sex-differentiating mechanisms. In *Mechanisms of sex differentiation in animals and man* (ed. C. R. Austin & R. G. Edwards), pp. 549–590. London: Academic Press.

Rao, S. R. V., Vasantha, K., Thelma, B. K., Juyal, R. C. & Jhanwar, S. C. 1983 Heterochromatin variation and sex chromosome polymorphism in *Nesokia indica*: a population study. *Cytogenet. Cell Genet.* **35**, 233–237.

Rathenberg, R. & Müller, D. 1973 X and Y chromosome pairing and disjunction in a male mouse with an XYY sex chromosome constitution. *Cytogenet. Cell Genet.* **12**, 87–92.

Refsdal, A. O. 1979 Undersokelse av kviger og kyr utsjaltet på grunn av ufruktbarhet. Kliniske, hormonelle, kromosomale og postmortelle funn. Dr. med. vet. – diss, Veterinary College of Norway.

Rieck, G. W. 1970 Das XXY-Syndrome beim Rind (Boviner Hypogonadismus). In *I. Europäisches Kolloquium über Zytogenetik* (*Chromosomenpathologie*) *in Veterinärmedizin und Säugetierkunde*, pp. 138–145. Giessen.

Rieck, G. W. & Herzog, A. 1984 *Allgemeine veterinärmedizinische Genetik*, *Zytogenetik unde allgemeine Teratologie.* Stuttgart: Ferdinand Enke Verlag.

Rieck, G. W., Höhn, H. & Herzog, A. 1970 X-Trisomie beim Rind mit Anzeichen familiärer Disposition für Meiosesstörungen. *Cytogenetics* **9**, 401–409.

Roberts, L. 1988 Zeroing in on the sex switch. *Science, Wash.* **239**, 21–23.

Russell, L. B. & Chu, E. H. Y. 1961 An XXY male in the mouse. *Proc. natn. Acad. Sci. U.S.A.* **47**, 571–575.

Satya Prakash, K. L. & Aswathanarayana, N. V. 1977 X-monosomy in the Indian black rat. *J. Heredity* **68**, 126–128.

Schempp, W., Wiberg, U. & Fredga, K. 1985 Correlation between sexual phenotype and X-chromosome inactivation pattern in the X*XY wood lemming. *Cytogenet. Cell Genet.* **39**, 30–34.

Schmid, W. 1967 Heterochromatin in mammals. *Arch. Julius Klaus-Stift. VererbForsch.* **42**, 1–60.

Scott, C. D. & Gregory, P. W. 1965 An XXY trisomic in an intersex of *Bos taurus*. *Genetics* **52**, 473–474.

Searle, J. B. 1984 A wild common shrew (*Sorex araneus*) with an XXY sex chromosome constitution. *J. Reprod. Fert.* **70**, 353–356.

Searle, J. B. & Wilkinson, P. J. 1986 The XYY condition in a wild mammal: an XY/XYY mosaic common shrew (*Sorex araneus*). *Cytogenet. Cell Genet.* **41**, 225–233.

Selden, J. R., Wachtel, S., Koo, G. C., Haskins, M. E. & Patterson, D. F. 1978 Genetic basis of XX male syndrome and XX true hermaphroditism: evidence in the dog. *Science, Wash.* **201**, 644–646.

Sharma, T. & Raman, R. 1971 An XO female in the Indian mole rat. *J. Hered.* **62**, 384–387.

Sharma, T. & Raman, R. 1973 Variation of constitutive heterochromatin in the sex chromosomes of the rodent *Bandicota bengalensis bengalensis* (Gray). *Chromosoma* **41**, 75–84.

Sharman, G. B., Robinson, E. S., Watson, S. M. & Berger, P. J. 1970 Sex chromosomes and reproductive anatomy of some intersexual Marsupials. *J. Reprod. Fert.* **21**, 57–68.

Soller, M., Padek, B., Wysoki, M. & Ayalon, N. 1969 Cytogenetics of Saanen goats showing abnormal development of the reproductive tract associated with the dominant gene for polledness. *Cytogenetics* **8**, 51–67.

Trommershausen Bowling, A., Millon, L. & Hughes, J. P. 1987 An update of chromosomal abnormalities in mares. *J. Reprod. Fert.* **35** (suppl.), 149–155.

Vitullo, A. D., Merani, M. S., Reig, O. A., Kajon, A. E., Scaglia, O., Espinosa, M. B. & Perez-Zapata, A. 1986 Cytogenetics of South American akodont rodents (Cricetidae): new karyotypes and chromosomal banding patterns of Argentinian and Uruguyan forms. *J. Mamm.* **67**, 69–80.

Vogel, W., Steinbach, P., Djalali, M., Mehnert, K., Ali, S. & Epplen, J. T. 1988 Chromosome 9 of *Ellobius lutescens* is the X chromosome. *Chromosoma* **96**, 112–118.

Vorontsov, N. N., Lyapunova, E. A., Borissov, Y. U. M. & Dovgal, V. E. 1980 Variability of sex chromosomes in mammals. *Genetica* **52–53**, 361–372.

Weiss, G., Weick, R. F., Knobil, E., Wolman, S. R. & Gorstein, F. 1973 An XO anomaly and ovarian dysgenesis in a rhesus monkey. *Folia primatol.* **19**, 24–27.

Welshons, W. J. & Russell, L. B. 1959 The Y chromosome as the bearer of male-determining factors in the mouse. *Proc. natn. Acad. Sci. U.S.A.* **45**, 560–566.

Wiberg, U. H. & Fredga, K. 1985 The H-Y transplantation antigen is present in XO and X* X female wood lemmings (*Myopus schisticolor*). *Immunogenetics* **22**, 495–501.

Wiberg, U. H. & Günther, E. 1985 Female wood lemmings with the mutant X*-chromosome carry the H-Y transplantation antigen. *Immunogenetics* **21**, 91–96.

Wiberg, U., Mayerova, A., Müller, U., Fredga, K. & Wolf, U. 1982 X-linked genes of the H-Y antigen system in the wood lemming (*Myopus schisticolor*). *Hum. Genet.* **60**, 163–166.

Winking, H., Gropp, A. & Fredga, K. 1981 Sex determination and phenotype in wood lemmings with XXY and related karyotypic anomalies. *Hum. Genet.* **58**, 98–104.

Wolf, M., Schempp, W. & Vogel, W. 1979 *Ellobius lutescens* Th. (Rodentia, Microtinae): Q-, R-, and replication banding pattern. *Cytogenet. Cell Genet.* **23**, 117–123.

Yong, H. S. 1971 Presumptive X monosomy in black rats from Malaya. *Nature, Lond.* **232**, 484–485.

Yosida, T. H. 1984 Studies on the karyotype differentiation of the Norway rat. IX. Translocation between pair nos. 4 and 7 occurred in a WM strain rat after γ-irradiation, with special regard to the segregation in F1 hybrids involving an XYY male. *Proc. Jap. Acad. Sci.* **60**, 88–91.

Yosida, T. H., Moriwaki, K. & Sagai, T. 1974 A female black rat (*Rattus rattus*) with a single X-chromosome. *Jap. J. Genet.* **49**, 49–52.

Zartman, D. L., Hinesley, L. L. & Gnatowski, M. W. 1981 A 53, X female sheep (*Ovis aries*). *Cytogenet. Cell Genet.* **30**, 54–58.

Discussion

M. G. BULMER (*Department of Biomathematics, University of Oxford, U.K.*). I should like to comment on the increased frequency of XY females in wood lemmings above the theoretical expectation of one third. Gileva (1987) has shown that there is a similar discrepancy in varying lemmings, and that it is due to preferential production or utilization of Y over X sperm. Might this also be happening in wood lemmings? Are there any relevant breeding data?

Reference

Gileva, E. A. 1987 Meiotic drive in the sex chromosome system of the varying lemming, *Dicrostonyx torquatus* Pall. (Rodentia, Microtinae). *Heredity* **59**, 383–389.

F. FREDGA. Yes, there are indications that offspring with a Y chromosome are born in excess also in the wood lemming. In *Myopus* 45% of the females are X*Y and not 33% as theoretically expected (Gropp & Winking 1982). The reason for this is unkown but I have data from my breeding colony showing that: (1) one XX line of females produced sons and daughters in a 2:1 ratio; in another XX line the ratio was the expected 1:1; (2) generally speaking, X*Y females give birth to more X*Y than X*X daughters. My breeding data are being analysed from different aspects, and experiments are in progress to elucidate the reason(s) for these deviations. Meiotic drive for the X* chromosome in X*X females may also account for a high frequency of X*Y females. Some X*X females produce a much higher frequency of daughters than the expected 3:1.

It should be mentioned that also in natural populations 45% of the females are X*Y ($n = 220$) (Fredga *et al.* 1989). This may, at least to some extent, be explained by differences in maturation rate, onset of reproduction and in pregnancy rate of the different female types. In all these attributes the X*Y was superior to X*X, which was superior to XX in a natural population studied by us (Bondrup-Nielsen *et al.* 1989).

References

Bondrup-Nielsen, S., Ims, R. A., Fredriksson, R. & Fredga, K. 1989 Demography of the wood lemming *Myopus schisticolor*. *Biol. J. Linn. Soc.* (In the press.)

Gropp. A. & Winking, H. 1982 Prospects for genetic manipulations of sex ratio in mammals. In *Prospects for sexing mammalian sperm* (ed. R. P. Amann & G. E. Seidel, Jr), pp. 253–270. Colorado University Press.

Phil. Trans. R. Soc. Lond. B **322**, 97–107 (1988) [97]
Printed in Great Britain

Sex inversion as a model for the study of sex determination in vertebrates

By U. Wolf

Institut für Humangenetik und Anthropologie der Universität, Albertstrasse 11, *D*-7800 *Freiburg i. Br., F.R.G.*

As a consequence of genetic sex determination, the indifferent gonadal blastema normally becomes either a testis or an ovary. This applies to mammals and to the majority of non-mammalian vertebrates. With the exception of placental mammals, however, partial or complete sex inversion can be induced in one sex by sexual steroid hormones of the opposite sex during a sensitive period of gonadogenesis. There is evidence that also during normal gonadogenesis in these species, in the XY/XX mechanism of sex determination testicular differentiation is induced by androgens, and in the ZZ/ZW mechanism, ovarian differentiation by oestrogens. In either case, the hormones may act via serological H-Y antigen as a morphogenetic factor. In contrast, in placental mammals including man, primary gonadal differentiation is independent of sexual steroid hormones, and factors directing differential gonadal development have not yet been conclusively identified. However, various mutations at the chromosome or gene level, resulting respectively in sex inversion or intersexuality, have provided clues as to some genes involved and their possible nature. In this context also, serological H-Y antigen is discussed as a possible factor acting on primordial gonadal cells and inducing differential growth or morphogenesis or both. The data available at present allow a tentative outline of the genetics of sex determination in placental mammals.

Introduction

Sex determination becomes manifest phenotypically when the indifferent gonadal blastema differentiates into either testis or ovary. The mechanism of sex determination resulting in differential gonadal development must include multiple steps which are to a large extent unknown. However, this multistep process can be disturbed either by mutation or by experimental interference, resulting in anomalous gonad differentiation and thus in partial or complete sex inversion. Spontaneous occurrence and experimental induction of sex inversion can therefore provide some insights into the mechanism of sex determination.

I present some examples of sex inversion pointing to a possible role of serological H-Y antigen in the mechanism of sex determination. The evidence is still circumstantial, and the gaps in our knowledge must be filled by hypotheses. However, these hypotheses can be tested, and it is therefore to be expected that the relevant experiments will be done in the near future. In this context, I should like to point also to the stimulating considerations of Polani (1985).

The serological H-Y antigen referred to here is identical with the Sxs antigen of Wiberg (1987). The problem of the existence of several H-Y antigens is not addressed in this paper. I use the term 'serological H-Y antigen' rather than SDM (serologically detected male) antigen because I deal with non-mammalian vertebrates as well as with mammals, so that the sex-specific antigen may be a female antigen (e.g. in birds).

It is well established that in normal sexual development, serological H-Y antigen is characteristic of the heterogametic sex (Ohno 1979; Wachtel 1983). In the XY/XX mechanism of sex determination the male, and in the ZZ/ZW mechanism the female, types H-Y positive, whereas the respective homogametic sexes are H-Y negative by definition. This definition does not exclude the possibility that some residual H-Y activity also occurs in the homogametic sex, but there is at least a distinct quantitative sex difference.

With the exception of placental mammals, it has been shown in various species belonging to different taxonomic categories of vertebrates that gonadal differentiation of one sex can be influenced by the sexual steroid hormone of the opposite sex (Mittwoch 1973). Taking the chicken as an example, administration of oestradiol to the male embryo at the indifferent stage of the gonadal anlage results in the transient formation of an ovotestis. However, the complementary experiment is not successful: administration of testosterone to the female chicken embryo does not change gonadal sex, and an ovary is formed. In this species, the female is the heterogametic (ZW) and the male the homogametic (ZZ) sex. Although in the female oestrogens are produced before ovarian differentiation, testosterone in the male is found only after the testis has developed. From these findings it may be assumed that, during normal development also, ovarian differentiation depends on oestrogens whereas testicular differentiation is independent of sexual steroid hormones. Thus in the ZZ/ZW mechanism of sex determination, the heterogametic female is the induced sex whereas the homogametic male is the constitutive sex. As oestradiol serves as an inducer in this case, it is also able to sex-invert the indifferent gonadal anlage of the male, at least to some extent, and an ovotestis is formed. In contrast, testosterone is not an inducer of primary gonadal development, and therefore has no influence on the female gonadal anlage (Taber 1964).

Because of the postulated role of serological H-Y antigen in primary gonad differentiation (Wachtel *et al.* 1975; Ohno 1976), and based on the findings mentioned above, it could be predicted that oestradiol controls the expression of serological H-Y antigen. If so, the female chicken embryo should be serological H-Y antigen negative at the indifferent stage of the gonad and before oestrogens occur physiologically. Moreover, the male which normally types negative for serological H-Y antigen should become positive after experimental sex inversion by oestradiol. Both predictions have been shown to be correct. The early female chicken embryo is negative for serological H-Y, and becomes positive at the time when ovarian development starts (Ebensperger *et al.* 1988*a*), whereas males, sex-inverted by oestradiol, become positive for serological H-Y antigen in their gonads. This has been shown not only in the chicken *in vivo* (Müller *et al.* 1979*b*) and *in vitro* (Ebensperger *et al.* 1988*b*), but also in other species with a ZW mechanism, e.g. the quail (Müller *et al.* 1980; Zaborski *et al.* 1981) and *Xenopus* (Wachtel *et al.* 1980). For a synopsis see Zaborski (1985).

In the XY mechanism of sex determination, one would expect the situation to be complementary to that in the ZW mechanism. Here, the male is the heterogametic (XY) and the female the homogametic (XX) sex. It is well known that in some teleostean and amphibian species with male heterogamety, the female can be sex-inverted by testosterone. Using the labrid fish *Coris julis* as a model, a hermaphroditic protogynous species with females and primary and secondary males, Reinboth (1975) has shown that females can be changed into secondary males by injections of testosterone. Our studies on serological H-Y antigen revealed that the female is negative whereas both types of male are positive for this antigen. We wondered if the female became positive after experimental sex inversion, and this was indeed the case

(Reinboth *et al.* 1987). Thus in this model, testosterone not only induces testicular development, but also appears to control the expression of serological H-Y antigen.

If, at this point, some generalizations are allowed, I could put forward the following hypothesis which, however, only apply to non-eutherian vertebrates.

1. In the ZZ/ZW mechanism of sex determination, oestrogens are the inducers of the ovary, and in the XY/XX mechanism, androgens are the inducers of the testis.
2. Primary gonadal development in the heterogametic sex is induced, whereas in the homogametic sex it is constitutive.
3. The sexual steroid hormones characteristic of the heterogametic sex control serological H-Y antigen, which has a functional role in the organization of the heterogametic gonad.

On these assumptions, either oestrogens or androgens control serological H-Y expression, depending on the type of sex determination. In addition, one and the same factor, serological H-Y antigen, is involved either in ovarian or in testicular morphogenesis, again depending on the type of sex determination. From this it can be concluded that this antigen serves the function of a non-specific signal to which the target cells, i.e. the somatic cells of the gonadal blastema, react in an autonomous way. However, the type of sex determination defines whether these cells react to the presence of the antigen by differentiating in a male or female direction.

In placental mammals, the mechanism of sex determination does not employ sexual steroid hormones (Jost 1947). Primary gonadal differentiation must have become hormone independent during evolution, presumably as a consequence of placentation. However, serological H-Y antigen is present in the heterogametic male sex and absent in the homogametic female sex (at least by definition based on serological criteria). Serological H-Y antigen is found in the early mammalian embryo already (Krco & Goldberg 1976), and therefore should be present in the male at the time of differential gonadal development also, before androgens are produced. Androgen independence of serological H-Y antigen follows also from the finding that in the syndrome of testicular feminization in man (Koo *et al.* 1977) and mouse (Bennett *et al.* 1975), owing to androgen resistance, this antigen is present. Thus serological H-Y antigen is not controlled by androgens in the mammalian male. This does not exclude, however, that it is controlled by sex-determining genes, and there is experimental evidence that this is indeed the case (Wolf (1985), and see below).

I shall not summarize here the various arguments supporting the hypothesis that serological H-Y antigen has a role in primary testicular differentiation in mammals including man, because there is abundant literature on this subject (for review, see Ohno 1979; Wachtel 1983). Instead, I shall concentrate on a special case: the occurrence of sex reversal in the mouse, when the Y chromosome of feral mice of the subspecies *Mus musculus domesticus* is transferred into the background of the C57BL laboratory strain. I have referred earlier to some preliminary findings on serological H-Y antigen in these mice carrying a foreign Y chromosome (Wolf 1985), and Eicher & Washburn (1986) were right to complain that detailed data on this important question were not yet published. In the meantime, we have finished our studies on this subject, and I shall present them briefly here because they may contribute to the problem of serological H-Y antigen and testis differentiation. (For details, an article is in preparation on this subject matter.)

The animals were provided by Dr Winking of Lübeck who mated feral male mice from four different localities (southern Germany, Switzerland, northern Italy and Yugoslavia) with

C57BL females, and who established four different lines by repeated back-crossing of hybrid males to C57BL females. From the second back-cross generation onwards a highly variable pattern of sexual differentiation occurred, and in general a quarter of all XY individuals developed as intersexes or females. With a few exceptions, XY females were sterile. I shall refer here to our findings on serological H-Y antigen only.

Serological H-Y antigen was determined by using two different assays: the Raji-cell cytotoxicity test (Fellous *et al.* 1978) and a urease-ELISA (Bradley *et al.* 1987). The results of both methods were essentially identical. In most animals, non-gonadal tissues (kidney, spleen, liver) were tested and gonadal sex was carefully analysed histologically. In some animals, gonads were used to absorb antisera raised against serological H-Y antigen, and here, gonadal sex was identified by morphological inspection. As can be seen in table 1, serological H-Y antigen status and gonadal differentiation were closely correlated. XY females with ovaries on both sides were negative for the antigen throughout, whereas true hermaphrodites with the simultaneous occurrence of testicular and ovarian tissue were positive, the titre being reduced compared with male controls in some cases.

TABLE 1. SEROLOGICAL H-Y ANTIGEN IN XY FEMALE AND HERMAPHRODITE MICE (C57BL-Y^{DOM})

no. individuals tested	gonads[a]	tissue studied[b]	H-Y antigen activity
6	O/O	gonads	not detectable
2	O/O	gonads	not detectable
		K	not detectable
15	O/O	S, K, Li, Lu, H	not detectable
3	O/T	gonads	intermediary
		Li	intermediary
12	O/T or O/OT	S, K, Li, Lu	intermediary or full positive
1	T/OT	Li	intermediary
1	T/T	Li	full positive

[a] O, ovary; T, testis; OT, ovotestis.
[b] S, Spleen; K, kidney; Li, liver; Lu, lung; H, heart.

Interestingly, similar findings were recently reported for the horse by Kent *et al.* (1988). In this species, an inherited trait is the occurrence of XY mares, showing a variable degree of sex-reversal. Some XY females are even fertile, others exhibit gonadal dysgenesis, and still others are virilized. Here again, the degree of sex inversion and the serological H-Y status were correlated; the nearly normal XY females and some females with gonadal dysgenesis were negative for the antigen whereas the more virilized animals were positive.

Whatever the genetic basis is for these two examples of sex inversion, the negative correlation between serological H-Y antigen and feminization is striking. In the general context that in mammals, males are positive for serological H-Y whereas females are not, these findings confirm the rule that, when testicular tissue is present in an individual, serological H-Y antigen is also present.

Up to this point, with respect to placental mammals, the following two hypotheses can be put forward.

1. Serological H-Y antigen expression has become independent of sexual steroid hormones, possibly in connection with the evolution of placentation, and may be under the direct control of sex-determining genes.

2. Serological H-Y antigen has kept its functional role in the primary differentiation of the heterogametic gonad, and this is the reason for the positive correlation between testicular tissue and this antigen.

As to the biological function of serological H-Y antigen, the evidence is still circumstantial, and we must await its biochemical characterization which is under way, before conclusive experiments can be done. It is to be said in this connection that the biological role of this antigen cannot be confined to primary testicular morphogenesis (if it has this function). It has been shown that the concentration of serological H-Y antigen in the mammalian testis increases towards puberty (Müller *et al.* 1978*b*), and also that early male germ cells are negative for this antigen and become positive when they differentiate (Zenzes *et al.* 1978; Bradley & Heslop 1988). Under this view it is tempting to speculate that serological H-Y antigen may interact also with testis maturation or spermatogenesis or both. In this connection, the postulate by Burgoyne (1987) that H-Y antigen as detected by cytotoxic T-cells (CML assay) plays a role in spermatogenesis is of interest. However, the molecular and functional relationships between the serological H-Y antigen and that detected by T-cells remains to be clarified first.

Sex inversion phenomena have also contributed to a delineation of the genetics of sex determination and serological H-Y antigen. I do not intend to review all the various data contributing to our present picture, but should rather like to discuss briefly my original conception (Wolf 1978) in the light of some recent findings pertaining to this problem.

My model postulates that the structural gene for serological H-Y antigen is autosomal. This is for various reasons. The Y chromosome can be excluded because serological H-Y antigen is found in individuals lacking this chromosome, e.g. XX true hermaphrodites (see, for example, Waibel *et al.* 1987) and possibly some XX males. A phylogenetic argument is that, in non-mammalian vertebrates, serological H-Y antigen can be induced in the homogametic sex, thus the structural gene is present in both sexes, whereas the Y chromosome is not. The X chromosome is not a good candidate because in polysomies of the X in the presence of the Y, titre of serological H-Y antigen decreases with an increasing number of X chromosomes (Fraccaro *et al.* 1982). If the structural gene were X-linked, H-Y activity should either show a positive gene–dose relation or remain on the same level, depending on whether or not the gene undergoes inactivation.

However, an autosomal localization is to be favoured not only by exclusion because there are various examples in mammals including man of autosomal mutations causing sex reversal. A particularly interesting case is the occurrence of XY females with ovaries in campomelic dysplasia, a condition with a probably autosomal recessive mode of inheritance. These sex-inverted patients lack serological H-Y antigen (Bricarelli *et al.* 1981), and the simultaneous occurrence, to a variable degree, of multiple malformations in these patients can be interpreted as the consequence of a submicroscopic chromosomal deletion including the structural gene for this antigen and one or several neighbouring genes. Autosomally caused sex-inversion is also known in the mouse (Eicher & Washburn 1986), the goat (Wachtel *et al.* 1978), and some other species. The recent reports by Lau *et al.* (1987, 1988), assigning a gene for a male-enhanced antigen which is a candidate gene for serological H-Y antigen to chromosome 6 of man and to chromosome 17 of the mouse, can be taken as further support for an autosomal localization of the structural gene for this antigen in mammals.

Obviously, the Y chromosome is involved in male determination, and a testis-determining factor (TDF) has for long been postulated to be encoded by this chromosome. The TDF gene

(*TDF*) has been mapped on the distal short arm of the human Y chromosome, and recently a DNA sequence which may code for a regulatory protein considered to be TDF has been cloned (Page *et al.* 1987). A gene exerting a positive control function on serological H-Y antigen has also been assigned to the Y-chromosome short arm. The assignment was based on deletion mapping on the one hand (Rosenfeld *et al.* 1979), and on the presence of this antigen in XX males on the other hand. XX males have been shown to carry various sized segments of the Y chromosome on one of their X chromosomes, but they all include the *TDF* region (Vergnaud *et al.* 1986, Affara *et al.* 1986, Müller *et al.* 1986). Assuming that all XX males are positive for serological H-Y (and there is no exception so far, see Wachtel 1983), presence of the *TDF* region and expression of this antigen would be correlated. From its chromosomal location as well as from its presumed function, the sequence of Page *et al.* (1987) could be part of or identical with the postulated Y-linked gene, exerting a positive control function on serological H-Y antigen (Wolf 1978). This control function could be exerted directly on the structural gene for serological H-Y, or indirectly by including several steps. Another possibility is that the presumed TDF gene and the serological H-Y controlling gene are separate entities located in the same chromosomal region of the Y chromosome.

Corresponding to this Y-linked gene controlling serological H-Y antigen, in my model an X-linked gene is postulated, acting antagonistically, i.e. suppressing serological H-Y activity in a dose-dependent way. This gene has been mapped on human Xp2.23 (Wolf *et al.* 1980). Interestingly, Page *et al.* (1987) identified a DNA sequence on the short arm of the X chromosome which seems to be very similar to the presumptive *TDF* sequence, raising the possibility that this X-linked sequence is part of or identical with the postulated gene exerting a negative control function on the autosomal structural gene for serological H-Y. However, according to regional mapping, this sequence is assigned now to a more proximal position on Xp, thus most probably excluding that possibility (D. Page, this symposium).

My model also includes a gene for a gonad-specific receptor for serological H-Y antigen. It has been shown that serological H-Y is secreted by testicular Sertoli cells and is therefore available as a soluble factor (Müller *et al.* 1978*a*, *b*; Brunner *et al.* 1984). It is able to bind to the somatic cells of the gonads of both sexes, but not to other cells, and this is most probably because of a gonad-specific receptor for serological H-Y (Müller *et al.* 1978*a*, 1979*a*). It can be imagined that mutations of the receptor gene occur, preventing the binding of antigen to the receptor and thus resulting in sex inversion. The X-linked form of XY gonadal dysgenesis in man is a candidate for this condition (Mann *et al.* 1983), and another candidate is the X*Y female wood lemming (Wiberg *et al.* 1982).

I realize that this is a rather straightforward and simplistic model; it does, however, allow for various modifications, and it still meets most of the data obtained in recent years. It may serve the purpose to do experiments aimed at its falsification.

I conclude with some general hypothetical considerations on the sex-determining mechanism in mammals. These considerations are essentially based on discussions with Professor Luis Izquierdo of the University of Chile.

My main premise is that serological H-Y antigen is instrumental for primary testis differentiation.

1. Up to the indifferent stage of the gonadal anlage and before sex-specific morphogenesis takes place, gonadal cells of both sexes differentiate and produce the receptor for serological H-Y antigen which is specific for these cells and not present on any other cells of the embryo. The serological H-Y receptor is the reason for the bipotency of the gonadal anlage.

2. *TDF* or a closely linked gene, which is present in XY cells only, controls serological H-Y antigen expression in all somatic cells of the male organism. Therefore the male types positive for this antigen in all somatic cells.

3.1. Sertoli-cell differentiation normally depends on TDF. Serological H-Y antigen is present on Sertoli cells as on other somatic cells, but because Sertoli-cell precursors are endowed with the receptor for serological H-Y, the antigen can bind to it and trigger Sertoli cell differentiation. By this process of self-differentiation, the Sertoli cells become able to produce serological H-Y in larger amounts which are then secreted.

3.2. In XX true hermaphrodites, Y-specific DNA has not been detected (Waibel *et al.* 1987; Page *et al.* 1987). Thus TDF is lacking, but nevertheless Sertoli cells are differentiated and testicular tissue is formed in these cases, and they are positive for serological H-Y. Therefore, expression of the autosomal serological H-Y antigen gene may have become independent of TDF, and once serological H-Y is synthesized, Sertoli-cell differentiation and testicular morphogenesis can take place.

4. Serological H-Y antigen, available as a soluble factor, acts via its gonad-specific receptor, inducing Sertoli cells to form seminiferous cords (and possibly also precursors of Leydig cells to become responsive to gonadotropins).

This model could be modified in several ways. One possibility is that the structural gene for serological H-Y is not controlled by TDF, but by another controlling gene located in the neighbourhood of *TDF*. In this case, the serological H-Y system would depend indirectly on TDF.

To my knowledge, the only obstacle for the serological H-Y hypothesis of gonadal differentiation may be the Sxr′ mutation in the mouse which results in XXSxr′ males (McLaren *et al.* 1984) that, in contrast to XXSxr males, are negative for H-Y antigen as defined by cytotoxic T-cells (Gordon *et al.* 1975) and by a transplantation assay (Simpson *et al.* 1986; Wiberg & Lattermann 1987). Definite results with a serological assay have not yet been obtained, but Dr Ellen Goldberg (this symposium) has evidence that non-gonadal cells of XXSxr′ males are negative for this antigen. Interestingly, Ulf Wiberg of our laboratory and Mark Bradley of the University of Otago have purified and characterized a male-specific protein that so far has been shown to be present in the liver of XXSxr and C57BL/6 (B6) male mice, B6, rat and sheep testis, but absent in B6 female and XXSxr′ male liver and ovaries of B6, rat and sheep. Antibodies raised to the purified sex-specific testis protein cross-react with the mouse male-specific liver protein on Western blots. The testis protein was purified on a female anti-male immunoaffinity column. Therefore it is possible that this protein is serological H-Y antigen (U. Wiberg and M. Bradley, personal communication).

These data may be interpreted as falsifying the hypothesis on the role of serological H-Y antigen in gonadal differentiation. However, to me it seems premature to give such an interpretation based on the present results. It cannot be excluded that serological H-Y antigen is present only during a certain time frame, such as the sensitive period of gonadal differentiation; or at the appropriate place, such as the milieu of the testicular Sertoli cells during this sensitive period. In this case, the Sxr′ mutation would affect the spatiotemporal regulation of the serological H-Y gene. Another possibility is that the serological H-Y protein has changed in such a way by this mutation, that it has escaped detection by the methods applied so far.

It must be envisaged that, if serological H-Y antigen is lacking entirely in the XXSxr′ and XSxr′ males, it would be neither necessary nor sufficient for primary male gonadogenesis. In this case it may serve the function of an enhancer of growth or differentiation (Heslop *et al.* 1988), or act on later stages of male differentiation as proposed by Burgoyne (1987).

Until the Sxr′ mutation is analysed closer and defined better, I see no reason to abandon the serological H-Y hypothesis of gonadal differentiation which is so strongly supported by various evidence obtained from different cases throughout the vertebrate phylum.

The sex-determining mechanism of placental mammals appears to be adapted to placentation, and it must have evolved from the more primitive mechanism employing sexual steroid hormones as major inducers of differentiation of the heterogametic gonad. Although in many taxonomic groups of non-eutherians serological H-Y is controlled by sexual steroids, in eutherians it may have come under the control of TDF. It can be debated whether, in non-eutherians, TDF has any function at all. However, from lower to higher vertebrates there appears to exist a decreasing responsiveness of indifferent gonadal cells to sexual steroids, whereas sex-determining genes like *TDF* appear to gain more influence. Thus in some fish species, sex can be inverted in either direction by the respective steroid hormone characteristic for the opposite sex. In amphibians, sex inversion can be induced experimentally only in one direction, from the homogametic to the heterogametic sex, but the sex inversion is still complete. In birds, sex inversion is also unidirectional, but transitional and incomplete (ovotestis). Finally, in eutherians sexual steroids remain without effect on primary gonadogenesis. It will be interesting to know if the presumptive *TDF* sequence, which can still be traced in birds (Page *et al.* 1987), is also preserved in lower vertebrates.

I thank Ulf Wiberg and Mark Bradley for making unpublished findings available to me, and I am most grateful to them, Luis Izquierdo and Cecilia Ebensperger for discussions and for reading the manuscript.

References

Affara, N. A., Ferguson-Smith, M. A., Tolmie, J., Kwok, K., Mitchell, M., Jamieson, D., Cooke, A. & Florentin, L. 1986 Variable transfer of Y-specific sequences in XX males. *Nucl. Acids Res.* **14**, 5375–5387.

Bennett, D., Boyse, E. A., Lyon, M. F., Mathieson, B. J., Scheid, M. & Yanagisawa, K. 1975 Expression of H-Y (male) antigen in phenotypically female Tfm/Y mice. *Nature, Lond.* **257**, 236–238.

Bradley, M. P., Ebensperger, C. & Wiberg, U. 1987 Determination of the serological H-Y antigen in birds and mammals using high-titer antisera and a sensitive urease ELISA. *Hum. Genet.* **76**, 352–356.

Bradley, M. P. & Heslop, B. F. 1988 The distribution of sex-specific (H-Y) antigens within the seminiferous tubules of the testis: an immunohistochemical study. *Hum. Genet.* (In the press.)

Bricarelli, F. D., Fraccaro, M., Lindsten, J., Müller, U., Baggio, P., Doria Lamba Carbone, L., Hjerpe, A., Lindgren, F., Meyerová, A., Ringertz, H., Ritzén, E. M., Rovetta, D. C., Sicchero, C. & Wolf, U. 1981 Sex-reversed XY females with campomelic dysplasia are H-Y negative. *Hum. Genet.* **57**, 15–22.

Burgoyne, P. S. 1987 The role of the mammalian Y chromosome in spermatogenesis. In *The mammalian Y chromosome: molecular search for the sex-determining factor* (ed. P. N. Goodfellow, I. W. Craig, J. C. Smith & J. Wolfe) (Development **101**(suppl.)), pp. 133–141. Cambridge: Company of Biologists.

Brunner, M., Moreira-Filho, C. A., Wachtel, G. & Wachtel, S. S. 1984 On the secretion of H-Y antigen. *Cell* **37**, 615–619.

Ebensperger, C., Drews, U., Mayerová, A. & Wolf, U. 1988*a* Serological H-Y antigen in the female chicken occurs during gonadal differentiation. *Differentiation* **37**, 186–191.

Ebensperger, C., Drews, U. & Wolf, U. 1988*b* An in vitro model of gonad differentiation in the chicken. Estradiol induced sex-inversion results in the occurrence of serological H-Y antigen. *Differentiation.* **37**, 192–197.

Eicher, E. M. & Washburn, L. L. 1986 Genetic control of primary sex determination in mice. *A. Rev. Genet.* **20**, 327–360.

Fellous, M., Günther, E., Kemler, R., Wiels, J., Berger, R., Guenet, J. L., Jakob, H. & Jacob, F. 1978 Association of the H-Y male antigen with β_2-microglobulin on human lymphoid and differentiated mouse teratocarcinoma cell lines. *J. exp. Med.* **148**, 58–70.

Fraccaro, M., Mayerová, A., Wolf, U., Bühler, E., Gebauer, J., Gilgenkrantz, S., Lindsten, J., Curto, F. L. & Ritzén, E. M. 1982 Correlation between the number of sex chromosomes and the H-Y antigen titer. *Hum. Genet.* **61**, 135–140.

Gordon, R. D., Simpson, E. & Samelson, L. E. 1975 In vitro cell-mediated immune responses to the male specific (H-Y) antigen in mice. *J. exp. Med.* **142**, 1108–1120.

Heslop, B. H., Bradley, M. P. & Baird, M. A. 1988 A proposed growth regulatory function for the serologically detectable sex-specific antigen, H-Ys. *Hum. Genet.* (In the press.)

Jost, A. 1947 Recherches sur la différenciation sexuelle de l'embryon de lapin. II. Action des androgènes de synthèse sur l'histogénèse génitale. *Archs Anat. microsc. Morph. exp.* **36**, 242–270.

Kent, M. G., Shoffner, R. N., Hunter, A., Elliston, K. O., Schroder, W., Tolley, E. & Wachtel, S. S. 1988 XY sex reversal syndrome in the mare: clinical and behavioural studies, H-Y phenotype. *Hum. Genet.* (In the press.)

Koo, G. C., Wachtel, S. S., Saenger, P., New, M., Dosik, H., Amarose, A. P., Dorus, E. & Ventruto, V. 1977 H-Y antigen: expression in human subjects with the testicular feminization syndrome. *Science, Wash.* **198**, 655–656.

Krco, C. J. & Goldberg, E. H. 1976 Detection of H-Y (male) antigen on 8-cell mouse embryos. *Science, Wash.* **193**, 1134–1135.

Lau, Y.-F. 1987 Localization of a gene for the male enhanced antigen on human and mouse chromosomes. In *Genetic markers of sex differentiation* (ed. F. P. Haseltine, M. E. McClure & E. H. Goldberg), pp. 161–167. New York and London: Plenum Press.

Lau, Y.-F. 1988 Molecular biology of a putative gene for serological H-Y antigen. In *Evolutionary mechanisms in sex determination* (ed. S. S. Wachtel). Boca Raton: CRC Press. (In the press.)

Mann, J. R., Corkery, J. J., Fisher, H. J. W., Cameron, A. H., Mayerová, A., Wolf, U., Kennaugh, A. A. & Woolley, V. 1983 The X linked recessive form of XY gonadal dysgenesis with a high incidence of gonadal germ cell tumours: clinical and genetic studies. *J. med. Genet.* **20**, 264–270.

McLaren, A., Simpson, E., Tomonari, K., Chandler, P. & Hogg, H. 1984 Male sexual differentiation in mice lacking H-Y antigen. *Nature, Lond.* **312**, 552–555.

Mittwoch, U. 1973 *Genetics of sex determination.* New York and London: Academic Press.

Müller, U., Aschmoneit, I., Zenzes, M. T. & Wolf, U. 1978*a* Binding studies of H-Y antigen in rat tissues. Indications for a gonad-specific receptor. *Hum. Genet.* **43**, 151–157.

Müller, U., Donlon, T., Schmid, M., Fitch, N., Richter, C. L., Lalande, M. & Latt, S. A. 1986 Deletion mapping of the testis determining locus with DNA probes in 46,XX males and in 46,XY and 46,X,dic(Y) females. *Nucl. Acids Res.* **14**, 6489–6505.

Müller, U., Guichard, A., Reyss-Brion, M. & Scheib, D. 1980 Induction of H-Y antigen in the gonads of male quail embryos by diethylstilbestrol. *Differentiation* **16**, 129–133.

Müller, U., Siebers, J. W., Zenzes, M. T. & Wolf, U. 1978*b* The testis as a secretory organ for H-Y antigen. *Hum. Genet.* **45**, 209–213.

Müller, U., Wolf, U., Siebers, J.-W. & Günther, E. 1979*a* Evidence for a gonad-specific receptor for H-Y antigen: binding of exogenous H-Y antigen in gonadal cells is independent of β_2-microglobulin. *Cell* **17**, 331–335.

Müller, U., Zenzes, M. T., Wolf, U., Engel, W. & Weniger, J.-P. 1979*b* Appearance of H-W (H-Y) antigen in the gonads of oestradiol sex-reversed male chicken embryos. *Nature, Lond.* **180**, 142–144.

Ohno, S. 1976 Major regulatory genes for mammalian sexual development. *Cell* **7**, 315–321.

Ohno, S. 1979 *Major sex-determining genes.* New York: Springer.

Page, D. C., Mosher, R., Simpson, E. M., Fisher, E. M. C., Mardon, G., Pollack, J., McGillivray, B., de la Chapelle, A. & Brown, L. G. 1987 The sex-determining region of the human Y chromosome encodes a finger protein. *Cell* **51**, 1091–1104.

Polani, P. E. 1985 The genetic basis of embryonic sexual dimorphism. In *Human sexual dimorphism* (*Symposium of the Society for the Study of Human Biology*, no. 24) (ed. J. Ghesquire, R. D. Martin & F. Newcombe), pp. 125–150. London: Taylor & Francis.

Reinboth, R. 1975 Spontaneous and hormone-induced sex-inversion in wrasses (Labridae). *Pubbl. Staz. zool. Napoli* II **39** (suppl.), 550–573.

Reinboth, R., Mayerová, A., Ebensperger, C. & Wolf, U. 1987 The occurrence of serological H-Y antigen (Sxs antigen) in the diandric protogynous wrasse *Coris julis* (L.) (Labridae, Teleostei). *Differentiation* **34**, 13–17.

Rosenfeld, R. G., Luzzatti, L., Hintz, R. L., Miller, O. J., Koo, G. C. & Wachtel, S. S. 1979 Sexual and somatic determinants of the human Y chromosome. Studies in a 46,XYp- phenotypic female. *Am. J. hum. Genet.* **31**, 458–468.

Simpson, E., Chandler, P., Hunt, R., Hogg, H., Tomonari, K. & McLaren, A. 1986 H-Y status of X/XSxr′ male mice: in vitro tests. *Immunology* **57**, 345–349.

Taber, E. 1964 Intersexuality in birds. In *Intersexuality in vertebrates including Man* (ed. C. N. Armstrong & A. W. Marshall), pp. 286–310. New York: Academic Press.

Vergnaud, G., Page, D. C., Simmler, M.-C., Brown, L., Ruyer, F., Noel, B., Botstein, D., de la Chapelle, A. & Weissenbach, J. 1986 A deletion map of the human Y chromosome based on DNA hybridization. *Am. J. hum. Genet.* **38**, 109–124.

Wachtel, S. S. 1983 *H-Y antigen and the biology of sex determination.* New York: Grune & Stratton.
Wachtel, S. S., Basrur, P. & Koo, G. C. 1978 Recessive male-determining genes. *Cell* **15**, 279–281.
Wachtel, S. S., Bresler, P. A. & Koide, S. S. 1980 Does H-Y antigen induce the heterogametic ovary? *Cell* **20**, 859–864.
Wachtel, S. S., Ohno, S., Koo, G. C. & Boyse, E. A. 1975 Possible role for H-Y antigen in the primary determination of sex. *Nature, Lond.* **257**, 235–236.
Waibel, F., Scherer, G., Fraccaro, M., Hustinx, T. W. J., Weissenbach, J., Wieland, J., Mayerová, A., Back, E. & Wolf, U. 1987 Absence of Y-specific DNA sequences in human 46,XX true hermaphrodites and in 45,X mixed gonadal dysgenesis. *Hum. Genet.* **76**, 332–336.
Wiberg, U. H. 1987 Facts and considerations about sex-specific antigens. *Hum. Genet.* **76**, 207–219.
Wiberg, U. & Lattermann, U. 1987 Syngeneic male graft rejection by B6 female mice primed with spleen and testes of Sxr and Sxr′ mice. *Expl clin. Immunogenet.* **4**, 167–173.
Wiberg, U., Mayerová, A., Müller, U., Fredga, K. & Wolf, U. 1982 X-linked genes of the H-Y antigen system in the Wood Lemming (*Myopus schisticolor*). *Hum. Genet.* **60**, 163–166.
Wolf, U. 1978 Zum Mechanismus der Gonadendifferenzierung. *Bull. schweiz. Akad. med. Wiss.* **34**, 357–368.
Wolf, U. 1985 Genes of the H-Y antigen system and their expression in mammals. In *The Y chromosome*, part A (*Basic characteristics of the Y chromosome*) (ed. A. A. Sandberg), pp. 81–91. New York: Alan R. Liss.
Wolf, U., Fraccaro, M., Mayerová, A., Hecht, T., Maraschio, P. & Hameister, H. 1980 A gene controlling H-Y antigen on the X chromosome. *Hum. Genet.* **54**, 149–154.
Zaborski, P., Guichard, A. & Scheib, D. 1981 Transient expression of H-Y antigen in quail ovotestis following early diethylstilbestrol (DES) treatment. *Biol. Cell.* **41**, 113–122.
Zaborski, P. 1985 H-Y antigen in non-mammalian vertebrates. *Archs Anat. microsc. Morph. exp.* **74**, 33–37.
Zenzes, M. T., Müller, U., Aschmoneit, I. & Wolf, U. 1978 Studies on H-Y antigen in different cell fractions of the testis during pubescence. Immature germ cells are H-Y negative. *Hum. Genet.* **45**, 297–303.

Discussion

M. ADINOLFI (*Guy's Hospital, London, U.K.*). I have detected great variations of the levels of serological H-Y antigen in human peripheral white blood cells from male and female subjects. In fact, in agreement with other investigations, I have observed – by using different techniques, including ELISA tests – an overlap of the H-Y values in about 5% of normal males and females. Is this Professor Wolf's experience as well? He seems to suggest that the serological H-Y is either present or absent. I think that small amounts of H-Y molecules can always be detected in normal females.

U. WOLF. We did not test larger samples of normal male and female subjects for inter-individual variation, but in my experience with controls, I have no doubt that such a variation exists. I cannot say, however, if there is an overlap between the ranges of serological H-Y titres of the two sexes, because I did not study this problem systematically. Yamada & Isurugi (1981) found inter-individual variation, but no overlap between sexes.

The question if there is residual serological H-Y activity in normal females, I would answer positively. I have evidence that patients with campomelic dysplasia and XY sex reversal differ from female controls. Although female control tissues usually absorb some anti-H-Y antiserum, tissues derived from these patients practically do not absorb at all. This may be explained by assuming that these patients have a deletion of the H-Y structural gene, whereas in normal females this gene is present.

Reference

Yamada, K. & Isurugi, K. 1981 H-Y antigen studies in thirty patients with abnormal gonadal differentiation: correlations among sex chromosome complement, H-Y antigen, and gonadal type. *Jap. J. hum. Genet.* **26**, 227–235.

U. Wiberg (*Institut für Humangenetik, Freiburg, F.R.G.*). Are there any results from Professor Wolf's laboratory as to the Sxs-status of, especially the testis, Sxr′ mice?

If it should turn out that all Sxr′ mice type Sxs negative, how would Professor Wolf interpret this in light of the hypothesis he presented to us?

U. Wolf. I shall answer these questions together. As I said in my paper, I do not consider the problem of whether or not these mice lack serological H-Y antigen of any kind at all as settled yet. Present evidence indicates that adult animals are negative for H-Y antigen in transplantation and serological tests in non-gonadal tissues. In my view, the following experiments must be performed before a definite answer on the serological H-Y status in this mutant can be given: (1) testing of gonads including embryonic gonads; (2) studies on the expression of the serological H-Y structural gene (which can be done after this gene has been cloned). If the results are negative, the serological H-Y hypothesis of gonadal differentiation must be modified.

Mary F. Lyon, F.R.S. (*M.R.C. Radiobiology Unit, Didcot, U.K.*). In Professor Wolf's studies on inversion experiments and so on, does serological H-Y appear before gonadal differentiation, or after, or can he not tell?

U. Wolf. In our studies on the chicken embryonic gonad, at day 6 of incubation of the eggs the gonads were still at the indifferent stage and they were serological H-Y negative; 12 h later, gonads showed a distinct sex-specific differentiation, and the ovaries were serological H-Y positive whereas the testes remained serological H-Y negative. For technical reasons, we worked with pooled gonads, and because the stages of gonadal development in individual embryos varied to some extent, we chose 12 h intervals for testing.

M. W. J. Ferguson (*Department of Cellular and Structural Biology, University of Manchester, U.K.*). What is the evidence that in vertebrates other than non-eutherian mammals, hormones control the sex differentiation? Are hormone experiments really sex-reversal experiments, i.e. downstream of the primary sex-determining mechanism and not the primary sex-determining mechanism?

Using staged embryos (as opposed to embryonic ages) does the appearance of serological H-Y antigen precede gonadal differentiation? If serological H-Y is a morphogen determining male gonadal organization one must demonstrate that it appears before the organization, if it appears at the same time as the organization cause and effect cannot be properly dissected!

U. Wolf. To answer the first question, I have no evidence that in eutherians primary gonadal differentiation is hormonally controlled. However, there is an interesting paper by Vigier *et al.* (1987) showing that anti-Müllerian hormone can induce a freemartin effect. In non-mammalian vertebrates, sexual steroid hormones may be the physiological inducers of the heterogametic gonad (acting via serological H-Y antigen?), but their role is definitely downstream of the primary sex-determining mechanism.

In reply to the second question, see my answer to Dr Lyon.

Reference

Vigier, B., Watrim, F., Magre, S., Tran, D. & Josso, N. 1987 Purified bovine AMH induces a characteristic freemartin effect in fetal rat prospective ovaries exposed to it *in vitro*. *Development* **100**, 43–55.

Phil. Trans. R. Soc. Lond. B **322**, 109–118 (1988) [109]
Printed in Great Britain

Autosomal genes involved in mammalian primary sex determination

BY EVA M. EICHER
The Jackson Laboratory, Bar Harbor, Maine 04609, *U.S.A.*

Beginning with findings made during the late 1950s and early 1960s, evidence continues to accumulate in support of the hypothesis that the mammalian Y chromosome carries a gene that induces the undifferentiated foetal gonad in XY individuals to develop as a testis. Recently a DNA sequence has been isolated from the human Y chromosome that appears to be the hypothesized Y-linked testis-determining gene, and advances have also been made toward identifying genes that interact with the Y-linked testis-determining (*Tdy*) gene to initiate testis formation. These loci have been identified in specific stocks of mice carrying the mutant T^{hp} or T^{Orl} allele at the *T* locus located on chromosome 17, and in crosses involving the transfer of a Y chromosome from two populations of *Mus domesticus* into the genomes of specific inbred strains of mice. The data in both cases support the hypothesis that there are several loci involved in testis determination and that abnormal interaction of these loci disrupts initiation of testis determination, resulting in development of ovarian tissue in XY individuals.

INTRODUCTION

Mammalian sex determination is one of the most interesting, yet least understood, developmental systems. The first suggestion that sex determination in mammals was under genetic control different from that in *Drosophila* came from discoveries made in the late 1950s that XO mice (Russell *et al.* 1959) and humans (Ford *et al.* 1959) develop ovaries. This information led to the hypothesis that the mammalian Y chromosome carries at least one gene involved in directing the bipotential foetal gonad to develop as a testis and the functional absence of this gene results in ovarian development (Welshons & Russell 1959). This hypothesis was further strengthened by the findings that XXY mice (Cattanach 1961; Russell & Chu 1961) and humans (Jacobs & Strong 1959) develop testes. In 1966 Jacobs & Ross (see review by Davis 1981) presented evidence that the Y-linked testis-determining locus was located on the short arm of the human Y chromosome, and Singh & Jones (1982) reported that this locus was located near the centromere on the mouse Y chromosome. Recently, Page *et al.* (1987) isolated a coding sequence from the short arm of the human Y chromosome that is absent in sex-reversed XY women and present in sex-reversed XX men, suggesting that this DNA sequence is the Y-linked testis-determining gene. Moreover, this Y-derived sequence is highly conserved in mammals, suggesting that it is involved in an important biological function. Also, recent unpublished work from A. McLaren's and C. E. Bishop's laboratories suggests that the testis-determining (*Tdy*) locus in the mouse is located on the short arm of the Y chromosome, not on the long arm, as previously thought. In summary, it has taken almost 30 years to travel from the observation that the mammalian Y chromosome is involved in testis determination to the accomplishment of obtaining a cloned DNA sequence from the mammalian Y chromosome that is most likely involved in testis determination. In some respects, we have come a long way towards understanding mammalian sex determination, and in other respects, we are just beginning.

What I hope to accomplish in this paper is to give a general review of mutant conditions in the mouse that cause complete or partial primary sex reversal. Specifically, I shall discuss two inherited conditions that involve the interaction of autosomal loci with the Y-linked testis determination (*Tdy*) gene. One of these conditions involves the transfer of a specific *Mus domesticus* Y chromosome onto the C57BL/6J inbred strain background. The other involves the interaction of two different deletions in chromosome (chr) 17 that cause sex reversal in the presence of a normal chr 17 derived from the C57BL/6J inbred strain and a Y chromosome derived from the AKR/J inbred strain. A more complete discussion of these and other conditions that cause sex reversal in the mouse can be found in a recent review of this subject by Eicher & Washburn (1986).

Mus domesticus Y chromosome placed on the C57BL/6J inbred strain background

In 1982 my laboratory reported that the transfer of the Y chromosome originally derived from a male *Mus domesticus* onto the C57BL/6J inbred strain caused XY mice to develop as females with two ovaries, or as hermaphrodites (an individual with both types of gonadal tissue) with an ovary accompanied by an ovotestis (a gonad containing ovarian and testicular tissue) or with two ovotestes. Our initial analysis indicated that the condition was Y-linked because only males transmitted the sex reversal trait to their offspring (Eicher *et al.* 1982). This inherited sex reversal was first identified in offspring derived during the course of transferring an unrelated dominant mutation, detected in a (C57BL/6J × POS A)F1 male, to the C57BL/6J inbred strain background. (The POS A was a partly inbred stock of mice that had been produced by sib matings derived from the mating of an NMRI female to a *Mus domesticus* male descended from mice captured in the Val Poschiavo, Switzerland.)

During the course of experiments designed to unravel the mode of inheritance of the above sex reversal, we were also transferring a Robertsonian translocation, originally identified in *Mus domesticus* mice trapped in Alpie Orobie, near Bergamo, northern Italy, to the C57BL/6J inbred strain background. After a few generations of backcrosses, we noted that the sex ratio was disturbed in favour of females and that overt hermaphrodites were present within litters derived from translocation carrier males. Analysis of this sex reversal condition also indicated that it was Y-linked. The simplest idea to account for the simultaneous occurrence of two Y-linked sex reversal conditions within a single colony of mice was that the Y chromosome derived from *Mus domesticus* mice trapped in the Val Poschiavo (hereafter designated Y^{POS} for Poschiavo) was 'identical' to the Y chromosome derived from *Mus domesticus* mice captured in Alpie Orobie (hereafter Y^{ORB} for Orobie). We further postulated that these two Y chromosomes carried an allele at the *Tdy* locus that was different from that carried by the C57BL/6J strain, and that the observed sex reversal was caused when the *Tdy* allele on the Y^{POS} or Y^{ORB} chromosomes was present with homozygous C57BL/6J-derived autosomal loci. (For purposes of further discussion, the *Tdy* allele derived from the Y^{POS} and Y^{ORB} chromosomes is designated Tdy^{do}, where '*do*' represents *Mus domesticus* and that from the C57BL/6J strain is designated Tdy^{b}.) The possibility that autosomal genes were involved in this inherited sex reversal was further strengthened by our finding that transfer of the Y^{POS} chromosome to the BALB/cBy, C58/J, or DBA/2J inbred strains did not cause either partial or complete sex reversal of XY individuals. In addition the normal interaction of the Y^{POS} chromosome on the BALB/cBy,

C58/J, and DBA/2J inbred backgrounds suggested that polymorphism for one or more of these autosomal loci existed among inbred strains of laboratory mice.

We decided to test our hypothesis as follows (Eicher & Washburn 1983). We had available a set of inbred strains that were each derived from strict sib matings of offspring obtained from mating an NMRI female to a male descendant of the *Mus domesticus* mice trapped in the Val Poschiavo. If our hypothesis was correct, each of these strains contained the Y^{POS} chromosome, thus the Tdy^{do} allele, and the transfer of this Y chromosome to the C57BL/6J strain background would cause sex reversal of XY offspring. We mated males from three of these strains (RB347BNR/Ei, RB156BNR/Ei, and RB16BNR/Ei) to C57BL/6J females and analysed foetuses at 14–16 days of development for gonad morphology and sex chromosome complement. This time of development was chosen for analysis because well-spread chromosomal preparations are easily obtained from liver and a small amount of one type of gonadal tissue within a majority of the other type is easy to ascertain (Eicher *et al.* 1980). For each cross, the sex ratio was normal and all F1 XY individuals contained two normal appearing testes.

We then mated F1 male offspring obtained from each of the crosses noted above to C57BL/6J females and, as before, analysed foetuses at 14–16 days of development. In addition we analysed foetuses produced from mating C57BL/6J females to F1 males that were derived from mating a POS A strain male to a C57BL/6J female. (The origin of the POS A strain is identical to that of the other three strains being analysed.) A total of 185 backcross foetuses from all crosses were successfully analysed, with the number of XY foetuses in each of the four crosses ranging from 19 to 97. The results indicated that for each backcross, half of the XY foetuses developed some ovarian tissue. We concluded that the C57BL/6J inbred strain contains an allele at an autosomal locus, designated testis-determining autosomal-1 (*Tda-1*), that results in ovarian tissue in XY individuals when this allele is homozygous and present with the Y-linked Tdy^{do} allele. (The *Tda-1* allele carried by C57BL/6J is designated $Tda\text{-}1^b$ and that carried by *Mus domesticus* is designated $Tda\text{-}1^{do}$).

We also mated a pure *Mus domesticus* male (derived from mice trapped in the Val Poschiavo) from the inbred strain ZALENDE/Ei to a C57BL/6J female and analysed F1 foetal offspring at 14–16 days of development. All XY mice contained two normal testes. Reciprocal (ZALENDE/Ei female × C57BL/6J male)F1 XY foetal mice were also analysed and found to be normal males. We then backcrossed (C57BL/6J × ZALENDE/Ei)F1 males to C57BL/6J females and found, as expected, that half of the backcross XY offspring developed some ovarian tissue. This finding was in agreement with the results obtained using the inbred strains derived from the C57BL/6J and *Mus domesticus* genomes and provided additional support for our suggestion that the C57BL/6J autosomal $Tda\text{-}1^b$ allele causes ovarian tissue development when present in the homozygous state with the Tdy^{do} allele.

Comparison of the data from the above crosses suggests that genes other than *Tda-1* also play a role in causing sex reversal of C57BL/6J-Y^{POS} XY mice. For example, all XY mice of the C57BL/6J-Y^{POS} strain develop either as females with two ovaries or as hermaphrodites, half of which have two ovotestes and half have an ovary and an ovotestis. No C57BL/6J-Y^{POS} XY mouse develops even a single testis. This result is in contrast to what was observed in first backcross XY offspring produced in matings involving C57BL/6J females mated to the F1 males obtained from mating C57BL/6J females to males of the POS A strain or one of the other three similar strains. In these cases, although half of the backcross XY mice developed ovarian tissue, the ovarian tissue was usually present in an ovotestis and more often accompanied by a testis or another ovotestis than an ovary. In terms of the actual types of gonads recorded, out of 102 backcross XY foetuses analysed, 6 developed two ovaries; 5 developed an ovary and an ovotestis; 63 developed two ovotestes; and 28 developed an ovotestis and a testis. To explain these contrasting results we have suggested that there are other C57BL/6J-derived alleles at autosomal loci that, when present in the homozygous state in a *Tda-1*^{b}/*Tda-1*^{b} XY^{POS} individual, increase the probability that ovarian tissue will develop.

The question arises as to why all XY mice of the C57BL/6J-Y^{POS} strain do not develop exclusively ovarian tissue. To perpetuate the C57BL/6J-Y^{POS} strain, we must breed mice from this strain that will transmit a Y^{POS} chromosome. As previously noted, all of the XY mice in this strain are either females or hermaphrodites. With the exception of one XY female, all XY females tested from this strain thus far have proven sterile (Eicher *et al.* 1983). Therefore we must use hermaphrodites that have developed a sufficient amount of testicular tissue to masculinize their external genitalia and at least one side of their internal reproductive tract completely, to transmit the Y^{POS} chromosome to the next generation. If, in the C57BL/6J-Y^{POS} strain, there still exists one autosomal gene that in the heterozygous state allows some testicular tissue to develop and in the homozygous state (homozygous for the C57BL/6J-derived allele) causes exclusively ovarian tissue to develop, by definition this gene is kept in a forced heterozygous state to perpetuate the C57BL/6J-Y^{POS} strain. Proof for this idea would come from finding that C57BL/6J-Y^{POS} XY females differ from XY hermaphrodites at an autosomal locus.

Although we have made a concerted effort to locate the chromosomal position of the *Tda-1* gene, we have been unsuccessful. Our initial approach to locate the chromosomal position of *Tda-1* was to utilize a set of recombinant inbred (RI) strains produced by Benjamin Taylor of The Jackson Laboratory. This is the BXD RI strain set, which has as progenitors the C57BL/6J (B) and DBA/2J (D) strains. Our experimental design involved mating C57BL/6J-Y^{POS} hermaphrodites to females of each of the BXD RI strains and analysing foetuses at 14–16 days of development for sex chromosome complement and gonad morphology. We chose the BXD set of RI strains because, as previously stated, the Y^{POS} chromosome does not cause sex reversal when placed on the DBA/2J inbred strain background, suggesting that DBA/2J carries an allele at the *Tda-1* locus that is different from the allele carried by C57BL/6J and interacts normally with the Y-linked *Tdy*^{do} locus. In addition, a sufficient number of BXD RI strains are available for analysis so that evidence for co-segregation of *Tda-1* with another locus would be strong evidence for the linkage of these two loci.

As expected, we recovered XY foetuses containing ovarian tissue in matings involving half of the BXD RI strains, again suggesting that C57BL/6J and DBA/2J carry different alleles at the *Tda-1* locus. Unfortunately, none of the potential linkages were confirmed when we attempted to verify the suggested chromosomal locations directly by analysing foetuses produced by mating (C57BL/6J × DBA/2J)F1 females to C57BL/6J-Y^{POS} hermaphrodites. In summary, although the chromosomal location of *Tda-1* remains unknown.

We have, however, been successful in locating the chromosomal position of another autosomal gene that interacts abnormally with the *Tdy*^{do} allele to cause sex reversal of XY mice. This finding was made during the course of trying to map the *Tda-1* gene by using another set of RI strains produced from the progenitor strains NZB/BLNJ (N) and SM/J (SM). We chose this RI strain set, designated NXSM, because hermaphrodites are produced by mating NZB/BLNJ females to C57BL/6J-Y^{POS} hermaphrodites whereas only normal XY males are produced if SM/J females are used. Analysis of the data indicates that a locus on chr 12 causes ovarian tissue to be formed when the NZB/BLNJ-derived allele for this gene is present in the F1 XY offspring. Because the autosomal sex-determining gene that we were attempting to map by using the BXD RI strains is not located on chr 12 (E. M. Eicher, L. L. Washburn & B. K. Lee, unpublished data), we conclude that the *Tda-1* locus we were trying to map by using the BXD RI strains is not the same locus that we have located on chr 12 with the NXSM RI strains. We have designated this locus on chr 12 testis-determining autosomal-2 (*Tda-2*).

In conclusion, what began as a simple story of Y-linked sex reversal has become increasingly complicated. Experiments are underway to analyse foetuses produced from mating C57BL/6J-Y^{POS} hermaphrodites to (NZB/BLNJ × SM/J)F1 females to confirm the mapping of one autosomal locus to chr 12; to (SM/J × C57BL/6J)F1 females to determine whether this chr 12 locus also segregates in this cross; and to (NZB/BLNJ × C57BL/6J)F1 females to determine whether all XY foetuses develop ovarian tissue.

Sex reversal caused by the T^{hp} and T^{Orl} deletions

The hairpin tail (T^{hp}) mutation, discovered by Dickie (1965) in an AKR/J male, was shown by Johnson (1974, 1975) to be an allele at the brachyury (T) locus, which is located in the proximal region of chr 17. As is the case for other T alleles, the presence of T^{hp} with a wild-type allele (+) causes a shortening of the tail and when present with most t haplotypes causes a tail-less condition. Of special interest was Johnson's findings that the $T^{hp}/+$ condition is lethal if offspring with this genotype inherit the T^{hp} allele from a female, but viable if they inherit T^{hp} from a male. Of importance to the effect of T^{hp} on primary sex determination is the fact that T^{hp} can only be transmitted through males. Thus, because T^{hp} occurred in the AKR/J inbred strain, all stocks of mice carrying T^{hp} contain an AKR/J-derived Y chromosome. Finally, T^{hp} is known to involve a deletion that includes the quaking (*qk*) locus (Bennett 1975) as well as several DNA sequences (Mann *et al.* 1986; see review by Silver 1985).

During the course of transferring T^{hp} onto the C57BL/6J inbred strain background, we noticed that the sex ratio of litters was skewed in favour of females and a number of $T^{hp}/+$ offspring were hermaphrodites (Washburn & Eicher 1983). A closer examination revealed that some $T^{hp}/+$ females were XY and all of the $T^{hp}/+$ hermaphrodites were XY. To investigate the inheritance of this sex reversal condition further, we mated C57BL/6J females to $T^{hp}/+$ males from the C57BL/6J-T^{hp} strain and analysed foetuses for sex chromosome complement, gonad morphology, and tail phenotype. Among a total of 95 foetuses analysed, 23 foetuses were XX, +/+ and 20 were XX, $T^{hp}/+$; all 43 of these foetuses had two normal ovaries. Of the 25 XY, +/+ foetuses analysed, all had two testes. The 27 XY, $T^{hp}/+$ foetuses, however, were different from expected: 15 had two ovaries, 7 had an ovary accompanied by an ovotestis, and 5 contained two ovotestes. We concluded from this data that on the C57BL/6J inbred strain background all XY, $T^{hp}/+$ offspring develop either exclusively ovarian tissue (completely sex reversed) or some ovarian tissue (partly sex reversed). We also determined that when C57BL/6J-$T^{hp}/+$ hermaphrodites are mated to C3H/HeJ females, all XY, $T^{hp}/+$ offspring develop as normal males.

From the above results we postulated that the inherited effect of T^{hp} on gonad determination was due to either (*a*) a pleiotropic effect of T^{hp}; (*b*) a mutation in a locus closely linked to T^{hp}, or (*c*) the effect of a locus on the normal chr 17 situated *trans* to the genetic deletion involving T^{hp}. For all of these possibilities, however, the presence of a chr 17 derived from the C57BL/6J inbred strain appeared essential for sex reversal to occur in XY, $T^{hp}/+$ mice, because if T^{hp} is placed onto another inbred strain background, such as C3H/HeJ, XY, $T^{hp}/+$ mice develop as normal males. We designated the inherited sex reversal associated with T^{hp} as T-associated sex reversal (*Tas*).

Through our work with the sex reversal that resulted from the transfer of the Y^{POS} chromosome to the C57BL/6J inbred strain background, we were aware that the transfer of a Y chromosome from one genetic background to another could affect testis determination. For this reason, we decided to analyse the *Tas* locus further by using another dominant mutation at the *T* locus that also involves a deletion of chr 17 including the *qk* locus (Moutier 1973*b*; Erickson *et al.* 1978) and loci identified by DNA sequences (Hermann *et al.* 1986; Sarvetnick *et al.* 1986; Mann *et al.* 1986; and review by Silver 1985). This mutation, designated T-Orleans (T^{Orl}) (Moutier 1973*a*), can, however, be transmitted to live offspring regardless of the sex of the $T^{Orl}/+$ parent. Thus, we could use T^{Orl} to investigate simultaneously (*a*) whether the presence of the deletion in the region of chr 17 common to T^{Orl} and T^{hp} caused sex reversal when accompanied by a normal chr 17 derived from the C57BL/6J inbred strain, and (*b*) whether substitution of the C57BL/6J Y chromosome for the AKR/J Y chromosome caused normal testis development in XY, $T^{Orl}/+$ mice. I shall present some of the results of these studies. The full study will be published elsewhere (Washburn & Eicher 1988).

Before initiating the experiments involving T^{Orl}, we transferred T^{Orl} onto the C57BL/6J inbred strain background. In addition, we constructed a C57BL/6J strain of mouse that contained an AKR/J Y chromosome (strain designated C57BL/6J.AKR/J-Y, abbreviated B6.AKR-Y). In one experiment we mated C57BL/6J-$T^{Orl}/+$ females to B6.AKR-Y males and, as before, analysed foetuses at 14–16 days of development for gonad morphology, sex chromosome complement, and tail phenotype. Of the 13 $T^{Orl}/+$ foetuses analysed, all contained two ovaries. Although 7 of these females were chromosomally XX, 6 were XY, thus completely sex-reversed. In another experiment, we mated C57BL/6J-T^{Orl} females to C57BL/6J males and analysed foetuses as before. Among the 22 $T^{Orl}/+$ foetuses recovered, 11 were XX and contained two ovaries, and 11 were XY and contained two testes.

From the results presented above, together with additional supporting evidence not presented in this review, we conclude that T^{hp} and T^{Orl} cause sex reversal of XY individuals when placed on a C57BL/6J inbred strain background, provided that the AKR/J Y chromosome is also present. These data also indicate that the *Tas* locus is located in the region of chr 17 common to T^{hp} and T^{Orl}. Finally, these results suggest that the *Tdy* allele carried by the AKR/J Y chromosome differs from the *Tdy* allele carried by the C57BL/6J Y chromosome.

Experiments are underway to define more precisely the position of *Tas* on chr 17. We are utilizing DNA probes that both identify loci deleted from the T^{hp} and T^{Orl} deletions and identify restriction fragment length polymorphisms (RFLPs) between C3H/HeJ and C57BL/6J. Specifically, we shall determine whether foetuses that are produced by mating C57BL/6J-T^{hp} /+ males to (C3H/HeJ × C57BL/6J)F1 females inherit a C3H/HeJ- or C57BL/6J-derived allele from their F1 parent. The sex chromosome complement, gonad morphology and T^{hp} phenotype of each foetus will also be determined. A similar experiment will also be done by using foetuses derived from the mating of C57BL/6J-T^{Orl}/+ females to (C3H/HeJ × B6.AKR-Y)F1 males. If we successfully position *Tas* between two closely linked DNA fragments, experiments will be initiated to clone the *Tas* locus.

General discussion

A model to account for the findings summarized in this review was first published in a paper by Eicher & Washburn (1983) and later expanded in a review published in 1986. We hypothesized that in mammals two primary sex determination pathways are available to a foetus: the ovary determination pathway and the testis determination pathway. In place at the time this decision is made are the primordia for both the male and female internal duct systems. Once gonadal sex is determined, barring secondary complications, the internal and external genitalia develop concordantly with the sex of the gonads.

We suggested that mammals evolved a genetic control mechanism that guarantees that an individual will utilize either the ovary or testis determination pathways. That is, each individual develops either ovaries or testes, but not both. This dichotomy was successfully accomplished when the first gene in the testis determination (TD) pathway, *Tdy*, became located on the chromosome that evolved into the Y chromosome, the only chromosome unique to males. We suggested that, to guarantee further that XY individuals develop only testes, the *Tdy* gene functions significantly earlier in development than the first gene in the ovarian determination (OD) pathway (gene symbolized *Od*). We also suggested that testis-only development in XY males is further guaranteed by inactivation of the *Od* locus by the *Tdy* gene product or another gene in the TD pathway. The outcome of this genetic control mechanism is that the presence of the *Tdy* locus in XY individuals guarantees development of only testicular tissue, and the functional absence of the *Tdy* locus, as is the case in XX individuals, guarantees that the *Od* locus initiates development of ovarian tissue.

We think that the mouse autosomal loci we have identified, *Tas*, *Tda-1* and *Tda-2*, are some of the loci constituting the TD pathway. We suggest that within a species all of the loci in the TD pathway are selected to function in a coordinated and sequential manner, with the *Tdy* locus functioning significantly earlier than the *Od* gene so as to 'lock in' the TD pathway before the OD pathway is initiated.

The genomes of the standard inbred strains of mice are a mixture from two different species of mice, *Mus domesticus* and *Mus musculus*, with each inbred strain having a unique set of alleles derived from *M. musculus* or *M. domesticus*. The Y chromosome carried by the C57BL/6J, C3H/HeJ, and DBA/2J strains is of *M. musculus* origin whereas the AKR/J Y chromosome is of *M. domesticus* origin. Interestingly, the Y chromosome carried by C57BL/6J is derived from a different source of *M. musculus* than are the Y chromosomes carried by C3H/HeJ and DBA/2J, which appear to be of identical origin (P. K. Tucker, B. K. Lee & E. M. Eicher, unpublished data). We suggest that the Tdy^{do} allele carried on the Y^{POS} chromosome, derived from *M. domesticus* trapped in Switzerland, functions later in development than does the Tdy^{b} allele carried on the C57BL/6J inbred strain, but not significantly different in time from the *Tdy* allele carried by the C3H/HeJ or DBA/2J Y chromosomes. Thus when the Tdy^{do} allele is transferred to the C57BL/6J inbred strain background, it now interacts with OD loci derived from C57BL/6J, which normally function earlier in time than the same loci derived from the *M. domesticus* genomes (or those carried in the C3H/HeJ or DBA/2J genomes). The result is that the OD pathway is set into motion before the TD pathway is 'locked in', causing development of ovarian tissue in XY individuals.

To account for the occurrence of sex reversal in C57BL/6J-$T^{hp}/+$ and C57BL/6J-$T^{Orl}/+$ mice carrying an AKR/J Y chromosome, we suggest that the presence of a single copy of a C57BL/6J-derived Tas^b allele, as occurs in the presence of the T^{Orl} or T^{hp} deletions, delays slightly the initiation of the TD pathway. In addition, the *Tdy* allele carried on the AKR/J Y chromosome functions slightly later in development than the *Tdy* allele carried on the C57BL/6J chromosome. Evidence for this suggestion comes from a preliminary observation in our laboratory that testis cord development is delayed at the ends of the foetal testis in B6.AKR-Y mice compared with C57BL/6J mice. In tandem, these two delays allow initiation of the OD pathway and formation of ovarian tissue in XY individuals (Washburn & Eicher 1988).

I thank Barbara K. Lee and Linda L. Washburn for their dedication to the research reported here. I also thank Muriel T. Davisson, Patricia A. Hunt, Barbara K. Lee, Joseph H. Nadeau, Priscilla K. Tucker and Linda L. Washburn for helpful suggestions concerning this manuscript, and Anne L. McLaren, F.R.S., and Colin E. Bishop for use of their unpublished results. The research reported in this paper was supported by grant GM 20919 from the National Institutes of Health. Its contents are solely the responsibility of the Jackson Laboratory and do not necessarily represent the official views of the National Institutes of Health. The Jackson Laboratory is fully accredited by the American Association for the Accreditation of Laboratory Animal Care.

References

Bennett, D. 1975 The *T*-locus of the mouse. *Cell* **6**, 441–454.

Cattanach, B. M. 1961 XXY mice. *Genet. Res.* **2**, 156–158.

Davis, R. 1981 Localization of male determining factors in man: a thorough review of structural anomalies of the Y chromosome. *J. med. Genet.* **18**, 161–195.

Dickie, M. M. 1965 *Mouse News Lett.* **32**, 43–44.

Eicher, E. M., Beamer, W. G., Washburn, L. L. & Whitten, W. K. 1980 A cytogenetic investigation of inherited true hermaphrodism in BALB/cWt mice. *Cytogenet. Cell Genet.* **28**, 104–115.

Eicher, E. M., Washburn, L. L., Whitney, J. B. III & Morrow, K. E. 1982 *Mus poschiavinus* Y chromosome in the C57BL/6J murine genome causes sex reversal. *Science, Wash.* **217**, 535–537.

Eicher, E. M. & Washburn, L. L. 1983 Inherited sex reversal in mice: identification of a new primary sex-determining gene. *J. exp. Zool.* **228**, 297–304.

Eicher, E. M. & Washburn, L. L. 1986 Genetic control of primary sex determination in mice. *A. Rev. Genet.* **20**, 327–360.

Erickson, R. P., Lewis, S. E. & Slusser, K. S. 1978 Deletion mapping of the *t* complex of chromosome 17 of the mouse. *Nature, Lond.* **274**, 163–164.

Ford, C. E., Jones, K. W., Polani, P. E., de Almeida, J. C. & Briggs, J. H. 1959 A sex chromosome anomaly in a case of gonadal dysgenesis (Turner's syndrome). *Lancet* i, 711–713.

Herrmann, B., Bucan, M., Mains, P. E., Frischauf, A.-M., Silver, L. M. & Lehrach, H. 1986 Genetic analysis of the proximal portion of the *t* complex: evidence for a second inversion within the *t* haplotypes. *Cell* **44**, 469–476.

Jacobs, P. A. & Strong, J. A. 1959 A case of human intersexuality having a possible XXY sex-determining mechanism. *Nature, Lond.* **183**, 302–303.

Jacobs, P. A. & Ross, A. 1966 Structural abnormalities of the Y chromosome in man. *Nature, Lond.* **210**, 352–354.

Johnson, D. R. 1974 Hairpin-tail: a case of post-reductional gene action in the mouse egg? *Genetics* **76**, 795–805.

Johnson, D. R. 1975 Further observations on the hairpin-tail (T^{hp}) mutation in the mouse. *Genet. Res.* **24**, 207–213.

Mann, E. A., Silver, L. M. & Elliott, R. W. 1986 Genetic analysis of a mouse *T* complex locus that is homologous to a kidney cDNA clone. *Genetics* **114**, 993–1006.
Moutier, R. 1973*a* *Mouse News Lett.* **48**, 38.
Moutier, R. 1973*b* *Mouse News Lett.* **49**, 42.
Page, D. C., Mosher, R., Simpson, E. M., Fisher, E. M. C., Mardon, G., Pollack, J., McGillivray, B., de la Chapelle, A. & Brown, L. G. 1987 The sex-determining region of the human Y chromosome encodes a finger protein. *Cell* **51**, 1091–1104.
Russell, L. B. & Chu, E. H. Y. 1961 An XXY male in the mouse. *Proc. natn. Acad. Sci. U.S.A.* **47**, 571–575.
Russell, W. L., Russell, L. B. & Gower, J. S. 1959 Exceptional inheritance of a sex-linked gene in the mouse explained on the basis that the X/O sex-chromosome constitution is female. *Proc. natn. Acad. Sci. U.S.A.* **45**, 554–560.
Sarvetnick, N., Fox, H. S., Mann, H. E., Mains, P. E., Elliott, R. W. & Silver, L. M. 1986 Nonhomologous pairing in mouse *t* haplotype heterozygotes can produce recombinant chromosomes with adjacent duplications and deletions. *Genetics* **113**, 723–734.
Silver, L. M. 1985 Mouse *t* haplotypes. *A. Rev. Genet.* **19**, 179–208.
Singh, L. & Jones, K. W. 1982 Sex reversal in the mouse (*Mus musculus*) is caused by a recurrent non-reciprocal crossover involving the X and an aberrant Y chromosome. *Cell* **28**, 205–216.
Washburn, L. L. & Eicher, E. M. 1983 Sex reversal in XY mice caused by dominant mutation on chromosome 17. *Nature, Lond.* **303**, 338–340.
Washburn, L. L. & Eicher, E. M. 1988 Normal testis determination in the mouse depends on genetic interaction of loci on chromosome 17 and the Y chromosome. *Genetics* (Submitted.)
Welshons, W. J. & Russell, L. B. 1959 The Y chromosome as the bearer of male determining factors in the mouse. *Proc. natn. Acad. Sci. U.S.A.* **45**, 560–566.

Discussion

URSULA MITTWOCH (*University College London, U.K.*). I have a question regarding the Y chromosome in the AKR/J strain, which promotes ovarian development when combined with the T^{Orl} allele. In their comparison of testis masses in inbred strains of mice, Shire & Bartke (1972) found males of the AKR/J strain to have the lowest relative testicular mass at eight weeks of age. Is it known whether a Y-linked allele is involved in the causation of this low testis mass?

Reference

Shire, K. & Bartke, Y. 1972 *J. Endrocrin.* **55**, 163–171.

EVA M. EICHER. I do not know. If this is unknown, it is certainly testable.

B. M. CATTANACH (*M.R.C. Radiobiology Unit, Didcot, U.K.*). On reviewing the literature on sex reversals a year or so ago I became concerned at the number of factors that appeared capable of reversing sex. Thus there is the information Dr Eicher has provided on the influence of the 'foreign' *domesticus* Y in C57BL/6J mice, the T^{hp} deletion with the AKR chromosome (and the T^{Orl} deletion), the X deletion in wood lemmings, certain autosomal translocations in humans, and perhaps the T16H translocation together with Sxr in the mouse. It seemed to me that perhaps these do not represent autosomal sex-determining genes but may only be non-specific interferences with male development in the presence of the Y. Any delay caused by such genetic changes might override the male-determining influence of the Y.

To test this hypothesis I have introduced the W^{19} deletion of chromosome 5 together with the AKR Y into the C57BL strain and have found from examination of both 15-day foetuses and adults that most W^{19} animals develop as phenotypic females or hermaphrodites, and that such males as appear possess very small testes as adults.

Do I conclude we have discovered by chance a W-associated sex reversal or could it not be that this observation supports the idea that sex-specific genetic events that perhaps delay or retard development may cause XY individuals to develop as females?

EVA M. EICHER. Dr Cattanach's ideas and observations are interesting. What they mean, however, must await further analysis. It is not known that the *Tda-1* locus is not located on mouse chromosome 5 near *W*.

Phil. Trans. R. Soc. Lond. B **322**, 119–124 (1988) [119]
Printed in Great Britain

Molecular aspects of sex determination in mice: an alternative model for the origin of the Sxr region

By C. E. Bishop[1], A. Weith[1], M.-G. Mattei[2] and C. Roberts[1]

[1]*Departement d'Immunologie, Unité d'Immunogénétique humaine, INSERM U-276, Institut Pasteur, 25 Rue du Dr Roux, Paris, France*

[2]*Groupe Hospitalier de la Timone, INSERM U-242, 13385 Marseille, Cedex 5, France*

Using a combination of *in situ* mapping and DNA analysis with recombinant DNA probes specific for the Sxr region of the mouse Y chromosome, we show that both the gene(s) controlling primary sex determination and the expression of the male-specific antigen H-Y (*Tdy* and *Hya* respectively) are located on the minute short arm of the mouse Y chromosome. We demonstrate that the H-Y$^-$ variant of Sxr (Sxr′) arose by a partial deletion within the Sxr region and propose an alternative model for the generation of the original Sxr region.

Introduction

Sex reversed (Sxr, Tp(Y)1Ct) is a small fragment of the mouse Y chromosome which has transposed to the distal pairing–recombination region (the pseudoautosomal region) of the Y in XYSxr mutant mice (Singh & Jones 1982; Evans *et al.* 1982; Hansmann 1982; Eicher & Washburn 1986). During male meiosis this fragment is regularly transferred by recombination to the paternal X, giving rise to sterile XXSxr (sex-reversed) males. It has been shown that Sxr contains the genes controlling primary sex-determination (*Tdy*) and the H-Y transplantation antigen (*Hya*) as defined by graft rejection and by the cytotoxic T-cell assay (Simpson *et al.* 1984). An H-Y negative variant (Sxr′) has also been described (McLaren *et al.* 1984) and it has been suggested that H-Y expression may play a role in spermatogenesis (Burgoyne *et al.* 1986). Sxr contains a high concentration of simple Bkm-related repeated sequences that, when used to probe the YSxr chromosome *in situ*, show a heavy concentration of grains in the pericentric region and another peak around the telomere (Singh & Jones 1982). This led to the conclusion that Sxr represented a fragment transposed from the subcentromeric region of the Y distal to the pseudoautosomal region. Hence *Tdy* and *Hya* were mapped to a region just below the centromere of the normal Y. We present here direct cytological and molecular data showing that Sxr is, in fact, derived from the normal Y-chromosome short arm.

Analysis of the Sxr region using DNA probes

Recently, we have isolated random DNA probes recognizing sequences within the Sxr region of the mouse and have used them to analyse this mutation at the molecular level (Bishop *et al.* 1987). One probe, pYCR8, is a 2Kb *Eco*RI fragment isolated from a Y-chromosome-enriched library. Figure 1*a* shows that, on genomic blots of *Taq*-1-restricted DNA, pYCR8 detects four bands in the XY and XYSxr males but fails to react with female DNA, showing them to be Y-located. All bands can be found in DNA from the XXSxr male, demonstrating that they are located within the Sxr region. In an analysis of over 100 backcross mice, co-segregation of Sxr

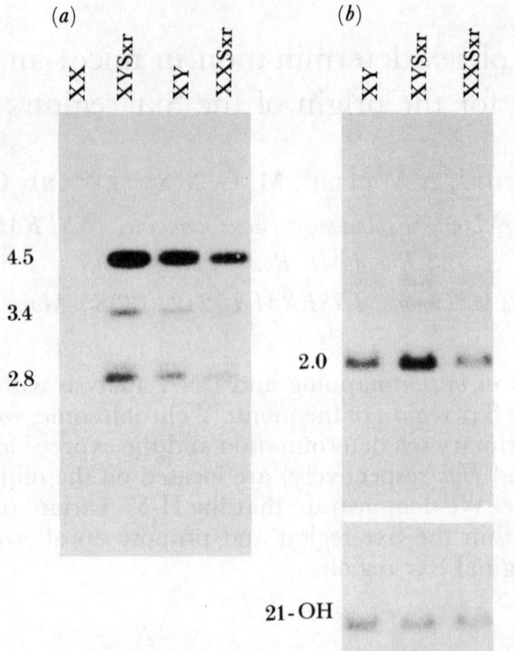

FIGURE 1. (*a*) Southern blot analysis of *Taq*1-restricted DNA from an XX female, XYSxr male, XY male and an XXSxr male by using pYCR8. (*b*) Southern analysis of the same DNAs as in (*a*) restricted by *Eco*RI. Lower panel shows the result of reprobing the same blot with the autosomal 21-OH probe to quantify the amount of DNA present. Methods: high molecular mass DNA was extracted from single mouse livers by standard procedures, 15 μg was digested with either *Taq*1 or *Eco*RI, separated on 0.8% agarose gels transferred to Hybond-N membranes (Amersham) and fixed by UV irradiation. Membranes were hybridized to [^{32}P]pYCR8 by random priming (Feinberg & Volgelstein 1984) (specific activity $> 5\times10^8$ counts min^{-1} μg^{-1}). The blots were then washed stringently (0.1×SSC†, 68 °C) and exposed moist to XAR-5 film (Kodak) with an intensifying screen at −80 °C for 18–24 h.

and pYCR8 was always observed (Nagamine *et al.* 1987). In addition, with Alu1- or HaeIII-digested DNA the probe did not hybridize to the Sxr-specific high molecular mass bands identified by Bkm, showing it to lie outside these sequences (data not shown). Figure 1*b* shows the result of probing *Eco*RI-digested DNA from XY, XYSxr and XXSxr males. pYCR8 detects the 2 kilobase cognate sequence and in addition two homologous bands of 2.6 and 2.8 kilobases, both of which map to the Sxr region. Densitometric scanning of the autoradiographs revealed that all three bands were twice as intense in the XYSxr carrier male as in the normal XY male or the XXSxr male. The amount of DNA in each lane was quantitated by reprobing with a steroid 21-hydroxylase probe (located on chromosome 17). Further dosage analysis showed the cognate band to be present as a single copy in normal male C57BL/6 XY DNA (not shown). Because of the unique nature of this probe we were able to use it to define accurately the region of the Y that has been duplicated in the YSxr chromosome. Figure 2 shows the results of *in situ* hybridization of pYCR8 to mouse metaphase chromosomes of a normal C57BL/6 male. Contrary to expectations the peak of hybridization on the normal Y was not underneath the centromere but above it. The silver grains in fact define the short arm of the Y. Although the

† 1×SSC = 0.15 M sodium chloride+0.015 M sodium citrate.

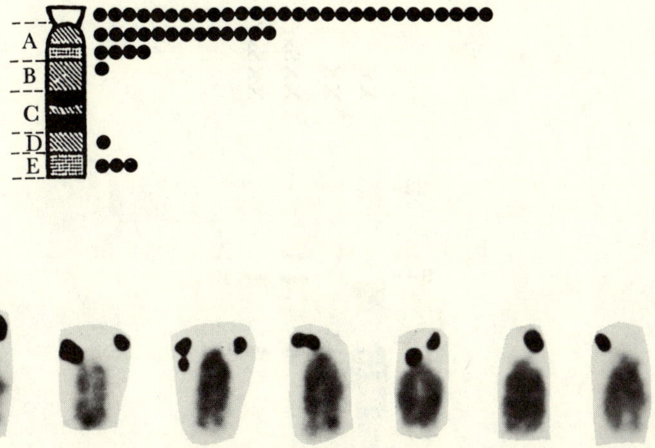

FIGURE 2. Hybridization *in situ* of probe pYCR8 to the Y chromosomes of a C57BL/6 normal male. Methods: the entire pYCR8 plasmid was tritium-labelled by nick translation to a specific activity of approximately 0.7×10^8 disintegrations min^{-1} μg^{-1}. Concanavalin-A-stimulated lymphocytes from C57BL/6, WMP and XYSxr male mice were cultured at 37 °C for 72 h and 5-bromodeoxyuridine added for the final 5.5 h of culture to ensure good post-hybridization chromosomal R-banding and optimal visualization of the Y short arm. Metaphase cells were hybridized by using a probe concentration of 10 ng ml^{-1} in the hybridization mixture as previously described (Dautigny *et al.* 1986). Slides were covered with kodak NTB2 nuclear track emulsion and exposed for 15 days at 4 °C. After development the chromosome spreads were first stained with buffered Giemsa solution and the metaphases photographed. R banding was then done by the fluorochrome-photolysis-Giemsa method and the metaphases rephotographed before analysis. More than 100 metaphases were examined.

existence of a Y short arm is not well documented, it was first described by Ford (1966) and is frequently used to identify the Y in cytogenetic studies (P. Burgoyne, E. Evans & E. Eicher, personal communications). This immediately suggests a simpler explanation for the origin of Sxr involving the relocation of the entire (or a portion) of the Y short arm containing *Tdy* and *Hya* to the pseudoautosomal region. This has the advantage of involving only one breakpoint and the mobilization of the short arm telomere.

With this model in mind we investigated the generation of the H-Y negative XXSxr′ mouse (McLaren *et al.* 1984). Probing the DNA of this mouse with pYCR8 revealed no differences in the hybridization profiles. Figure 3, however, shows the result of probing *Bam*HI-digested DNA from an XY male, XX female (C57BL/6 strain), XXSxr, XXSxr′ (latter two from an N9 generation backcrossed onto C57BL/6) with the probe pY291. This probe is a 2.6 kilobase *Eco*RI fragment taken from a Y chromosome microcloned library (A. Weith & C. E. Bishop, unpublished data). Four Y-located bands are detected in the normal XY male at approximately 12.0 kilobases (band A), 9.0 kilobases (band B), 6.0 kilobases (band C) and 3.0 kilobases (band D). These bands are not present in female DNA. All four are present in XXSxr although 291B and 291C are reduced in intensity. This suggests that 291B and C are repeated on the Y but only a limited fraction of them map within Sxr. A comparison of the banding pattern of XXSxr with XXSxr′ reveals a deletion of band 291A whereas the other bands remain unchanged. These data clearly show that the generation of the Sxr′ ($H\text{-}Y^-$) mouse from Sxr ($H\text{-}Y^+$) was not merely because of a point mutation in *Hya* (leading to loss of H-Y expression) but involved a partial deletion event within Sxr itself.

Based on these data we propose the following model for the origin of Sxr and Sxr′ (see figure 4):

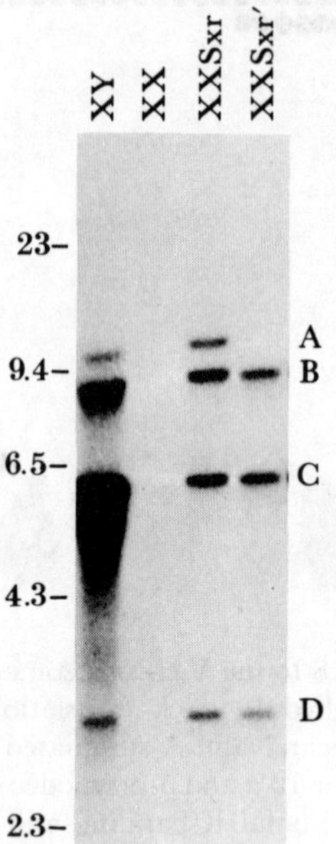

FIGURE 3. Southern blot analysis of *Bam*HI digested DNA from XY male (CB′ strain), XX female (C57BL/6 strain), XXSxr and XXSxr′ males with pY291. With the exception of the XX female all mice were kindly provided by Anne McLaren.

the Sxr region containing the genes (structural or controlling) for *Tdy* and *Hya* maps to the short arm of the mouse Y chromosome (figure 4*a*). Sxr was generated by the relocation of the whole or part of this arm from one chromatid to the distal pairing region of the sister chromatid by transposition or non-homologous exchange. Hence only one chromosomal break need be postulated and the short-arm telomere would then become the telomere of the YSxr chromosome long arm. At the DNA level this Sxr fragment would contain Sxr-specific sequences recognized by pYCR8 and pY291 (represented by an □ and ○ respectively in figure 4), a concentration of simple repeats (GATA/GACA) and several Y-specific (but not Sxr-specific) repeats recognized by pY291 (represented by a closed circle in figure 4). The placing of the ancestral Sxr region on the short arm of the Y is not in conflict with the results of Bkm hybridization *in situ*, as this latter probe is too highly repeated on the Y to resolve the short arm. The generation of Sxr′ from Sxr was a relatively simple event bearing in mind that the original father was carrying Sxr on both the X and the Y chromosomes (XSxr/YSxr). An unequal recombination event could have occurred between the two Sxr regions during male meiosis, leading to the deletion of DNA carrying all or part of the H-Y gene *Hya* (figure 4*b*). At the DNA level this would involve the loss of Sxr-specific unique sequences recognized by pY291. Consistent with this model are the surprisingly high rates of unequal crossover recently reported by Harbers *et al.* (1986) for the mouse pseudoautosomal region.

Finally, the detection of this DNA deletion within the Sxr region correlated with the loss of H-Y antigen expression may open the way to the molecular cloning of *Hya* itself (or its controlling gene) and allow one to test the hypothesis that it is involved in spermatogenesis. To this end we are at present constructing a long-range map of the Sxr region by using pulsed-field

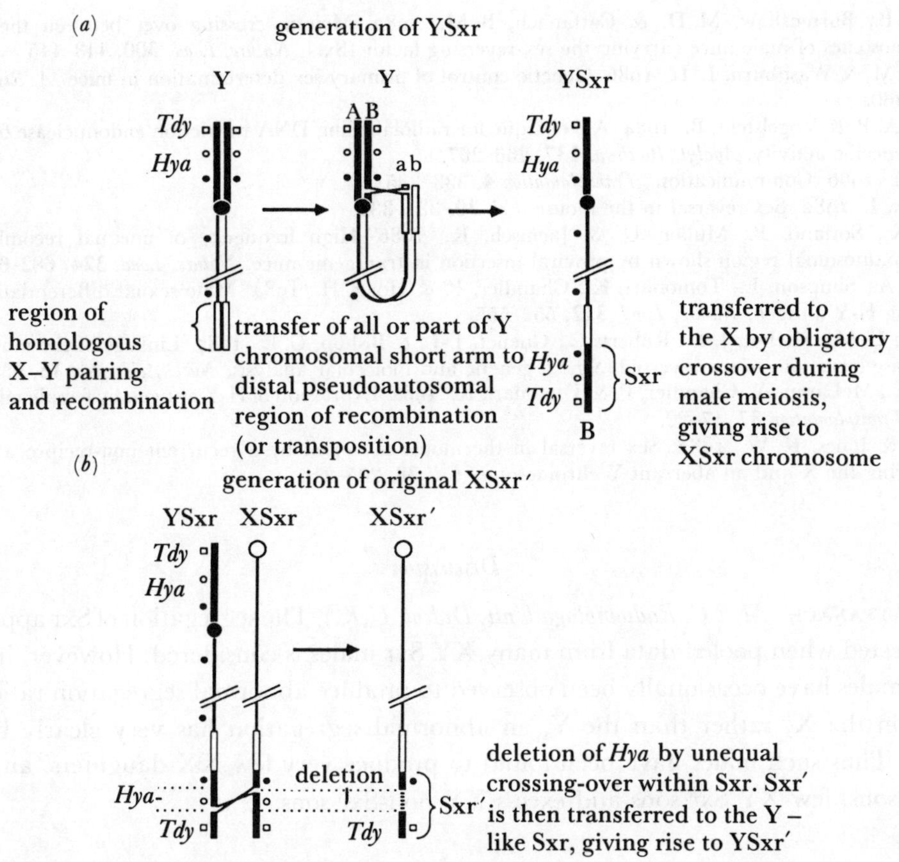

FIGURE 4. Proposed origin of Sxr and Sxr′. Open box (Â) represents the unique Sxr-specific sequence recognized by pYCR8. (○) The unique sequence detected by pY291 which is deleted in Sxr′; (●) the repeated sequences detected with this probe. The exact location of these sequences relative to each other has yet to be determined. Similarly the order of *Tdy* and *Hya* is arbitrary.

gel electrophoresis and multiple Sxr-specific DNA probes. This should allow a minimum size estimate of the deletion to be made as a first step to cloning the Y-located gene.

We acknowledge the continuous interest and support of Dr M. Fellous, Dr P. Avner, Dr C. Rijnders and Dr D. Traud during the course of this work, J. Weissenbach for critical comments, J.-L. Guenet for the WMP strain and Anne McLaren, F.R.S., for the Sxr′ mice. We acknowledge the financial support of the Fondation pour la Recherche Médicale (C.R.), the Deutsche Forschungsgemeinschaft (A.W.) and INSERM.

References

Bishop, C. E., Roberts, C., Michot, J.-L., Nagamine, C., Winking, H., Guenet J.-L. & Weith, A. 1987 The use of specific DNA probes to analyse the Sxr mutation in the mouse. *Development* **101** (suppl.), 167–175.

Bishop, C. E. & Hatat, D. 1987 Molecular cloning and sequence analysis of a mouse Y chromosome transcript expressed in the testis. *Nucl. Acids Res.* **15**, 2959–2969.

Burgoyne, P., Levy, E. & McLaren, A. 1986 Spermatogenic failure in male mice lacking H-Y antigen. *Nature, Lond.* **320**, 170–172.

Dautigny, A., Mattei, M.-G., Morrello, D., Alliel, P. M., Pham-Dinh, D., Amar, L., Arnaud, D., Simon, D., Mattei, J.-F., Guenet, J.-L., Jolles, P. & Anver, P. 1986 The structural gene coding for the myelin-associated proteolipid protein is mutated in *jimpy* mice. *Nature, Lond.* **321**, 867–869.

Evans, E. P., Burtenshaw, M. D. & Cattanach, B. M. 1982 Meiotic crossing over between the X and Y chromosomes of male mice carrying the sex-reversing factor (Sxr). *Nature, Lond.* **300**, 443–445.

Eicher, E. M. & Washburn, L. L. 1986 Genetic control of primary sex determination in mice. *A. Rev. Genet.* **20**, 327–360.

Feinberg, A. P. & Vogelstein, B. 1984 A technique for radiolabelling DNA restriction endonuclease fragments to high specific activity. *Analyt. Biochem.* **137**, 266–267.

Ford, C. E. 1966 Communication. *Transplantation* **4**, 333–335.

Hansmann, I. 1982 Sex reversal in the mouse. *Cell* **30**, 331–332.

Harbers K., Soriano, P., Muller, U. & Jaenisch, R. 1986 High frequency of unequal recombination in pseudoautosomal region shown by proviral insertion in transgenic mice. *Nature, Lond.* **324**, 682–685.

McLaren, A., Simpson, E., Tomonari, K., Chandler, P. & Hogg, H. 1984 Male sexual differentiation in mice lacking H-Y antigen. *Nature, Lond.* **312**, 552–555.

Nagamine, C. M., Michot, J.-L., Roberts C., Guenet, J.-L. & Bishop, C. E. 1987 Linkage of the murine steroid sulfatase locus, *Sts*, to sex reversed, *Sxr*,: a genetic and molecular analysis. *Nucl. Acids Res.* **15**, 9227–9238.

Simpson, E., McLaren, A., Chandler, P. & Tomonari, K. 1984 Expression of H-Y antigen by female mice carrying Sxr. *Transplantation* **37**, 17–22.

Singh, L. & Jones, K. W. 1982 Sex reversal in the mouse is caused by a recurrent non-reciprocal cross-over involving the X and an aberrant Y chromosome. *Cell* **28**, 205–216.

Discussion

B. M. CATTANACH (*M.R.C. Radiobiology Unit, Didcot, U.K.*). The segregation of Sxr appears to be that expected when pooled data from many XY Sxr males is considered. However, individual XY Sxr males have occasionally been observed to produce abnormal segregation ratios. When carried on the X, rather than the Y, an abnormal segregation has very clearly been seen recently. Thus such males have been found to produce very few XX daughters, an excess of XX Sxr sons, few XY Sxr sons and excess XY non-Sxr sons.

Phil. Trans. R. Soc. Lond. B **322**, 125–131 (1988) [125]
Printed in Great Britain

Mapping the human Y chromosome

By J. Weissenbach

Unité de recombinaison et expression génétique, INSERM U-163, CNRS UA-271, Institut Pasteur, 75015 Paris, France

This paper reviews past and present trends in mapping the human Y chromosome. So far, mapping has essentially used a combination of cytogenetic and molecular analyses of Y-chromosomal anomalies and sex reversal syndromes. This deletion mapping culminated recently in the isolation of the putative sex-determining locus *TDF*. With the availability of new separation and cloning techniques suited for large size fragments (over 100 kilobases), the next step will consist rather in the establishment of a physical map of fragments of known physical sizes. This may allow the definition of several variants of the human Y chromosome differing by the order or location of DNA sequences along the molecule.

1. Introduction

Sex chromosomes which first and foremost control sex determination can be observed when they are heteromorphic. This heteromorphism appears almost exclusively, though not necessarily, in species with male or female heterogamety. It reflects a difference in the constitution of the X and Y or Z and W chromosomes. But sex chromosomes may also differ from the autosomes. The X or Z is generally typical of autosomes and the Y or W is rather unusual and at least in part heterochromatic. This atypical aspect of the Y chromosome usually reflects its low genetic activity. The mammalian Y chromosome fits this general description. It is well established that the mammalian Y chromosome exerts a key function in sex determination through the testis-determining factor (TDF in man, Tdy in mouse) which triggers testis differentiation of undifferentiated gonads. However, other functions may be coded by loci on the mammalian Y chromosome, but so far have not been traced by classical genetics. With the advent of molecular cloning, isolation of functions known simply by their phenotype has become feasible in man by the procedures of reverse genetics (Orkin 1986). This approach has recently culminated in the cloning of DNA sequences probably representing the TDF locus (*TDF*) (Page *et al.* 1987*a*). Isolation of this gene opens a new way of analysing early development pathways in mammals. But molecular approaches have also provided a wealth of structural information on the human Y chromosome and evolution of mammalian sex chromosomes. Most of these conclusions are again derived from mapping studies using DNA probes. This paper briefly reviews some general aspects of mapping the human Y chromosome.

2. Mapping procedures using molecular probes

(*a*) *General remarks*

Although usual mapping procedures have been successfully applied to the human Y chromosome, some specific problems need to be overcome. (i) Very few genes have been mapped to the Y chromosome, confirming that it codes for a limited number of functions.

(ii) In addition, mutations in the most important of these functions may prevent their transmission to further generations. Unlike dominant or recessive X-linked genes, there is so far no definite evidence for a truly holandric transmission from fathers to sons. Even the case of hypertrychosis of the ear remains questionable. (iii) Because of its haploid state, most of the chromosome does not lend itself to recombination mapping.

(*b*) *Probe sources*

Single or low copy number Y-specific probes have been produced from two main sources: Y-only somatic-cell hybrid lines and chromosome preparations enriched by flow-sorting. An improvement in the use of somatic hybrids, allowing the isolation of more targetted probes, has been used by Pritchard & Goodfellow (1986). This procedure consists of a selection of fragments of the human Y chromosome, based on expression after chromosome-mediated gene transfer of a cell-surface antigen encoded by a Y-located gene (*MIC2*). A resistance marker had been integrated at a random location in the Y chromosome beforehand and could be used to preselect those cells that had incorporated Y-chromosomal fragments.

(*c*) *Mapping procedures*

(i) *Deletion mapping*

The present procedures combine cytogenetic and molecular methods. Mapping is essentially based on a fragmentation of the whole molecule. This breaking up can occur naturally and the resulting chromosomal deletions can be readily observed in routine karyotyping. These deletions are then probed by DNA analysis using Y-specific DNA fragments. Cytogenetic differences can be correlated with molecular differences, but the resolving power of molecular analysis allows discrimination even among cytogenetically undistinguishable anomalies. A combination of cytogenetics and molecular studies has led to the construction of the first deletion map of the human Y chromosome. This method has been extended even to cases of sex reversal in which the sex chromosomes showed no microscopic structural anomalies. It was first shown that the genome of males with an apparently 46,XX karyotype contained some Y-specific DNA (Guellaen *et al.* 1984). In such individuals (designated as Y(+) XX males) the presence of testicular tissue results from the effect of *TDF*, which is thus located in that part of the Y chromosome that they carry. The size of this chromosomal portion is variable among the different individuals analysed, but a map of overlapping fragments (nested series) could be derived and *TDF* was located in the region of shortest overlap. According to the established polarity of the map, *TDF* was in the distal interval of Yp (Vergnaud *et al.* 1986). This location was confirmed by analysis of XY women (pure gonadal dysgenesis) who lacked DNA from distal Yp (Disteche *et al.* 1986; Müller *et al.* 1986; Affara *et al.* 1987). Using this kind of approach Page *et al.* (1987*a*) were able to define an interval of 160 kilobases of Yp deleted in an XY female and present in an XX male. DNA sequences probably corresponding to exons of the TDF locus have been isolated within that interval. Using the same type of sex-reversal anomalies (Y(+) XX males and Yp- XY females), Simpson *et al.* (1987) were able to show that the H-Y locus defined by T-cell killing does not map to Yp and is thus, as in mouse, distinct from *TDF*.

(ii) *Recombination mapping*

A region of strict homology shared by the tips of the short arms of the X and Y chromosomes (Cooke *et al.* 1985; Simmler *et al.* 1985; Buckle *et al.* 1985) has only recently been found, some fifty years after its prediction by Koller & Darlington (1934). It corresponds to the telomeric part of the X–Y pairing region observed at male meiosis (Pearson & Bobrow 1970; Chen & Falek 1971). Exchange of polymorphic loci from that region through meiotic crossing-over in male gametogenesis has been observed between the two sex chromosomes (Cooke *et al.* 1985; Simmler *et al.* 1985). Genetic segregation of such loci is thus reminiscent of autosomal behaviour and was therefore termed pseudoautosomal (Burgoyne 1982). Existence of this pairing region has split the human sex chromosomes into two distinct parts: the pseudoautosomal region located at the tip of the short arm and the much larger sex-specific part which does not recombine at male meiosis.

X–Y crossing-over appears as a single, obligatory but not uniquely localized event at male meiosis (Rouyer *et al.* 1986*a*, *b*; Goodfellow *et al.* 1986; Page *et al.* 1987*b*). Loci from the pseudoautosomal region can therefore be readily mapped by family studies. The obligatory character of this X–Y crossing over facilitates accurate mapping. In addition, pseudoautosomal recombination distances measured in male meiosis appear to be 10- to 20-fold higher than in female meiosis (Rouyer *et al.* 1986*a*, *b*; Goodfellow *et al.* 1986; Page *et al.* 1987*b*), making recombination mapping in this region far more accurate than elsewhere in the genome. Mapping of the pseudoautosomal loci relative to each other can also be achieved by measuring linkage to *TDF*. Loci will be ordered from the most distal telomeric to the most proximal according to an increasing gradient of sex linkage (table 1).

TABLE 1. SEX LINKAGE OF PSEUDOAUTOSOMAL LOCI

(Compilation of data collected from Rouyer *et al.* (1986*b*); Goodfellow *et al.* (1986); Page *et al.* (1987*b*); M. C. Simmler, F. Rouyer & J. Weissenbach, unpublished results. Locus *DXYS60* is located distal to *DXYS28* on the basis of a recombination between those two loci (Rouyer *et al.* 1987). Other loci show the same order on recombination and physical maps (Petit *et al.* 1988).)

loci	meioses	recombinations	θ (%)	sex-linkage, $1-\theta$ (%)
DXYS14/DXYS20	363	172	47.4	52.6
DXYS60	37	13	35.1	64.9
DXYS28	179	68	38.0	62.0
DXYS59	38	14	36.8	63.2
DXYS15	85	28	32.9	67.1
DXYS17	145	18	12.4	87.6
MIC2	99	2	2.0	98.0

So far, no male meiosis with a double recombination event in the human pseudoautosomal region has been observed. As a consequence of this complete interference, genetic distances between loci, when measured directly, are practically identical to the recombination intervals deduced from sex-linkage values. Contrary to human, it has been shown recently that double recombination events are not infrequent in the mouse pseudoautosomal region (Keitges *et al.* 1987; Soriano *et al.* 1987). The occurrence of double events in the mouse would imply that telomeric loci recombine at a rate below 50% in this species.

(*d*) *Genes located on the Y chromosome*

So far, three clearly defined genes have been mapped to the human Y chromosome, namely *TDF* (Page *et al.* 1987*a*) and the surface antigens 12E7, specified by gene *MIC2* (Buckle *et al.* 1985), and H-Y (Simpson *et al.* 1987). These localizations are more accurate than the best resolved cytogenetic maps. *MIC2* is pseudoautosomal (Goodfellow *et al.* 1986). Another pseudoautosomal gene, the *XGR* locus, has been proposed by Goodfellow *et al.* 1987) on genetic grounds. The *XGR* locus controls in cis, expression of the *MIC2* and *XG* loci on red blood cells. On the Y chromosome, this locus was previously termed *YG* and was shown to control 12E7 red-cell quantitative polymorphism (Goodfellow & Tippett 1981; Tippett *et al.* 1986). Similarly, *XGR* is polymorphic with two alleles. In cis the same allele induces XGa antigen expression from the *XG* locus and high level 12E7 antigen expression from the *MIC2* locus. However, a recombination between *TDF* and *XGR* (*YG*) suggested that this latter is pseudoautosomal (Goodfellow *et al.* 1987). It has also been proposed that the Y chromosome carries some other functions controlling growth (Alvesalo & de la Chapelle 1981) and fertility (Tiepolo & Zuffardi 1976).

(*e*) *Limitations*

Recombination and deletion mapping have provided reliable structural data allowing ordering of numerous anonymous DNA loci and location of a few genes. But these methods are subject to several limitations. (i) They do not provide physical distances. (ii) Is the order deduced from chromosomal anomalies identical to that of a 'normal' Y chromosome? Some deletions that appear to result from single breaks on cytogenetic criteria have actually occurred through complex rearrangements and give rise to chromosomal blocks irrelevant to any single contiguous part of the original chromosome. Such rearrangements are often associated with duplications due to fusions consequent upon a primary break (Magenis *et al.* 1985). In other instances an inversion may occur before the break. (iii) Is there a 'normal' or typical Y chromosome? The order of loci is practically immutable within an autosome of a given species and its disruption suppresses recombination as illustrated by the T-locus inversions in the mouse (Artzt *et al.* 1982). Such disruption may therefore lead to progressive genetic isolation, and may have caused divergence of mammalian sex chromosomes simultaneously with crossover suppression (Muller 1964). As long as new rearrangements of the Y-chromosome-specific part do not impair its essential functions (sex determination and fertility), they can be regarded as neutral mutations. Thus it is theoretically possible to observe several orders of the different loci, though the initial mapping by molecular analysis was based on existence of a single map. The first mapping results were consistent with a unique order but soon several discrepancies were reported. In some Y(+) XX males presence of proximal Yp is found in the absence of distal Yp sequences (Affara *et al.* 1986, 1987; G. Vergnaud & J. Weissenbach, unpublished data). Similar reciprocal results have been observed in a 46,XYp- female (Disteche *et al.* 1986; Page 1986). It was proposed to ascribe such variants to inversion polymorphisms, but this still needs further confirmation by physical mapping of Y chromosomes from normal males (see below).

3. Estimating physical distances

The advent of pulsed-field electrophoretic procedures (Schwartz & Cantor 1984; Carle & Olson 1984; Carle *et al.* 1986; Chu *et al.* 1986) resolving fragments up to several megabases opens the possibility of establishing maps of large chromosomal segments and evaluating physical distances. This may make it possible to map directly Y chromosomes without anomalies and to confirm the existence of several variants of the Y chromosome differing by gross rearrangements.

The first tentative estimations of physical distances of defined areas of the Y chromosome with pulsed-field gel electrophoresis have been focused on the centromeric alphoid repetitive sequence *DYZ3* (Wolfe *et al.* 1985) and on the boundary of the pseudoautosomal region (Pritchard *et al.* 1987). All *DYZ3* repeats are clustered within a single block of variable size of approximately 500 kilobases (Tyler-Smith & Brown 1987). A long-range restriction map covering approximately 1.1 megabases of DNA including this *DYZ3* cluster has been proposed (Tyler-Smith & Brown 1987). Another map frames the proximal boundary of the pseudoautosomal region between two *HTF* islands. The most distal island corresponds to the 5′ end of gene *MIC2*. On its 3′ end this gene is linked to Y-specific DNA up to a second *HTF* island adjacent to the *TDF* locus (Pritchard *et al.* 1987; Page *et al.* 1987*a*).

This second embryonic map can now be extended to the entire pseudoautosomal region (Brown 1988; Petit *et al.* 1988; Rappold & Lehrach 1988). The pseudoautosomal region spans a chromosomal segment of almost 3 Mb which fits well with a 15- to 20-fold higher recombination frequency in male than in female meiosis. In male meiosis 1 cM† would thus represent about 60 kilobases of pseudoautosomal DNA. The region is characterized in its terminal part by a very high density of CpG doublets. Several other more classical *HTF* islands are scattered throughout the region. At the present level of resolution there is no obvious distortion between the physical and recombination maps, suggesting that recombination occurs either at random or in very many preferential points.

4. Future challenges in mapping the human Y chromosome

Some important genes of the mammalian Y chromosome remain to be isolated. The H-Y antigen will be mapped with increased accuracy and possibly cloned in the forthcoming years. This may shed some new light on the possible involvement of H-Y in spermatogenesis (Burgoyne *et al.* 1986). Restriction maps of large chromosomal segments should enable variants to be distinguished among apparently identical chromosomes and hence gross rearrangements to be detected by comparison with other primates. This may help to establish a patriarchal phylogeny of the human Y chromosome with some relevance to population genetics. Similarly, the evolution of mammalian sex chromosomes could be approached through detailed structural analysis of some specific sites, such as the pseudoautosomal boundary, with respect to their stability or variation in human populations and those of closely related species.

The dearth of genetic functions has not seriously hampered the first attempts at mapping. Paradoxically, the chromosome bearing the fewest genes has the relatively most extended physical map at present!

References

Affara, N. A., Ferguson-Smith, M. A., Tolmie, J., Kwok, K., Mitchell, M., Jamieson, D., Cooke, A. & Florentin, L. 1986 Variable transfer of Y-specific sequences in XX males. *Nucl. Acids Res.* **14**, 5375–5387.

Affara, N. A., Ferguson-Smith, M. A., Magenis, R. E., Tolmie, J., Cooke, A., Boyd, E., Jamieson, D., Kwok, K., Mitchell, M. & Snadden, L. 1987 Mapping the testis determinants by an analysis of Y-specific sequences in males with apparent XX and XO karyotypes and females with XY karyotypes. *Nucl. Acids Res.* **15**, 7325–7342.

† The morgan is the unit of relative distance between genes on a chromosome. One centimorgan represents a crossover value of 1%.

Alvesalo, L. & de la Chapelle, A. 1981 Tooth size in two males with deletions of the long arm of the Y chromosome. *Ann. hum. Genet.* **54**, 49–54.

Artzt, K., McCormick, P. & Bennett, D. 1982 Gene mapping within the T/t complex of the mouse. I. t-lethal genes are nonallelic. *Cell* **28**, 463–470.

Brown, W. R. A. 1988 A physical map of the human pseudoautosomal region. *EMBO J.* **7**. (In the press.)

Buckle, V., Mondello, C., Darling, S., Craig, I. W. & Goodfellow, P. N. 1985 Homologous expressed genes in the human sex chromosome pairing region. *Nature, Lond.* **317**, 739–741.

Burgoyne, P. S. 1982 Genetic homology and crossing over in the X and Y chromosomes of mammals. *Hum. Genet.* **61**, 85–90.

Burgoyne, P. S., Levy, E. R. & McLaren, A. 1986 Spermatogenetic failure in male mice lacking H-Y antigen. *Nature, Lond.* **230**, 170–172.

Carle, G. F. & Olson, M. V. 1984 Separation of chromosomal DNA molecules from yeast by orthogonal-field-alternation gel electrophoresis. *Nucl. Acids Res.* **12**, 5647–5656.

Carle, G. F., Frank, M. & Olson, M. V. 1986 Electrophoretic separations of large DNA molecules by periodic inversion of the electric field. *Science, Wash.* **232**, 65–68.

Chen, A. & Falek, A. 1971 Cytological evidence for the association of the short arms of the X and Y in the human male. *Nature, Lond.* **232**, 555–556.

Chu, G., Vollrath, D. & Davies, R. W. 1986 Separation of large DNA molecules by contour-clamped homogeneous electric fields. *Science, Wash.* **234**, 1582–1585.

Cooke, H. J., Brown, W. R. A. & Rappold, G. A. 1985 Hypervariable telomeric sequences from the human sex chromosomes are pseudoautosomal. *Nature, Lond.* **317**, 687–692.

Disteche, C. M., Casanova, M., Saal, H., Friedman, C., Sybert, V., Graham, J., Thuline, H., Page, D. C. & Fellous, M. 1986 Small deletions of the short arm of the Y chromosome in 46,XY females. *Proc. natn. Acad. Sci. U.S.A.* **83**, 7841–7844.

Goodfellow, P. J., Darling, S. M., Thomas, N. S. & Goodfellow, P. N. 1986 A pseudoautosomal gene in man. *Science, Wash.* **234**, 740–743.

Goodfellow, P. J., Pritchard, C., Tippett, P. & Goodfellow, P. N. 1987 Recombination between the X and Y chromosomes: implications for the relationship between MIC2, XG and YG. *Ann. hum. Genet.* **51**, 161–167.

Goodfellow, P. N. & Tippett, P. 1981 A human quantitative polymorphism related to Xg blood groups. *Nature, Lond.* **289**, 404–405.

Guellaen, G., Casanova, M., Bishop, C., Geldwerth, D., Andre, G., Fellous, M. & Weissenbach, J. 1984 Human XX males with Y single-copy DNA fragments. *Nature, Lond.* **307**, 172–173.

Keitges, E. A., Schorderet, D. F. & Gartler, S. M. 1987 Linkage of the steroid sulfatase gene to the Sex-reversed mutation in the mouse. *Genetics, Princeton* **116**, 465–468.

Koller, P. C. & Darlington, C. D. 1934 The genetical and mechanical properties of the sex chromosomes. 1. *Rattus norvegicus*. *J. Genet.* **29**, 159–173.

Magenis, R. E., Brown, M. G., Donlon, T., Olson, S. B., Sheehy, R. & Tomar, D. 1985 Structural aberrations of the Y chromosome, including the nonfluorescent Y: cytologic origin and consequences. In *The Y chromosome* (ed. A. A. Sandberg), part A, pp. 537–574. New York: Alan R. Liss.

Muller, H. J. 1964 The relation of recombination to mutational advance. *Mutat. Res.* **1**, 2–9.

Müller, U., Donlon, T., Schmid, M., Fitch, N., Richer, C. L., Lalande, M. & Latt, S. A. 1986 Deletion mapping of the testis determining locus with DNA probes in 46,XX males and in 46,XY and 46,Xdic(Y) females. *Nucl. Acids Res.* **14**, 6489–6505.

Orkin, S. H. 1986 Reverse genetics and human disease. *Cell* **47**, 845–850.

Page, D. C. 1986 Sex reversal: deletion mapping the male-determining function of the human Y chromosome. *Cold Spring Harb. Symp. quant. Biol.* **51**, 229–235.

Page, D. C., Mosher, R., Simpson, E. M., Fisher, E. M. C., Mardon, G., Pollack, J., McGillivray, B., de la Chapelle, A. & Brown, L. G. 1987*a* The sex-determining region of the human Y chromosome encodes a finger protein. *Cell* **51**, 1091–1104.

Page, D. C., Bieker, K., Brown, L. G., Hinton, S., Leppert, M., Lalouel, J. M., Lathrop, M., Nystrom-Lahti, M., de la Chapelle, A. & White, R. 1987*b* Linkage, physical mapping, and DNA sequence analysis of pseudoautosomal loci on the human X and Y chromosomes. *Genomics* **1**, 243–256.

Pearson, P. L. & Bobrow, M. 1970 Definitive evidence for the short arm of the Y chromosome associating with the X chromosome during meiosis in the human male. *Nature, Lond.* **226**, 959–961.

Petit, C., Levilliers, J. & Weissenbach, J. 1988 Physical mapping of the human autosomal region; comparison with genetic linkage map. *EMBO J.* **7**. (In the press.)

Pritchard, C. A. & Goodfellow, P. N. 1986 Development of new methods in human gene mapping: selection for fragments of the human Y chromosome after chromosome-mediated gene transfer. *EMBO J.* **5**, 979–985.

Pritchard, C. A., Goodfellow, P. J. & Goodfellow, P. N. 1987 Mapping the limits of the human pseudoautosomal region and a candidate sequence for the male-determining gene. *Nature, Lond.* **328**, 273–275.

Rappold, G. A. & Lehrach, H. 1988 A long range restriction map of the pseudoautosomal region by partial digest PFGE analysis from the telomere. *Nucl. Acids Res.* **16**, 5361–5377.

Rouyer, F., Simmler, M. C., Johnsson, C., Vergnaud, G., Cooke, H. J. & Weissenbach, J. 1986*a* A gradient of sex linkage in the pseudoautosomal region of the human sex chromosomes. *Nature, Lond.* **319**, 291–295.

Rouyer, F., Simmler, M. C., Vergnaud, G., Johnsson, C., Levilliers, J., Petit, C. & Weissenbach, J. 1986*b* The pseudoautosomal region of the human sex chromosomes. *Cold Spring Harb. Symp. quant. Biol.* **51**, 221–228.

Rouyer, F., Simmler, M. C., Page, D. C. & Weissenbach, J. 1987 A sex chromosome rearrangement in a human XX male caused by Alu–Alu recombination. *Cell* **51**, 417–425.

Schwartz, D. C. & Cantor, C. R. 1984 Separation of yeast chromosome-sized DNAs by pulsed field gradient gel electrophoresis. *Cell* **37**, 67–75.

Simmler, M. C., Rouyer F., Vergnaud, G., Nyström-Lahti, M., Ngo, K. Y., de la Chapelle, A. & Weissenbach, J. 1985 Pseudoautosomal DNA sequences in the pairing region of the human sex chromosomes. *Nature, Lond.* **317**, 692–697.

Simpson, E., Chandler, P., Goulmy, E., Disteche, C. M., Ferguson-Smith, M. A. & Page, D. C. 1987 Separation of the genetic loci for the H-Y antigen and for testis determination on human Y chromosome. *Nature, Lond.* **326**, 876–878.

Soriano, P., Keitges, K. A., Schorderet, D. F., Harbers, K., Gartler, S. M. & Jaenisch, R. 1987 High rate of recombination and double crossovers in the mouse pseudoautosomal region during male meiosis. *Proc. natn. Acad. Sci. U.S.A.* **84**, 7218–7220.

Tiepolo, L. & Zuffardi, O. 1976 Localization of the factors controlling spermatogenesis in the non-fluorescent portion of the human Y chromosome long arm. *Hum. Genet.* **34**, 119–124.

Tippett, P., Shaw, M. A., Green, C. A. & Daniels, G. L. 1986 The 12E7 red cell quantitative polymorphism: control by the Y-borne locus, Yg. *Ann. hum. Genet.* **50**, 339–347.

Tyler-Smith, C. & Brown, W. R. A. 1987 Structure of the major block of alphoid satellite DNA on the human Y chromosome. *J. molec. Biol.* **195**, 457–470.

Vergnaud, G., Page, D. C., Simmler, M. C., Brown, L., Rouyer, F., Noël, B., Botstein, D., de la Chapelle, A. & Weissenbach, J. 1986 A deletion map of the human Y chromosome based on DNA hybridization. *Am. J. hum. Genet.* **38**, 109–124.

Wolfe, J., Darling, S. M., Erickson, R. P., Craig, I. W., Buckle, V. J., Rigby, P. W. J., Willard, H. F. & Goodfellow, P. N. 1985 Isolation and characterization of an alphoid centromeric repeat family from the human Y chromosome. *J. molec. Biol.* **182**, 477–485.

Phil. Trans. R. Soc. Lond. B **322**, 133–144 (1988) [133]
Printed in Great Britain

Accidental X–Y recombination and the aetiology of XX males and true hermaphrodites

By M. A. Ferguson-Smith, F.R.S., and N. A. Affara
Department of Pathology, University of Cambridge, Tennis Court Road, Cambridge CB2 1QP, U.K.

Accidental recombination between the differential segments of the X and Y chromosomes in man occasionally allows transfer of Y-linked sequences to the X chromosome leading to testis differentiation in so-called XX males. Loss of the same sequences by X–Y interchange allows female differentiation in a small proportion of individuals with XY gonadal dysgenesis. A candidate gene responsible for primary sex determination has recently been cloned from within this part of the Y chromosome by Page and his colleagues. The observation that a homologue of this gene is present on the short arm of the X chromosome and is subject to X-inactivation, raises the intriguing possibility that sex determination in man is a quantitative trait. Males have two active doses of the gonad determining gene, and females have one dose. This hypothesis has been tested in a series of XX males, XY females and XX true hermaphrodites by using a genomic probe, CMPXY1, obtained by probing a Y-specific DNA library with synthetic oligonucleotides based on the predicted amino-acid sequence of the sex-determining protein. The findings in most cases are consistent with the hypothesis of homologous gonad-determining genes, *GDX* and *GDY*, carried by the X and Y chromosomes respectively. It is postulated that in sporadic or familial XX true hermaphrodites one of the *GDX* loci escapes X-inactivation because of mutation or chromosomal rearrangement, resulting in mosaicism for testis and ovary-determining cell lines in somatic cells. Y-negative XX males belong to the same clinical spectrum as XX true hermaphrodites, and gonadal dysgenesis in some XY females may be due to sporadic or familial mutations of *GDX*.

Introduction

From the early days of chromosome cytology the X and Y chromosomes of several species, including man, were described as having paired homologous segments and non-homologous differential segments (Darlington 1976). The male testis determining factors (*TDF*) are contained in the differential part of the Y chromosome. The paired segments are kept homologous by synapsis, chiasma formation and crossing over, and these processes ensure the proper segregation during first meiosis of the X and Y chromosomes into different gametes and thus an approximately equal sex ratio. In man, failure of synapsis and chiasma formation within the pairing segment leads to non-disjunction (or non-conjunction) of the sex chromosomes and the production of sterile individuals with the 45, X and 47, XXY syndromes of Turner & Klinefelter respectively. The maintenance of an approximately normal sex ratio and normal sex determination and differentiation also depends on the absence of crossing over within the differential segments which might allow transfer of *TDF* from Y to X. Such accidental crossing over outside the X–Y pairing segment was postulated in an earlier paper (Ferguson-Smith, 1966) as the most likely cause of Klinefelter's syndrome in sterile males with an apparently normal female karyotype and of gonadal dysgenesis in females with an apparently normal male karyotype. The rare occurrence of this form of X–Y interchange could be regarded as the price paid by the species for the comparatively low frequency of 47, XXY and 45, X individuals.

Evidence from the XG blood group

The evidence that X–Y interchange might be involved in the aetiology of XX males came first from studies of the sex-linked dominant XG blood group which was later found to map to the tip of the short arm of the X (Ferguson-Smith *et al.* 1982). Several of the earlier cases were observed who had failed to inherit the XG^a allele from their father. Data are now available on 102 XX males, 71.6% of whom are Xg(a+), a frequency significantly different from the 88.4% expected in a sample of normal females, and rather more than the 65.9% expected in normal males (R. Sanger & P. Tippett, unpublished observations). This is consistent with loss of the *XG* locus from the paternal X in many XX males. The reciprocal situation, namely the transmission of the father's XG^a allele to an XY female on an interchanged Y, has not been demonstrated and it is not known what proportion of XY females are Xg(a+).

Evidence from chromosome analysis and flow cytometry

With the improvement of cytogenetic techniques, several authors reported that one X chromosome was slightly larger than the other in some XX males (Madan 1976; Wachtel *et al.* 1976; Evans *et al.* 1979) and, later, that this was due to transfer of Yp11.2 → pter from the Y (Magenis *et al.* 1982). It has been possible to measure the DNA content of X chromosomes by flow cytometry in a series of XX males and this reveals an increase of 3.8% (equivalent to approximately 6 million base pairs) in one of the two Xs in 12 of 20 cases (Ferguson-Smith 1988); in the other 8 cases the two X chromosomes are indistinguishable in total DNA content. As far as XY females are concerned, a much smaller proportion of cases have been found to have loss of Y chromosome material. In one case the Y chromosome is about 10% smaller than the father's Y chromosome indicating a loss of about 6 megabases from the Y short arm (Affara *et al.* 1987).

Evidence from molecular genetics studies

Confirmation of transfer of Y material from the Y to the X came with the demonstration that the Y-linked locus *MIC2*, associated with high expression of the 12E7 cell-surface antigen on red cells (see Goodfellow *et al.*, this symposium), was present in an Xg(a−) XX male who had failed to inherit the paternal Xg(a+) allele (de la Chapelle *et al.* 1984). The *MIC2* locus on the Y had apparently been interchanged with the *XG* locus. This report was followed by several studies in which the presence of Y-specific DNA sequences was demonstrated in the DNA of an increasing proportion of XX males by using DNA probes isolated from Y-chromosome-specific libraries in Southern blotting experiments (Guellaen *et al.* 1984; Page *et al.* 1985; Muller *et al.* 1986*a*; Affara *et al.* 1986*a*). However, these studies could not determine whether or not the Y sequences had been transferred to Xp in proximity to the pairing segment and this was not clarified until Y-specific probes were annealed direct to metaphase chromosomes by using the technique of *in situ* hybridization (Magenis *et al.* 1984; Andersson *et al.* 1986; Buckle *et al.* 1987; Kalaitzidakis *et al.* 1987). In our own series of XX males, all nine cases known to have Y-specific sequences so far tested have these sequences located at the proximal tip of one of the two X chromosomes (Kalaitzidakis *et al.* 1987). Similarly, loss of Y-specific sequences has been demonstrated in several XY females (Disteche *et al.* 1986; Muller *et al.* 1986*b*; Affara *et al.* 1987).

Several XX males are described in which no Y-specific sequences have been demonstrated and there are, similarly, many XY females without any apparent loss of Y sequences. It is therefore likely that mechanisms other than X–Y interchange are responsible for the sex reversal in these exceptions. There seem to be some interesting clinical differences between those XX males with and without evidence of X–Y interchange (see below).

Cloning the sex determining factors on Yp

The primary signal for male (testis) differentiation has long been regarded as a Y-linked dominant trait determined by a gene (*TDF*) or genes located on the short arm of the Y chromosome. Thus testicular differentiation occurs only in individuals who have a specific segment of the short arm of the Y chromosome containing *TDF* in at least some of their somatic cells. Y-negative XX males and XX true hermaphrodites remain the only exceptions to this rule. Attempts by several groups to isolate and clone *TDF* have therefore focused on the Y-specific sequences carried by XX males and deleted in some XY females. It is almost certain that this has now been accomplished. Page *et al.* (1987*a*) have reported details of a likely candidate for *TDF*, some sequences of which were cloned from an X–Y interchange male and found to be missing in a female patient who had a reciprocal translocation between the short arm of the Y and chromosome 22 associated with the loss of a 160 kilobase segment from Yp. The gene codes for a DNA binding protein, characterized by a series of zinc fingers, which presumably acts in the regulation of transcription of a key substance in the pathway to testis differentiation. The DNA sequence is highly conserved in mammals and an important finding is that there is a homologous sequence carried on the short arm of the X. The X-linked sequence is located in Xp21–22.3 and is therefore likely to be subject to X-inactivation. If both X and Y genes code for the same sex-determining protein, normal male somatic cells have a double dose and normal female somatic cells a single active dose of the *TDF* product. Similarly, females with abnormal sex chromosome constitutions including X0, XXX or XXXX have one active dose, males with XXY, XXXY and XXXXY have two active doses and males with XYY, XXYY have three active doses (suggesting that more than one dose is male determining). XX males have two doses because *TDY* is transferred to part of the X that normally escapes X-inactivation. The implication is that man now falls into line with many other invertebrate species including *Drosophila*, where the primary sex-determining system depends on gene dosage (see McLaren, this symposium). In fact, all mammalian species so far tested have X and Y homologues of *TDF*. As the sex difference depends on X-inactivation in female somatic cells, the suggestion of Chandra (1985) that X-inactivation has evolved in mammals primarily as a sex-determining device seems highly plausible. In chickens, where there is no mechanism for dosage compensation analogous to X inactivation, it seems likely that the Z chromosome but not the W chromosome carries *TDF* so that the ZZ male has two doses and the ZW female only one.

If it is confirmed that the testis-determining signal is not a Y-linked dominant trait, but as suggested above, a quantitative trait determined by X and Y homologous gonad-determining genes, it would seem preferable to drop the *TDF* symbol and in future follow German (1988) and refer to the X and Y loci as *GDX* and *GDY* respectively.

The contribution of X–Y interchange males and females to mapping the X and Y chromosomes

The results quoted above strongly support the concept of accidental recombination of *GDY* as an important factor in the aetiology of XX males and XY females. A substantial number of patients have now been studied with a variety of X- and Y-specific probes, and data are accumulating on the extent of X–Y interchange and on the chromosomal sites of interchange in both X and Y. Most data come from the study of XX males, and considerable variation has been found in the amount of Y material transferred to the X from case to case. On the assumption that the interchange involves a single terminal transfer of Y short arm to the X, preliminary maps of the differential part of the Y chromosome have been constructed (Vergnaud *et al.* 1986; Affara *et al.* 1986*a*; Muller *et al.* 1986*b*). Affara *et al.* 1986*b* (updated in Ferguson-Smith *et al.* 1987) have used 58 DNA probes that recognize 76 Y-specific DNA fragments to construct deletion maps of the Y chromosome in two groups of patients, namely those with structural Y chromosome aberrations defined by classical cytogenetic analysis, and those with X–Y interchange. The results show that both maps are approximately consistent and that all Y sequences involved in 18 patients with X–Y interchange map to the short arm of the Y. There are a few exceptions to the consensus order that can be explained by inversion polymorphisms. These polymorphisms may be comparatively common in the differential part of the Y chromosome, as there is, of course, no mechanism of synapsis and chiasma formation to maintain any particular order of loci on the non-pairing part of the Y. Chromosome mutations that change the order of loci are likely to be tolerated provided they do not disturb reproductive fitness.

Different approaches have led to the isolation of DNA sequences from the homologous pairing (or pseudoautosomal) segment of the sex chromosomes (Cooke *et al.* 1985; Simmler *et al.* 1985; Rouyer *et al.* 1986; Goodfellow *et al.* 1986). Those sequences that identify X- and Y-specific restriction fragment length polymorphisms have been used to study recombination between the X and Y (partial sex linkage). The results are consistent with a single obligate cross-over in male meiosis (that is probably essential for segregation of the X and Y) and show that recombination is much higher in male meiosis than in female meiosis. Most work has been accomplished using probes at four pseudoautosomal loci: *DXYS14* (p29C1), *DXYS15* (p113), *DXYS17* (p601, 602) and *MIC2* (pSG1, p19B). Linkage analysis reveals a gradient of partial sex linkage, the most proximal locus (*MIC2*) recombining with sex infrequently (2.5%) whereas the most distal locus DXYS14 shows virtually no sex linkage (Rouyer *et al.* 1986). No examples of double recombination have been found within the pairing segment. A comparison of recombination between males and females demonstrates that, between the most proximal and most distal loci, there is 45% recombination in male meiosis compared with 2.0% recombination in female meiosis. The high frequency of recombination within the pairing segments is also associated with hypervariability of several of the sequences (e.g. *DXYS14* and *DXYS15*) used as probes. This is the result of variation in copy number of small repeats or minisatellites, and makes the probes particularly informative in family studies.

These pseudoautosomal probes can therefore be used to study X–Y interchange, first to determine the X or Y origin of the pairing segment contributed by the father, and secondly to help map the breakpoints of the interchange. Thus Petit *et al.* (1987) have studied six Y-positive XX males and have shown that in each case the complete pseudoautosomal region of the father's Y chromosome had been transferred to the paternal X. In addition, the authors demonstrated loss of Xp sequences tightly linked to the pairing segment in the paternal X. The three Y-negative XX males studied showed inheritance of proximal pseudoautosomal loci from the paternal X, indicating that terminal X–Y interchange had not occurred.

In another XX male (Page *et al.* 1987*b*) not only the entire pseudoautosomal region from the paternal Y chromosome but the proximal part of the pseudoautosomal region from the paternal X was present in the interchange showing that the X breakpoint involved in the interchange had occurred within the pseudoautosomal region. The molecular basis of X–Y interchanges can thus be studied with existing mapping data, and now reveals considerable heterogeneity. The interesting paper of Rouyer *et al.* (1987) shows that in one XX male the abnormal homologous recombination occurred between two Alu sequences, one in the pseudoautosomal region of the paternal X, the other located in the differential segment of Yp. Cloning of the breakpoints in other examples of XX males should indicate if this type of homology is commonly found to be associated with X–Y interchange.

Our own studies in a series of 23 XX males provide information about the variation in the location of X and Y breakpoints in X–Y interchange.

(*a*) *Xg studies*

Five patients are informative for *XG*. Four are Xg(a−) negative and have failed to inherit the father's XG^a allele; in each case they show high expression of 12E7 indicating that the *MIC2* locus has been transferred to the X from the paternal Y. The X breakpoint is thus proximal to the *XG* locus on the paternal X in these cases. One Y-negative XX male, is Xg(a+) positive and has inherited his father's XG^a allele, indicating that if X–Y interchange has occurred the breakpoint is distal to the *XG* locus.

(*b*) *STS studies*

Eleven patients have had steroid sulphatase activity (STS) assayed in hair roots. The locus for this enzyme maps to the end of Xp within measurable distance of *XG* and escapes inactivation. Seven XX males have levels of STS consistent with the double dose expected in normal female controls, and three have considerably elevated levels approximately twice the levels found in normal female controls. No explanation for the increased activity in these cases has been found, other than a suggestion that there may have been some disturbance at a regulatory locus. None of the patients have an STS activity in the male range, as would be expected if the STS locus had been included in the interchange. One such case with reduced STS activity has been noted previously (Wieaker *et al.* 1983).

(*c*) *Variation in transfer of Y-specific sequences*

We have tested our series of 23 XX males with 27 DNA probes that recognize 30 Y short arm sequences. All except one of the 17 Y+XX males have retained GMGY3 (table 1), which is therefore regarded as being that most closely linked of our probes to the *GDY* locus (Affara *et al.* 1987). The studies of Page *et al.* (1987*a*) show that GMGY3 is distal to *GDY* but proximal to *MIC2Y*. GMGY3 is the only sequence found to be transferred in two cases. Eight cases appear to have transferred 28 Y sequences (approximately 70% of the Y short arm sequences) and in these cases the breakpoint is in exactly the same interval, suggesting a possible recombination 'hot-spot'. In four cases, six to eight Y sequences have been transferred,

Table 1. Pattern of Y sequences in XX males

(The table summarizes the results of Southern blot analysis on genomic DNA on an extensive group of XX males by using a series of DNA probes that detect Y linked fragments. The order of sequences given on the table reflects the order derived with this series of patients and a series of patients with deletions of Yp (Affara *et al.* 1986*b*). CMPXY1 recognizes X and Y fragments of the sex-determining locus.)

probe....		KS	RH	JM	TA	AG	JT	GA	WB	DR	NI	NE	OP	AP	RS	MM	TK	GC	HM	MS	AN	RT	PP	DC
GMGY3		+	+	+	+	+	+	+	+	+	+	+	+	+	+	+	+	−	−	−	−	−	−	−
CMPXY1		+	+	+	+	+	+	+	+	+	+	+	+	+	+	+	+	−	.	−	−	−	−	−
47z		+	+	+	+	+	+	+	+	+	+	+	+	+	+	−	−	−	−	−	−	−	−	−
GMGXY7		+	+	+	+	+	+	+	+	+	+	+	+	+	−	−	−	−	−	−	−	−	−	−
GMGXY6		+	+	+	+	+	+	+	+	+	+	+	+	+	−	−	−	−	−	−	−	−	−	−
115i		+	+	+	+	+	+	+	+	+	+	+	+	+	−	−	−	−	−	−	−	−	−	−
GMGXY4		+	+	+	+	+	+	+	+	+	+	+	+	+	−	−	−	−	−	−	−	−	−	−
13d		+	+	+	+	+	+	+	+	+	+	+	+	−	−	−	−	−	−	−	−	−	−	−
GMGXY9		+	+	+	+	+	+	+	+	+	+	+	−	−	−	−	−	−	−	−	−	−	−	−
GMGXY5		+	+	+	+	+	+	+	+	+	−	−	−	−	−	−	−	−	−	−	−	−	−	−
GMGY10	E	−	+	+	+	+	+	+	+	+	−	−	−	−	−	−	−	−	+	−	−	−	−	−
GMGXY2		−	+	+	+	+	+	+	+	+	−	−	−	−	−	−	−	−	+	−	−	−	−	−
GMGY7	A	−	+	+	+	+	+	+	+	+	−	−	−	−	−	−	−	−	−	−	−	−	−	−
	C	−	+	+	+	+	+	+	+	+	−	−	−	−	−	−	−	−	−	−	−	−	−	−
	D	−	+	+	+	+	+	+	+	+	−	−	−	−	−	−	−	−	−	−	−	−	−	−
50f2	A	−	+	+	+	+	+	+	+	+	−	−	−	−	−	−	−	−	−	−	−	−	−	−
	B	−	+	+	+	+	+	+	+	+	−	−	−	−	−	−	−	−	−	−	−	−	−	−
118	D	−	+	+	+	+	+	+	+	+	−	−	−	−	−	−	−	−	−	−	−	−	−	−
	E	−	+	+	+	+	+	+	+	+	−	−	−	−	−	−	−	−	−	−	−	−	−	−
GMGY46	A	−	+	+	+	+	+	+	+	+	−	−	−	−	−	−	−	−	−	−	−	−	−	−
GMGY22		−	+	+	+	+	+	+	+	+	−	−	−	−	−	−	−	−	−	−	−	−	−	−
GMGXY10		−	+	+	+	+	+	+	+	+	−	−	−	−	−	−	−	−	−	−	−	−	−	−
GMGY41		−	+	+	+	+	+	+	+	+	−	−	−	−	−	−	−	−	−	−	−	−	−	−
GMGY10	B	−	+	+	+	+	+	+	+	+	−	−	−	−	−	−	−	−	−	−	−	−	−	−
118e	C	−	+	+	+	+	+	+	+	+	−	−	−	−	−	−	−	−	−	−	−	−	−	−
118e	A	−	+	+	+	+	+	+	+	−	−	−	−	−	−	−	−	−	−	−	−	−	−	−
	B	−	+	+	+	+	+	+	+	−	−	−	−	−	−	−	−	−	−	−	−	−	−	−
GMGY23		+	+	+	+	+	+	+	+	+	−	−	−	−	−	−	−	−	−	−	−	−	−	−
GMGY46	B	+	+	+	+	+	+	+	+	+	−	−	−	−	−	−	−	−	−	−	−	−	−	−
GMGY7	B	+	−	−	−	−	−	−	−	−	−	−	−	−	−	−	−	−	−	−	−	−	−	−
	D′	+	?	?	?	?	?	?	?	?	−	−	−	−	−	−	−	−	−	−	−	−	−	−
GMGY10	E′	+	?	?	?	?	?	?	?	?	−	−	−	−	−	−	−	−	−	−	−	−	−	−
GMGY46	C	+	−	−	−	−	−	−	−	−	−	−	−	−	−	−	−	−	−	−	−	−	−	−
GMGXY8		+	−	−	−	−	−	−	−	−	−	−	−	−	−	−	−	−	−	−	−	−	−	−
pDP34		+	−	−	−	−	−	−	−	−	−	−	−	−	−	−	−	−	−	−	−	−	−	−
p2F(2)		+	−	−	−	−	−	−	−	−	−	−	−	−	−	−	−	−	−	−	−	−	−	−
50f2	D	−	−	−	−	−	−	−	−	−	−	−	−	−	−	−	−	−	−	−	−	−	−	−
GMGY10	A	−	−	−	−	−	−	−	−	−	−	−	−	−	−	−	−	−	−	−	−	−	−	−
	C	−	−	−	−	−	−	−	−	−	−	−	−	−	−	−	−	−	−	−	−	−	−	−
GMGY4(a)		−	−	−	−	−	−	−	−	−	−	−	−	−	−	−	−	−	−	−	−	−	−	−
centromere																								
GMGYl		−	−	−	−	−	−	−	−	−	−	−	−	−	−	−	−	−	−	−	−	−	−	−
50f2	C	−	−	−	−	−	−	−	−	−	−	−	−	−	−	−	−	−	−	−	−	−	−	−
	E	−	−	−	−	−	−	−	−	−	−	−	−	−	−	−	−	−	−	−	−	−	−	−
pY3.4		−	−	−	−	−	−	−	−	−	−	−	−	−	−	−	−	−	−	−	−	−	−	−

suggesting a further recombination 'hot-spot'. It is noteworthy that all cases with a large X chromosome by flow cytometry have transferred at least six Y-specific sequences.

More recently, we have tested the same XX males with a DNA probe (CMPXY1), which we believe maps within the locus reported by Page *et al.* (1987*a*) to be a likely candidate for *GDY* and which recognizes both X- and Y-specific sequences. CMPXY1 was obtained by probing a Y-specific DNA library with a series of synthetic oligonucleotides constructed from the predicted amino-acid sequence of the DNA binding protein described by Page *et al.* (1987*a*). Sixteen of the seventeen XX males who have previously been found to be Y-positive also have the Y sequence recognized by CMPXY1, which proves to be absent in the six previously Y-negative XX males (figure 1). The exception has normal-sized X chromosomes and ambiguity of the external genitalia, and otherwise seems similar to Y-negative XX males.

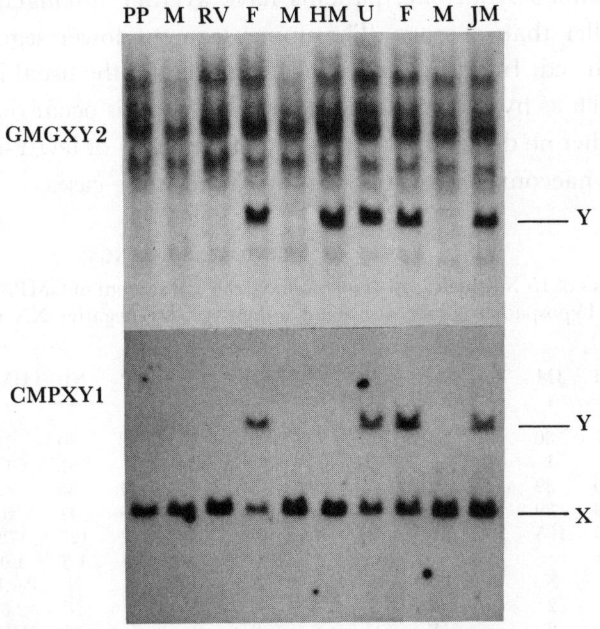

FIGURE 1. Eight micrograms of genomic DNA from patients and their relatives were digested with the restriction enzyme *Eco*RI and subjected to Southern blot analysis in the usual manner. DNA blots were successively probed with GMGXY2 and CMPXY1. From left to right: PP, Y-negative XX male; M, mother of PP; RV, XX true hermaphrodite; F, father of RV; M, mother of RV; HM, Y-positive XX male; U, uncle of HM; F, father of HM; M, mother of HM; JM, Y-positive XX male. Note that although HM has the Y-specific fragment of GMGXY2 he lacks the Y fragment of CMPXY1. JM has both Y-specific fragments, and PP and RV have neither.

(*d*) *DNA analysis using X-specific probes*

The DNA from our series of Y-positive XX males was probed with several probes that map to the distal end of the X chromosome, either within or outside the pairing segment, to look for evidence of deletion or duplication of X-linked sequences. The probes used include 782(*DSX85*), dic56 (*DXS143*), GMGX9 (*DXS237*); GMGXY19, GMGXXY3 and p19B (*MIC2*). There is no evidence for loss of any of these sequences in the 17 patients tested. Dosage studies in the 17 patients tested with p19B, however, strongly suggest that there are three alleles at the *MIC2* locus in five cases, indicating that the breakpoint in the paternal X is distal to *MIC2* as in the case described by Page *et al.* (1987*b*). It is therefore clear that several XX males have retained both the paternal *MIC2* locus and X-linked loci proximal to it, including *XG*. With regard to the cluster of probes tightly linked to the *STS* locus (GMGX9, GMGXXY3 and GMGXY19), all patients tested show no evidence of either duplication or deletion, indicating that *STS* is not commonly deleted in XX males, and that the increased *STS* activity noted above in some patients cannot be ascribed to triple dose of the *STS* allele.

Genotype-phenotype correlations in XX males and XY females

The majority of XX males have the same type of prepubertal testicular atrophy and endocrinological features described in XXY Klinefelter's syndrome (Ferguson-Smith 1965*a*). Gynaecomastia is a more frequent feature, present in 11 of 14 post-pubertal patients in our series (table 2). All patients have azoospermia and most show clinical and biochemical evidence of androgen insufficiency with reduced body hair and lack of temporal recession. Unlike XXY Klinefelter's syndrome, patients have average intelligence and are smaller in stature instead of taller than average. The upper segment:lower segment ratio tends to be normal instead of reduced. Infertility and gynaecomastia are the usual indications for referral. Genital anomalies such as hypospadias and undescended testis occur only among those of our patients who have either no detectable (three out of four cases) or few Y-specific sequences (one out of two cases). Gynaecomastia is present in all Y-negative cases.

Table 2. Clinical Findings

(Clinical features in a series of 15 XX males, 10 of whom have the Y fragment of CMPXY1 (*GDY*) in their genomic DNA samples. Note that hypospadias is present in four of the five *GDY*-negative XX males, but not in any of the *GDY*-positive XX males.)

	RH	JM	TA	AG	JT	GA	WB	KS	AP	NE	HM	GC	AN	RT	PP
CMPXY 1	+	+	+	+	+	+	+	+	+	+	–	–	–	–	–
age at examination	45	30	32	15	27	30	34	27	23	10	21	17	20	39	20
reason for referral	I	I	I	G	G	G	G	G	I	SSE	GC	HG	H	I	HG
maternal age at birth	30	39	29	26	·	22	·	35	27	35	32	·	25	22	·
paternal age at birth	29	39	37	25	·	23	·	36	28	41	29	·	32	24	·
height	163	165	161	163	166	166	166	170	172	127	172	·	160	172	·
US:LS ratio	0.9	·	·	1.0	0.9	·	0.9	1.0	0.9	1.3	1.0	·	1.1	0.9	
external genitalia	N	N	N	N	N	N	N	N	N	N	Per.H	Pen.H	GH	SP	Per.H
testes right/cm	2	2	·	2	S	2	S	2	2	N	2.5	3.5	S	2.5	2
testes left/cm	2	2	·	2	S	2	S	2	2	N	UND	2	S	2.5	2
gynaecomastia	0	0	+	++	+(R)	+	+	+	0	–	++	++	+	++	++
pubic & axillary hair	↓	+	·	↓	↓	+	+	↓	+	–	+	+	↓	+	+
chest hair	+	0	·	0	·		0	+	0	–	0	+	0	+	+
temporal recession	+	0	·	0	·	0	0	+	0	–	0	0	0	+	+
shaving frequency (per week)	1	3	1	2	1	1	0	3	7	–	2	·	0	7	7
plasma testosterone	·	↓	↓	·	↓	·	↓	N	↓	·	·	·	↓	·	↓
intelligence	N	N	N	N	N	N	N	N	N	N	N	N	N	N	N

Key to abbreviations used: I, infertility; G, gynaecomastia; SSE, short stat., epilepsy; GC, gynaecomastia, cryptorchidism; HG, hypospadias, gynaecomastia; H, hypogonadism; Per.H, perineal hypospadias; Pen.H, penile hypospadias; GH, glandular hypospadias; SP, small penis; S, small; N, normal; +, present; 0, absent; –, not applicable; ·, no information; ↓, less than normal.

One can speculate that the phenotypic differences between XXY and Y-positive XX males are directly related to the amount of Y material present. Karyotype–phenotype correlations in patients with the Klinefelter and Turner syndromes (Ferguson-Smith 1965*b*) show that determinants for skeletal growth are carried by the short arms of both the X and Y chromosomes. Patients with 47, XXY and XYY are taller and 45, X and 46, XXp- are smaller than average. However, patients with a 47, XXX karyotype are of average stature (Johnston *et al.* 1961) and it is clear that loss of Xp or the addition of a Y have a more profound effect on stature than gain of an X. On the other hand, the gain of either an X or Y seems to have a more harmful effect on intellectual function than loss of an X. It is possible that the normal intelligence of a Y+XX male is in fact due to the presence of a normal complement of

X/Y homologous segments and his smaller than average male stature is due to absence of skeletal growth determinants from the proximal part of the short arm of the Y.

The phenotype of the few XY females who have been shown to have both X and Y pairing segments but who lack Yp sequences, have in addition to gonadal dysgenesis (including bilateral gonadoblastoma in some cases) some features of Turner's syndrome, such as webbed neck, peripheral lymphoedema, short IVth metacarpals, hypoplasia of the nails, etc. However, they are unlike patients with Turner's syndrome in that they are not short in stature. In other words, those determinants on the Y which normally prevent Turner's stigmata in normal males have been lost along with *GDY*, although the determinants for stature are retained, presumably because they are located proximal to the breakpoint of the X–Y interchange in the Y. It is therefore concluded that the main Y-linked determinants for stature are excluded from these abnormal X–Y interchanges.

The aetiology of true hermaphroditism

Testis differentiation in the absence of Y chromosome material occurs also in XX true hermaphrodites. These are individuals who have ambiguity of the external and internal genitalia associated with either bilateral ovotestes, unilateral testis and ovary, ovary and ovotestis, or testis and ovotestis. There is variable regression of the Müllerian ducts depending on the extent of testicular differentiation. An identical phenotype in man can result from XX/XY chimerism or in the mouse from experimental chimerism induced by injecting embryonic XY cells into an XX blastocyst. In these chimeras the somatic cells are of two types: those with an XY complement are testis determining and those with an XX complement are ovary determining. X–Y interchange with random inactivation of the interchanged X could well account for the gonadal findings (Ferguson-Smith 1966) but so far Y-specific sequences have not been found in XX true hermaphrodites. Wiberg & Scherer (1987) have investigated 7 cases with Y-specific probes and we have tested 12 others with 14 Yp probes including CMPXY1 (*GDY*). Other hypotheses must be sought for the presence of both ovarian and testicular tissues in the same individual. One that would satisfy the current gene-dosage theory of sex determination involves the possibility of escape from X-inactivation at the *GDX* locus in one of the two X chromosomes. This release of a *GDX* allele from the normal constraints of random X-inactivation might be achieved by mutation involving a regulatory sequence close to *GDX* or by an inversion or transposition that moves *GDX* into the distal end of Xp (which normally escapes inactivation). Random X-inactivation during early embryogenesis would lead to somatic-cell mosaicism in which some cells would have two doses of *GDX* whereas others have only one dose. The former would be testis determining and the latter ovary determining. The hypothesis is testable by a combination of molecular genetic techniques including pulsed-field gradient electrophoresis, restriction mapping and DNA sequencing, which might reveal changes in the locus of one *GDX* allele or mutations in adjacent sequences.

It seems likely that Y-negative XX males have a similar aetiology to XX true hermaphrodites if only because spontaneous and experimental XX/XY chimeras sometimes have bilateral testes and a male phenotype. It may also be significant that Y-negative XX males may have abnormalities of the external genitalia, such as hypospadias (page 140). In our exceptional Y+XX male (HM) with hypospadias and unilateral cryptorchidism but without *GDY* (table 1), the transfer of other Y sequences from Yp to the X may have been the event that led to the escape from X-inactivation of the *GDX* locus on one X chromosome. The *GDX* activation hypothesis could also account for the occurrence of familial cases in which siblings are affected with XX true hermaphroditism, or XX Klinefelter's syndrome, or both in the same sibship. In these cases the activated *GDX* allele might be transmitted by unaffected fertile XX mothers or fertile XY fathers as an X-linked dominant trait with incomplete penetrance. All known pedigrees with multiple affected relatives (see de la Chapelle 1987) can be interpreted in this way without invoking autosomal inheritance, and this would seem to be a powerful argument in favour of the gene-dosage hypothesis of sex determination.

The gene-dosage hypothesis may also help to explain the origin of some cases of gonadal dysgenesis in XY females. If *GDY* and *GDX* are truly homologous and have an identical gene product, loss or mutation of *GDX* should have the same consequence as loss or mutation of *GDY*. We have so far tested nine patients with XY gonadal dysgenesis by using CMPXY1 and only one (case AM in Affara *et al.* (1987)) shows loss of *GDY*. None shows loss of *GDX* but a 'null' mutation in either *GDX* or *GDY* has not yet been excluded. Once again, familial cases showing X-linked recessive inheritance could conceivably be due to a familial mutation of *GDX*.

References

Affara, N. A., Ferguson-Smith, M. A., Tolmie, J., Kwok, K., Mitchell, M., Jamieson, D., Cooke, A. & Florentin, L. 1986*a* Variable transfer of Y specific sequences in XX males. *Nucl. Acids Res.* **14**, 5375–5387.

Affara, N. A., Florentin, L., Morrison, N., Kwok, K., Mitchell, M., Cooke, A., Jamieson, D., Glasgow, L., Meredith, L., Boyd, E. & Ferguson-Smith, M. A. 1986*b* Regional assignment of Y linked DNA probes by deletion mapping and their homology with X-chromosome and autosomal sequences. *Nucl. Acids Res.* **14**, 5353–5373.

Affara, N. A., Ferguson-Smith, M. A., Magenis, R. E., Tolmie, J. L., Boyd, E., Cooke, A., Jamieson, D., Kwok, K., Mitchell, M. & Snadden, L. 1987 Mapping the testis determinants by an analysis of Y specific sequences in males with apparent XX and XO karyotypes and females with XY karyotypes. *Nucl. Acids Res.* **15**, 7325–7342.

Andersson, M., Page, D. C. & de la Chapelle, A. 1986 Chromosome Y-specific DNA is transferred to the short arm of X chromosome in human XX males. *Science, Wash.* **233**, 786–788.

Buckle, V. J., Boyd, Y., Fraser, N., Goodfellow, P. N., Wolfe, J. & Craig, I. W. 1987 Localisation of Y chromosome sequences in normal and XX males. *J. med. Genet.* **24**, 197–203.

Chandra, H. S. 1985 Is human X chromosome inactivation a sex determining device? *Proc. natn. Acad. Sci. U.S.A.* **82**, 6947–6949.

Cooke, H. J., Brown, W. R. A. & Rappold, G. A. 1985 Hypervariable telomeric sequences from the human sex chromosomes are pseudoautosomal. *Nature, Lond.* **317**, 687–692.

Darlington, C. D. 1976 Chromosomes, meiosis and man. *Chromosomes Today* **5**, 1–12.

de la Chapelle, A. 1987 The Y chromosomal and autosomal testis determining genes. *Development* **101** (suppl.), 33–38.

de la Chapelle, A., Tippett, P. A., Wetterstrand, G. & Page, D. C. 1984 Genetic evidence of X–Y interchange in a human XX male. *Nature, Lond.* **307**, 170–171.

Disteche, C. M., Casanova, M., Saal, M., Friedman, C., Sybert, V., Graham, J., Thuline, M., Page, D. C. & Fellous, M. 1986 Small deletions of the short arm of the Y chromosome in 46, XY females. *Proc. natn. Acad. Sci. U.S.A.* **83**, 7841–7844.

Evans, H. J., Buckton, K. E., Spowart, G. & Carothers, A. D. 1979 Heteromorphic X chromosomes in 46 XX males: evidence for the involvement of X-Y interchange. *Hum. Genet.* **49**, 11–31.

Ferguson-Smith, M. A. 1965*a* Sex chromatin, Klinefelter's syndrome and mental deficiency. In *The sex chromatin* (ed. K. L. Moore), pp. 277–315. Philadelphia: W. B. Saunders.

Ferguson-Smith, M. A. 1965*b* Karyotype–phenotype correlations in gonadal dysgenesis and their bearing on the pathogenesis of malformations. *J. med. Genet.* **2**, 142–155.

Ferguson-Smith, M. A. 1966 X-Y chromosomal interchange in the aetiology of true hermaphroditism and of XX Klinefelter's syndrome. *Lancet* ii, 475–476.

Ferguson-Smith, M. A. 1988 Progress in the molecular cytogenetics of man. *Phil. Trans. R. Soc. Lond.* B **319**, 239–248.

Ferguson-Smith, M. A., Affara, N. A. & Magenis, R. E. 1987 Ordering of Y specific sequences by deletion mapping and analysis of X–Y interchange males and females. *Development* **101** (suppl.), 41–50.

Ferguson-Smith, M. A., Sanger, R., Tippett, P., Aitken, D. A. & Boyd, E. 1982 A familial t(X;Y) translocation which assigns the Xg blood group locus to the region Xp22.3 → pter. *Cytogenet. Cell Genet.* **32**, 273–274.

German, J. L. 1988 Gonadal dimorphism explained as a dosage effect of a locus on the sex chromosomes, the gonad-differentiation locus (GDL) *Am. J. hum. Genet.* **42**, 414–421.

Goodfellow, P. J., Darling, S. M., Thomas, N. S., Goodfellow, P. N. 1986 A pseudoautosomal gene in man. *Science, Wash.* **234**, 740–743.

Guellaen, G., Casanova, M., Bishop, C., Geldworth, D., Andre, E., Fellous, M. & Weissenbach, J. 1984 Human XX males with Y single copy DNA fragments. *Nature, Lond.* **307**, 172–173.

Johnston, A. W., Ferguson-Smith, M. A., Handmaker, S. D., Jones, H. W. & Jones, G. S. 1961 The triple-X syndrome: clinical, pathological and chromosomal studies in three mentally retarded cases. *Br. med. J.* **2**, 1046–1052.

Kalaitsidakis, M., Theriault, A., Boyd, E., Affara, N. A., Cooke, A. & Ferguson-Smith, M. A. 1987 The destination of Y specific sequences in X–Y interchange males. *Development* **101** (suppl.), 195.

Madan, K. 1976 Chromosome measurements on an XXp+male. *Hum. Genet.* **32**, 141–142.

Magenis, R. E., Tomar, D., Sheehy, R., Fellous, M., Bishop, C. & Casanova, M. 1984 Y short arm material translocated to distal X short arm in XX males: evidence from *in situ* hybridisation of a Y specific single copy DNA probe. *Am. J. hum. Genet.* **36**, 1025.

Magenis, R. E., Webb, M. J., McKean, R. S., Tomar, D., Allen, L. J., Kammer, H., van Dyke, D. L. & Lovrien, E. 1982 Translocation (X;Y) (p22.33;p11.2) in XX males etiology of male phenotype. *Hum. Genet.* **62**, 271–276.

Muller, U., Lalande, M., Donlon, T. & Latt, S. A. 1986*a* Moderately repeated DNA sequences specific for the short arm of the human Y chromosome are present in XX males and reduced in copy number in an XY female. *Nucl. Acids Res.* **14**, 1325–1340.

Muller, U., Donlon, T., Schmid, M., Fitch, N., Richer, C. L., Lalande, M. & Latt, S. A. 1986*b* Deletion mapping of the testis determining locus with DNA probes in 46, XX males and in 46, XY and 46X, dic(Y) females. *Nucl. Acids Res.* **14**, 6489–6505.

Page, D. C., de la Chapelle, A. & Weissenbach, J. 1985 Chromosome Y-specific DNA in related human XX males. *Nature, Lond.* **315**, 224–226.

Page, D. C., Mosher, R., Simpson, E. M., Fisher, E. M. C., Mardon, G., Pollack, J. & McGillivray, B., de la Chapelle, A. & Brown, L. G. 1987*a* The sex determining region of the human Y chromosome encodes a finger protein. *Cell* **51**, 1091–1104.

Page, D. C., Brown, L. G. & de la Chapelle, A. 1987*b* Exchange of terminal portions of X and Y chromosomal short arms in human XX males. *Nature, Lond.* **328**, 437–440.

Petit, C., de la Chapelle, A., Levilliers, J., Castillo, S., Noel, B. & Weissenbach, J. 1987 An abnormal X–Y interchange accounts for most but not all cases of human XX maleness. *Cell* **49**, 595–602.

Rouyer, F., Simmler, M. C., Johnsson, C., Vergnaud, G., Cooke, H. J. & Weissenbach, J. 1986 A gradient of sex linkage in the pseudoautosomal region of the human sex chromosomes. *Nature, Lond.* **319**, 291–295.

Rouyer, F., Simmler, M. C., Page, D. C. & Weissenbach, J. 1987 A sex chromosome rearrangements in a human XX male caused by ALU-ALU recombination. *Cell* **51**, 417–425.

Simmler, M. C., Rouyer, F., Vergnaud, G., Nystrom-Lahti, M., Ngo, K. Y., de la Chapelle, A. & Weissenbach, J. 1985 Pseudoautosomal DNA sequences in the pairing region of the human sex chromosomes. *Nature, Lond.* **317**, 692–697.

Vergnaud, G., Page, D. C., Simmler, M. C., Brown, L., Rouyer, F., Noel, B., Botstein, D., de la Chapelle, A. & Weissenbach, J. 1986 A deletion map of the human Y chromosome based on DNA hybridisation. *Am. J. hum. Genet.* **38**, 109–124.

Wachtel, S. S., Koo, G. C., Breg, W. R., Thaler, H. T., Dilord, G. M., Rosenthal, I. M., Dosik, H., Gerald, P. S., Saenger, P., New, M., Lieber, E. & Iller, O. J. 1976 Serologic detection of a Y linked gene in XX males and XX true hermaphrodites. *New Engl. J. Med.* **295**, 750–754.

Wiberg, U. H. & Scherer, G. 1987 Evidence for the presence of testicular tissue and sxs antigen in the absence of Y-derived sequences. *Development* **101** (suppl.), 163–166.

Wieaker, P., Vioculescu, J., Muller, C. R. & Ropers, H. H. 1983 An XX male with a single STS gene dose. *Cytogenet. Cell. Genet.* **35**, 72–74.

Discussion

P. N. Goodfellow (*Imperial Cancer Research Fund, London, U.K.*). Could Professor Ferguson-Smith's Yp^+, CMPXY1 (−) XX males represent intragenic breaks, so explaining maleness and the specific phenotype he identifies?

M. A. Ferguson-Smith, F.R.S. Yes. If that part of *GDY* without the CMPXY1 homology was transferred to the X and was functional, it would be possible to generate a Y-positive, CMPXY1-negative XX male. However, because of the phenotypic similarity of our patient to XX true hermaphroditism, other possibilities seem more likely.

B. M. Cattanach (*MRC Radiobiology Unit, Didcot, U.K.*). The situation regarding STS expression in the mouse may provide a model for Professor Ferguson-Smith's hypothesis. Thus recent data from Harwell clearly establish that the locus in the pseudo-autosomal segment is subject to the X-inactivation process in females and, because there are functional X and Y loci in this species that are equally expressed, there is a 1:2 ratio of STS expression in females and males.

M. A. Ferguson-Smith, F.R.S. This new observation on STS expression in the mouse is of great interest. A 1:2 ratio of sex-determining protein expression in females and males is exactly what I propose. The STS locus is also unusual in man, although not comparable to the mouse. The 1.7:1 ratio of STS expression is due to its partial escape from X-inactivation because it maps sufficiently close to the pairing segment, and also because the STS allele is non-functional on the Y.

D. C. Deeming (*Department of Cell and Structural Biology, University of Manchester, U.K.*). Is Professor Ferguson-Smith suggesting that sex determination in *Drosophila*, nematodes, reptiles and humans is essentially the same?

M. A. Ferguson-Smith, F.R.S. Yes, in that in all these species primary sex determination seems to depend on quantitative effects, rather than the effect of a Y-linked dominant gene as was previously thought for mouse and man.

However, in *Drosophila* and *Caenorhabditis*, females and hermaphrodites have two doses of the sex-determining factors whereas males have only one. In mammals and birds, females seem to have only one dose and males have two.

D. C. Deeming. Intersexes in turtles could also be explained by a dosage–mosaic model.

M. Hulten. (*Regional Cytogenetics Laboratory, East Birmingham Hospital, U.K.*). This is a question not only for Professor Ferguson-Smith but also for others who have done molecular investigations on parents and sibs of XX males. I wondered if there is now enough data to tell whether or not the XpYp meiotic recombination in fathers of XX males is generally occurring in aberrant positions. One of the reasons I am asking this question is that many years ago, I had the opportunity to investigate meiosis in a father of an XX male. In air-dried preparations about 30% of cells at diakinesis/MI showed a clear XY chiasma. A chiasma is not normally seen in this position as the X and Y appear associated end to end. I have taken the occurrence of a visible chiasma in this father of an XX male to indicate a proximalization of the XY recombination. I was wondering if he is exceptional or if other fathers might also show a general tendency to proximalization of their XpYp meiotic recombination?

M. A. Ferguson-Smith, F.R.S. The information is mounting (see table 1) that the Y breakpoint in X–Y interchange may be non-random, but it appears at present that the X breakpoint may be at any position either within the pairing segment or even proximal to the *STS* locus, if the results of STS activity in XX males can be interpreted as evidence of gene dosage. It is tempting to speculate that the observed variation in the order of gene loci in the differential segment of the Y may sometimes lead to proximalization of recombination sites, thus providing an alternative explanation of the high frequency of cells in diakinesis showing an XY chiasma mentioned by Dr Hulten.

Phil. Trans. R. Soc. Lond. B **322**, 145–154 (1988) [145]
Printed in Great Britain

MIC2: a human pseudoautosomal gene

By P. N. Goodfellow[1], B. Pym[1], C. Pritchard[1,2], N. Ellis[1], M. Palmer[1], M. Smith[1] and P. J. Goodfellow[1]

[1] *Human Molecular Genetics Laboratory, Imperial Cancer Research Fund, Lincoln's Inn Fields, London WC2A 3PX, U.K.*

[2] *Department of Physiology, University of California Medical Centre, San Francisco, California* 94143, *U.S.A.*

MIC2 and *XGR* are the only known pseudoautosomal genes in man. *MIC2* encodes the 12E7 antigen, a human cell-surface molecule of unknown function. *XGR* regulates, in *cis*, the expression of the *XG* and *MIC2* genes.

DNA probes derived from the *MIC2* locus have been used in the construction of a meiotic map of the pseudoautosomal region and a long range restriction map into the X- and Y-specific chromosome domains. *MIC2* is the most proximal marker in the pseudoautosomal region and recombination between the sex chromosomes only rarely includes the *MIC2* locus. Our long-range restriction maps and chromosome walking experiments have localized the pseudoautosomal boundary within 40 kilobases adjacent to the 3′ end of the *MIC2* gene. The same maps have been used to predict the chromosomal location of *TDF*.

Introduction

The Y chromosome of man and other mammals is highly adapted for its role in male sex determination. It is composed of two distinct regions with antithetical genetic properties (Koller & Darlington 1934). One region is Y-chromosome-specific and encodes *TDF*, a gene required for male sex determination. Sequences derived from this region do not normally recombine with the X chromosome. Abnormal recombination, which occurs infrequently, leads to the generation of XX males or XY females and the breakdown of the chromosomal basis of sex determination (Ferguson-Smith 1966). The second region of the Y chromosome is shared by the X and Y chromosomes and is responsible for correct sex chromosome pairing and segregation in male meiosis. Sequences in this region are exchanged between the sex chromosomes by recombination and fail to show classical sex-linked inheritance. This behaviour has been described as 'pseudoautosomal', and the shared part of the sex chromosomes is known as the pseudoautosomal region (Burgoyne 1982).

Very few genes are encoded by the Y chromosome (Goodfellow *et al.* 1985). This is a direct consequence of the role of the Y chromosome in male sex determination and the evolution of dosage compensation by X-inactivation in mammals (Lyon 1974). To maintain gene dosage, genes shared by the sex chromosomes must either escape inactivation on the X chromosome or undergo inactivation on the Y chromosome. The X-located homologues of pseudoautosomal genes are known to escape X-inactivation (Goodfellow *et al.* 1984). There is no evidence for inactivation of Y-located genes. These considerations have led to the prediction that the genes encoded by the Y-specific region are either directly required for the male phenotype or are deleterious to the female phenotype. In contrast there is no obvious *a priori* restriction on the function of genes encoded by the pseudoautosomal region.

The paucity of genetic markers has in the past hindered the analysis of the human Y chromosome and most studies have been restricted to correlation of phenotype with gross chromosomal rearrangements (Davis 1981). The introduction of molecular cloning techniques has provided an unlimited supply of genetic markers for the Y chromosome and has led to construction of genetic maps of both the pseudoautosomal and the Y-specific regions (Davies *et al.* 1988). In addition, molecular cloning techniques have resulted in the isolation of the pseudoautosomal gene *MIC2* (Darling *et al.* 1986*a*, *b*) and a candidate sequence for *TDF* (Page *et al.* 1987).

In this review we consider the molecular cloning of *MIC2* and the use of *MIC2*-derived probes for investigating the genetics of the Y chromosome.

The 12E7 antigen

The monoclonal antibody 12E7 recognizes a human cell-surface molecule with a wide tissue distribution. The 12E7 antigen is found in man, gorilla and chimpanzee, but is not found in orangutan, gibbon or any other species tested (Goodfellow 1983). This species specificity was exploited to investigate the genetics of the 12E7 antigen. Human–rodent hybrids that retain the human X chromosome or the human Y chromosome express the 12E7 antigen; retention of no other human chromosome in the hybrids correlates with expression of the 12E7 antigen. These results define the X-located gene *MIC2X* and the Y-located gene *MIC2Y* (Goodfellow *et al.* 1980, 1983). Biochemical studies demonstrated that the 12E7 antigen is associated with a 32.5 kDa cell-surface molecule with a pI of 5.0. No differences were detected between the putative products of the *MIC2X* and *MIC2Y* loci (Banting *et al.* 1985).

Human–rodent somatic-cell hybrids that retain the inactive X chromosome also express the 12E7 antigen, implying that the *MIC2X* locus escapes X-inactivation (Goodfellow *et al.* 1984). These experiments suggested that *MIC2* is a pseudoautosomal gene, the first pseudoautosomal gene defined in man. Proof of this contention required cloning of the *MIC2* gene.

Molecular cloning and analysis of *MIC2*

φλgt11 is a cloning vector that allows expression of eukaryotic proteins as fusion products in bacterial cells (Young & Davis 1983). A φλgt11 library was constructed with complementary DNA (cDNA) sequences prepared from the human T cell line J6 and this library was screened with a mixture of two monoclonal antibodies that reacted with the 12E7 antigen (Darling *et al.* 1986*a*). A positive clone, designated SG1, was isolated and shown to be derived from the *MIC2* locus by three independent methods.

1. *In situ* hybridization of the cDNA clone to human chromosomes identified two sites of hybridization in the human genome: the end of the X chromosome short arm, Xp22.3-pter, and the Y chromosome short arm, Yp11-pter (Buckle *et al.* 1985).

2. Mouse cells were transfected with genomic human DNA and transfectants expressing the 12E7 antigen were isolated by using the fluorescence-activated cell sorter. DNA prepared from the antigen-positive transfectants reacted with the *MIC2* cDNA clone in Southern blot analysis (Darling *et al.* 1986*a*).

3. A monoclonal antibody, MSGB1, was raised against a peptide, the sequence of which was derived from a conceptual translation of the cDNA clone. The MSGB1 antibody recognizes the 12E7 antigen (Darling *et al.* 1986*b*).

The cDNA clone has been used to isolate further cDNA clones and genomic sequences. The DNA sequence of one full length (or close to full length) cDNA clone is presented in figure 1, with its conceptual translation. A preliminary sequence of a partial cDNA clone has been published previously (Darling *et al.* 1986*b*). The published sequence contains an error that resulted in the premature termination of the coding region.

```
CGTGGAGGCC GGGGCGGGGC GGGCGCAGCC GGCGCTGAGC TTGCAGGGCC GCTCCCCTCA CCCGCCCCCT TCGAGTCCCC GGGCTTCACC

CCACCCGGCC CGTGGGGGAG TATCTGTCCT GCCGCCTTCG CCCACGCCCT GCACTCCGGG ACCGTCCCTG CGCGCTCTGG GCGCACC

ATG GCC CGC GGG GCT GCG CTG GCG CTG CTG CTC TTC GGC CTG CTG GGT GTT CTG GTC GCC GCC CCG GAT GGT GGT
MET Ala Arg Gly Ala Ala Leu Ala Leu Leu Leu Phe Gly Leu Leu Gly Val Leu Val Ala Ala Pro Asp Gly Gly

TTC GAT TTA TCC GAT GCC CTT CCT GAC AAT GAA AAC AAG AAA CCC ACT GCA ATC CCC AAG AAA CCC AGT GCT GGG
Phe Asp Leu Ser Asp Ala Leu Pro Asp Asn Glu Asn Lys Lys Pro Thr Ala Ile Pro Lys Lys Pro Ser Ala Gly

GAT GAC TTT GAC TTA GGA GAT GCT GTT GTT GAT GGA GAA AAT GAC GAC CCA CGA CCA CCG AAC CCA CCC AAA CCG
Asp Asp Phe Asp Leu Gly Asp Ala Val Val Asp Gly Glu Asn Asp Asp Pro Arg Pro Pro Asn Pro Pro Lys Pro

ATG CCA AAT CCA AAC CCC AAC CAC CCT AGT TCC TCC GGT AGC TTT TCA GAT GCT GAC CTT GCG GAT GGC GTT TCA
Met Pro Asn Pro Asn Pro Asn His Pro Ser Ser Ser Gly Ser Phe Ser Asp Ala Asp Leu Ala Asp Gly Val Ser

GGT GGA GAA GGA AAA GGA GGC AGT GAT GGT GGA GGC AGC CAC AGG AAA GAA GGG GAA GAG GCC GAC GCC CCA GGC
Gly Gly Glu Gly Lys Gly Gly Ser Asp Gly Gly Gly Ser His Arg Lys Glu Gly Glu Glu Ala Asp Ala Pro Gly

GTG ATC CCC GGG ATT GTG GGG GCT GTC GTG GTC GCC GTG GCT GGA GCC ATC TCT AGC TTC ATT GCT TAC CAG AAA
Val Ile Pro Gly Ile Val Gly Ala Val Val Val Ala Val Ala Gly Ala Ile Ser Ser Phe Ile Ala Tyr Gln Lys

AAG AAG CTA TGC TTC AAA GAA AAT GCA GAA CAA GGG GAG GTG GAC ATG GAG AGC CAC CGG AAT GCC AAC GCA GAG
Lys Lys Leu Cys Phe Lys Glu Asn Ala Glu Gln Gly Glu Val Asp Met Glu Ser His Arg Asn Ala Asn Ala Glu

CCA GCT GTT CAG CGT ACT CTT TTA GAG AAA TAGAAGATTG TCGGCAGAAA CAGCCCAGGC GTTGGCAGCA GGGTTAGAAC
Pro Ala Val Gln Arg Thr Leu Leu Glu Lys

AGCTGCCTG AGGCTCCTCCC TGAAGGACAC CTGCCTGAGA GCAGAGATGG AGGCCTTCTG TTCACGGCGG ATTCTTTGTT TTAATCTTGC

GATGTGCTTT GCTTGTTGCT GGGCGGATGA TGTTTACTAA CGATGAATTT TACATCCAAA GGGGGATAGG CACTTGGACC CCCATTCTCC

AAGGCCCGGG GGGGCGGTTT CCCATGGGAT GTGAAAGGCT GGCCATTATT AAGTCCCTGT AACTCAAATG TCAACCCCAC CGAGGCACCC

CCCCGTCCCC CAGAATCTTG GCTGTTTACA AATCACGTGT CCATCGAGCA CGTCTGAAAC CCCTGGTAGC CCCGACTTCT TTTTAATTAA

AATAAGGTAA GCCCTTCAAT TTGTTTCTTC AATATTTCTT TCATTTGTAG GGATATTTGT TTTTCATATC AGACTAATAA AAAGAAATTA

GAAACCAAAA
```

FIGURE 1. Nucleotide sequence of the *MIC2* cDNA clone, NT23. The conceptual translation of the cDNA is shown. NT23 was isolated from a cDNA library constructed with mRNA from a human testicular teratocarcinoma cell line by screening with a previously described cDNA, SG1 (Darling *et al.* 1986*a*, *b*). DNA sequence analysis was done on both strands by using the dideoxy chain termination procedure (Sanger *et al.* 1977) after cloning into M13 vectors (Messing 1983). Synthetic oligonucleotide primers were used to confirm the sequence in areas of ambiguity.

The *MIC2* product contains two hydrophobic regions corresponding to an N-terminal signal sequence and a putative transmembrane domain adjacent to the C terminus. Unusual features of the protein sequence include a high concentration of proline residues in the middle region of the molecule and many charged pairs of amino acids. These features of the sequence present no obvious clue as to the function of the *MIC2* gene. A search of available protein and nucleic acid sequence data bases has failed to find related sequences (Banting *et al.* 1988).

The cDNA clone has been used to isolate genomic sequences derived from the *MIC2* locus. These sequences have been used for an investigation of the promoter region at the 5′ end of the gene and as a source of polymorphic probes for family studies. The *MIC2* gene is unusually large for the size of the transcript. The mRNA is about 1.3 kilobases (the cDNA clone in figure 1 is 1242 base pairs (b.p.) long) and this derives from over 50 kilobases of genomic DNA. The

5′ end of the gene contains a region that is high in G+C content (67%) and shows no suppression of the occurrence of CpG dinucleotide pairs (Goodfellow *et al.* 1988). These features are characteristic of the 5′ regions of many mammalian genes and may have functional importance for gene expression (Bird 1986). Another feature of these CpG-rich regions is the lack of methylation of the cytosine in the CpG pair. The absence of 5-methyl cytosine residues allows cleavage by methylation-sensitive restriction enzymes such as *Hpa*II, generating multiple small *Hpa*II fragments (hence the name HTF island or *Hpa*II tiny fragment island). These regions are also cleaved by methylation-sensitive enzymes used in long-range restriction mapping (Brown & Bird 1986). Several X-located genes have CpG-rich 5′ regions; these regions are unmethylated on the active X and methylated on the inactive X (Yen *et al.* 1984; Keith *et al.* 1986). This correlation suggests that methylation of CpG-rich regions may play a role in X-inactivation. Consistent with this view the *MIC2* CpG-rich region is unmethylated on the inactive X as well as on the active X and Y chromosome (Goodfellow *et al.* 1988). In this case escape from inactivation is correlated with lack of methylation at the CpG-rich region. Methylation at CpG sites within the body of the gene is variable and shows a poor correlation with X-inactivation (Mondello *et al.* 1988).

The *MIC2* cDNA clones recognize many restriction-fragment polymorphisms in genomic DNA; however, the patterns generated with most restriction enzymes are difficult to analyse. Single-copy probes derived from genomic *MIC2* sequences have proved to be more convenient tools for use in family studies and the construction of meiotic maps of the pseudoautosomal region (Goodfellow *et al.* 1986*a*). *MIC2* probes have also been used in the construction of deletion maps and long-range restriction maps of the Y chromosome.

Mapping the Y chromosome with *MIC2* probes

DNA probes, derived from sequences isolated at random from the human Y chromosome, were used to demonstrate recombination between the X and Y chromosomes and to construct a meiotic map of the pseudoautosomal region (Simmler *et al.* 1985; Cooke *et al.* 1985; Rouyer *et al.* 1986; Goodfellow *et al.* 1986*a*). The most distal sequence, *DXYS14*, exchanges in 50% of cases, implying that an obligate recombination occurs in the pseudoautosomal region in each male meiotic event. In an initial search for recombination events that included the *MIC2* locus we studied 46 informative male meioses and found one exchange between the X and Y chromosomes. This constitutes formal proof that *MIC2* is a pseudoautosomal gene (Goodfellow *et al.* 1986*a*).

Figure 2 summarizes the meiotic maps of the pseudoautosomal region for both male and female meioses. There are dramatic differences in the rates of recombination between the pseudoautosomal marker loci in male versus female meioses. The most proximal marker, *MIC2*, shows no detectable linkage with the most distal marker, *DXYS14*, in male meioses. In female meioses, however, *MIC2* and *DXYS14* recombine at a rate of only 2.4% ($\theta = 0.024$, $Z_1 = 20.0$, one lod unit† confidence interval 0.00–0.05) (combined data of Weissenbach *et al.* (1987) and our unpublished data). Whereas *MIC2* and *DXYS17* recombine at a rate of 15% in male meioses, no recombination between the pair of markers is observed in female meioses. The male map is more than ten times larger than the female map and emphasizes the high levels of recombination in this region in males. Both indirect evidence (Mondello *et al.* 1987;

† A lod score represents the $\log_{10}$ of the likelihood (L) ratio: L (recombination fraction)/L (0.5).

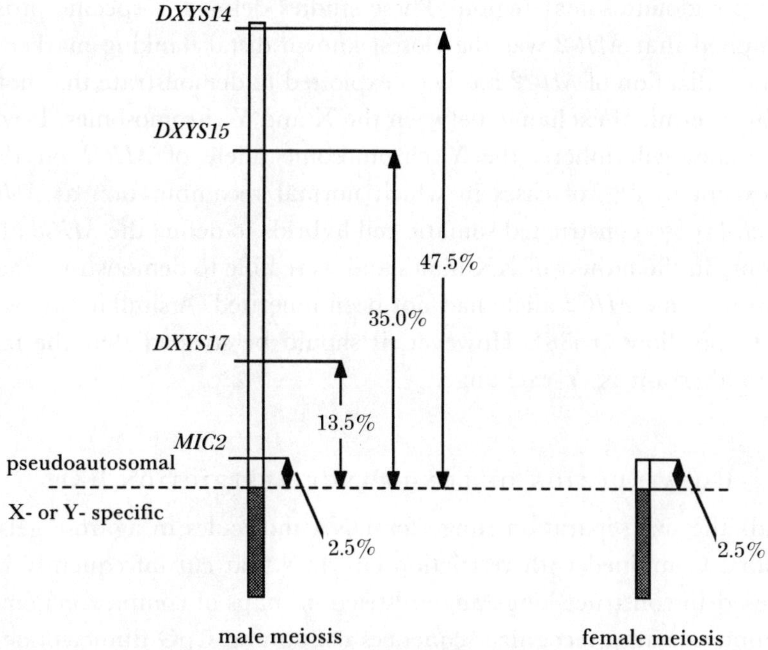

FIGURE 2. Meiotic maps of the pseudoautosomal region for male and female meiosis. Recombination rates with respect to sex-specific sequences and marker loci *DXYS14*, *DXYS15*, *DXYS17* and *MIC2* are given for male meioses. The distances between pairs of markers in male meioses are additive and consistent with values relative to sex-specific sequences. Few recombinants are observed in female meioses and only the estimated genetic size of the region in females is shown. Data are a further compilation of our unpublished results with those compiled by Weissenbach *et al.* (1987).

Rouyer *et al.* 1986) and direct measurement using pulsed field gel electrophoresis (PFGE) (J. Weissenbach, this symposium) suggest that the pseudoautosomal region is about 3.0×10^6 b.p. in size. In man, one unit of recombination is on average equated with approximately 1×10^6 b.p. (Renwick 1969). The genetic size of the pseudoautosomal region when measured in female meiosis is consistent with the physical size of the region. In male meiosis, one unit of recombination in the region is equivalent to 1×10^5 b.p. (100 kilobases) or less. Recombination in the pseudoautosomal region in male meiosis therefore occurs at a frequency greater than ten times the genome average.

In summary, *MIC2* only rarely exchanges between the sex chromosomes and is the most proximal of the pseudoautosomal markers in man.

A DELETION MAP OF THE Y CHROMOSOME

The genomes of the majority of XX males contain Y chromosome sequences (Affara *et al.* 1986*a*, *b*; Guellaen *et al.* 1984; Petit *et al.* 1987). These sequences derive from an abnormal exchange between the X and Y chromosomes resulting in the transfer of Y sequences, including *TDF*, to the tip of the X chromosome (Andersson *et al.* 1986; Buckle *et al.* 1987). The amount of Y-derived sequences transferred is variable but, by definition, must always include *TDF*. Analysis of the variable amounts of Y sequences present in XX males has allowed construction of deletion maps of the Y chromosome (Affara *et al.* 1986*a*; Vergnaud *et al.* 1986). From these maps it was concluded that *TDF* is located on the distal part of the short arm of Y chromosome adjacent to the pseudoautosomal region. These studies defined Y-specific proximal flanking markers and implied that *MIC2* was the closest known distal flanking marker for *TDF*.

The regional localization of *MIC2* has been exploited to demonstrate that not all XX males are generated by a terminal exchange between the X and Y chromosomes. It was argued that exchange XX males will inherit the Y chromosome allele of *MIC2* on the paternal X chromosome (except in 2% of cases in which normal recombination at *MIC2* might also occur). Petit *et al.* (1987) constructed somatic cell hybrids to define the *MIC2* allele present on the Y chromosome in the fathers of XX males and were able to demonstrate that in three XX males the Y chromosome *MIC2* allele had not been inherited. A similar case was reported by Goodfellow & Goodfellow (1988). However, it should be stressed that the majority of XX males are due to aberrant X–Y exchange.

Construction of long-range restriction maps

PFGE extends the size separation range for DNA molecules in agarose gels up to several million base pairs. Combined with restriction enzymes that cut infrequently in the genome, PFGE can be used to construct long-range restriction maps of complex genomes. Most 'rare cutting' restriction enzymes recognize sequences containing CpG dinucleotide pairs and are sensitive to cytosine methylation. In consequence, 'rare cutting' enzymes frequently cleave the CpG-rich regions found at the 5′ end of many genes (Brown & Bird 1986).

From a series of experiments designed to facilitate 'reverse genetic' approaches to cloning *TDF*, a Y-specific sequence, *DYS104*, was isolated from the region adjacent to *TDF* (Pritchard *et al.* 1987*a*). Another sequence, *DYS13*, with similar properties, was isolated by Affara *et al.* (1986*a*, *b*). Using probes for *MIC2*, *DYS104* and *DYS13*, a long-range restriction map was constructed (Pritchard *et al.* 1987*b*). The starting point for this map was the CpG-rich region at the 5′ end of *MIC2*. This region has been sequenced (Goodfellow *et al.* 1988) and several sites for 'rare cutting' restriction enzymes were demonstrated to be unmethylated in genomic DNA, providing an 'anchor point' upon which a long-range restriction map was based. The map we obtained contained several features of interest (figure 3).

1. For several enzymes all three sequences are located on the same restriction fragments. As *MIC2* is pseudoautosomal and *DYS104* and *DYS13* are Y-specific these fragments must span the boundary of the pseudoautosomal region. This conclusion was confirmed by demonstrating that *MIC2* probes recognize different restriction fragments on the X and the Y chromosomes. The smallest fragment that differs between the X and Y chromosomes is 150 kilobases. This defines the maximum distance between the *MIC2* CpG-rich region and the boundary. The position of the boundary has been further localized, by chromosome-walking experiments, to a region within 40 kilobases of the 3′ end of the *MIC2* gene.

The genetic distance between *MIC2* and the boundary is approximately 2.5 cM†. This recombination occurs in a physical distance of only 100 kilobases. Thus there is no evidence for suppression of recombination in the immediate vicinity of the boundary.

2. On the Y chromosome there are two clusters of 'rare cutting' cleavage sites detected by the probes. The first cluster is at the 5′ end of *MIC2*, the second cluster is approximately 260 kilobases proximal to *MIC2*. We suggested that this cluster was defining a gene and, on

† The morgan is the unit of relative distance between genes on a chromosome. One centimorgan (cM) represents a crossover value of 1%.

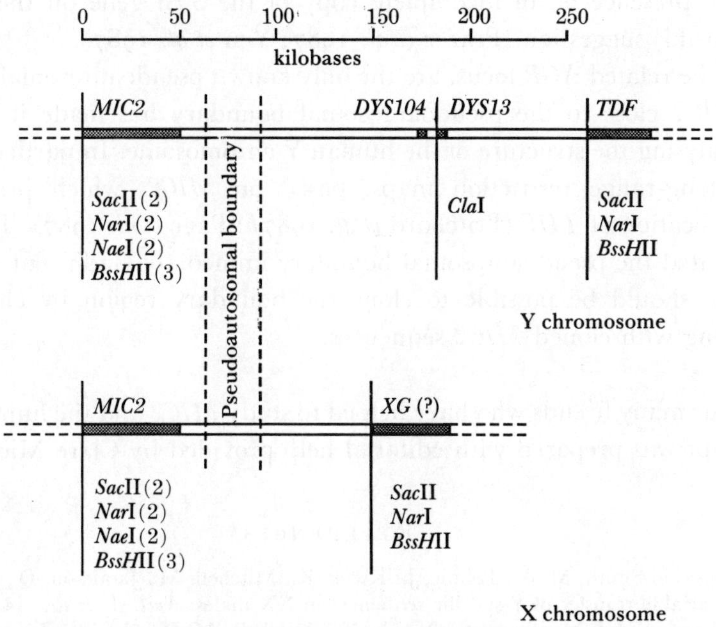

FIGURE 3. Long-range restriction map across the pseudoautosomal boundary. Rare-cutting restriction-enzyme recognition sites in the *MIC2* HTF-island and the X- and Y-specific cluster of sites are shown. The number of sites at the *MIC2* island are given in parentheses. The *ClaI* site that separates *DYS104* and *DYS13* and their positions relative to it are shown. The positions of *DYS104*, *DYS13* and the pseudoautosomal boundaries were refined by chromosomal walking experiments (our unpublished observations).

the basis of chromosomal location, we predicted that this gene was *TDF*. This prediction appears to have been confirmed by the elegant studies of Page *et al.* (1987).

3. On the X chromosome there are also two clusters of 'rare cutting' cleavage sites detected by the *MIC2* probe. The second cluster is specific to the X chromosome and we have suggested that this may represent the structural gene for the Xg blood-group antigen. This prediction is based on the finding of genetic interaction between *MIC2*, *XG* and a third locus *XGR* (Goodfellow *et al.* 1986*b*). On red blood cells, expression of the *XG* antigen and the 12E7 antigen is coordinately regulated in *cis* by *XGR*, a pseudoautosomal locus. This locus was previously believed to be Y-specific and was named *YG* (Goodfellow & Tippett 1981; Tippett *et al.* 1986). Recombination occurs between *XGR* and *XG*, but *XGR* has not been separated from *MIC2* and it is possible that *XGR* is a polymorphism at the *MIC2* locus. Nevertheless, the *cis* interaction between *XGR*, *MIC2* and *XG* is easier to understand if *XG* and *MIC2* are in close proximity.

CONCLUSIONS

Two pseudoautosomal genes have been defined in mammals: *Sts* in mouse and *MIC2* in man. The murine *Sts* locus encodes the enzyme steroid sulphatase and this locus exchanges with a high frequency between the sex chromosomes in male meiosis (Keitges *et al.* 1985). The equivalent locus in man, *STS*, is not pseudoautosomal, but is located on the X chromosome adjacent to the pseudoautosomal region (Geller *et al.* 1986; Mondello *et al.* 1987). *STS* is subject to only partial X-inactivation (Migeon *et al.* 1982) and this might imply that *STS* was originally pseudoautosomal and has been lost recently from the Y chromosome during evolution. The presence of an incomplete copy of the *STS* gene on the Y chromosome is consistent with this suggestion (Frazer *et al.* 1987; Yen *et al.* 1987).

MIC2, and the related *XGR* locus, are the only known pseudoautosomal genes in man. The position of *MIC2* close to the pseudoautosomal boundary has made it a valuable genetic marker for analysing the structure of the human Y chromosome. In particular, it was possible to construct long-range restriction maps, based on *MIC2*, which precisely defined the chromosomal location of *TDF* (Pritchard *et al.* 1987*b*; Page *et al.* 1987). The same restriction maps have located the pseudoautosomal boundary immediately adjacent to the 3′ end of the *MIC2* gene. It should be possible to clone the boundary region by chromosome-walking methods starting with cloned *MIC2* sequences.

We thank our many friends who have helped to study *MIC2* and the human Y chromosome. This manuscript was prepared with editorial help provided by Clare Middlemiss.

References

Affara, N. A., Ferguson-Smith, M. A., Tolmie, J., Kwok, K., Mitchell, M., Jamieson, D., Cooke, A. & Florentin, L. 1986*a* Variable transfer of Y-specific sequences in XX males. *Nucl. Acids Res.* **14**, 5375–5387.

Affara, N. A., Florentin, L., Morrison, N., Kwok, K., Mitchell, M., Cooke, A., Jamieson, D., Glasgow, L., Meredith, L., Boyd, E. & Ferguson-Smith, M. A. 1986*b* Regional assignment of Y-linked DNA probes by deletion mapping and their homology with X-chromosome and autosomal sequences. *Nucl. Acids Res.* **14**, 5353–5373.

Andersson, M., Page, D. C. & de la Chapelle, A. 1986 Chromosome Y-specific DNA is transferred to the short arm of the X chromosome in human XX males. *Science, Wash.* **233**, 786–788.

Banting, G. S., Pym, B. & Goodfellow, P. N. 1985 Biochemical analysis of an antigen produced by both human sex chromosomes. *EMBO J.* **4**, 1967–1972.

Banting, G. S., Pym, B., Darling, S. M. & Goodfellow, P. N. 1988 The *MIC2* gene product: epitope mapping and structural prediction analysis define an integral membrane protein. (Submitted.)

Bird, A. P. 1986 CpG-rich islands and the function of DNA methylation. *Nature, Lond.* **321**, 209–213.

Brown, W. R. A. & Bird, A. P. 1986 Long-range restriction site mapping of mammalian genomic DNA. *Nature, Lond.* **322**, 477–481.

Buckle, V., Mondello, C., Darling, S., Craig, I. W. & Goodfellow, P. N. 1985 Homologous expressed genes in the human sex chromosome pairing region. *Nature, Lond.* **317**, 739–741.

Buckle, V., Boyd, Y., Fraser, N., Goodfellow, P. N., Goodfellow, P. J., Wolfe, J. & Craig, I. W. 1987 Localisation of Y chromosome sequences in normal and 'XX' males. *J. med. Genet.* **24**, 197–203.

Burgoyne, P. S. 1982 Genetic homology and crossing over in the X and Y chromosomes of mammals. *Hum. Genet.* **61**, 85–90.

Cooke, H. J., Brown, W. R. A. & Rappold, G. 1985 Hypervariable telomeric sequences from the human sex chromosome are pseudoautosomal. *Nature, Lond.* **317**, 688–692.

Darling, S. M., Banting, G. S., Pym, B., Wolfe, J. & Goodfellow, P. N. 1986*a* Cloning an expressed gene shared by the human sex chromosomes. *Proc. natn. Acad. Sci. U.S.A.* **83**, 135–139.

Darling, S. M., Goodfellow, P. J., Pym, B., Banting, G. S., Pritchard, C. & Goodfellow, P. N. 1986*b* Molecular genetics of *MIC2*: a gene shared by the human X and Y chromosomes. *Cold Spring Harb. Symp. quant. Biol.* **51**, 205–212.

Davies, K. E., Mandel, J.-L., Weissenbach, J. & Fellous, M. 1987 Report of the committee on the genetic constitution of the X and Y chromosome. HGM9. *Cytogenet. Cell Genet.* **46**, 277–315.

Davis, R. M. 1981 Localization of male determining factors in man: a thorough review of structural anomalies of the Y chromosome. *J. med. Genet.* **18**, 161–195.

Ferguson-Smith, M. A. 1966 X–Y chromosomal interchange in the aetiology of true hermaphroditism and of XX Klinefelter's syndrome. *Lancet* ii, 475–476.

Frazer, N., Ballabio, A., Zollo, M., Persico, G. & Craig, I. 1987 Identification of incomplete coding sequences for steroid sulphatase on the human Y chromosome: evidence for an ancestral pseudoautosomal gene? *Development* **101**(suppl.), 127–132.

Geller, R. L., Shapiro, L. J. & Mohandas, T. K. 1986 Fine mapping of the distal short arm of the human X chromosome using X/Y translocations. *Am. J. hum. Genet.* **38**, 884–890.

Goodfellow, P. N. 1983 Expression of the 12E7 antigen is controlled independently by genes on the human X and Y chromosomes. *Differentiation* **23** (suppl.), 35–39.

Goodfellow, P. N. & Goodfellow, P. J. 1988 The pseudoautosomal region of man. In *Mechanisms of sex determination* (ed. S. S. Wachtel). Boca Raton, Florida: CRC Press. (In the press.)

Goodfellow, P. N. & Tippett, P. 1981 A human polymorphism related to Xg blood groups. *Nature, Lond.* **289**, 404–405.

Goodfellow, P. N., Banting, G., Levy, R., Povey, S. & McMichael, A. 1980 A human X-linked antigen defined by a monoclonal antibody. *Somatic Cell Genet.* **6**, 777–787.

Goodfellow, P. N., Banting, G., Sheer, D., Ropers, H.-H., Caine, A., Ferguson-Smith, M. A., Povey, S. & Voss, R. 1983 Genetic evidence that a Y-linked gene in man is homologous to a gene on the X chromosome. *Nature, Lond.* **302**, 346–349.

Goodfellow, P. N., Pym, B., Mohandas, T. & Shapiro, L. J. 1984 The cell surface antigens locus, *MIC2X*, escapes X-inactivation. *Am. J. hum. Genet.* **36**, 777–782.

Goodfellow, P. N., Darling, S. & Wolfe, J. 1985 The human Y chromosome. *J. med. Genet.* **22**, 329–344.

Goodfellow, P. J., Darling, S. M., Thomas, N. S. & Goodfellow, P. N. 1986*a* A pseudoautosomal gene in man. *Science, Wash.* **234**, 740–743.

Goodfellow, P. J., Pritchard, C., Tippett, P. & Goodfellow, P. N. 1986*b* Recombination between the X and Y chromosomes at the *YG* locus: implications for the relationship between *MIC2*, *XG* and *YG*. *Ann. hum. genet.* **51**, 161–167.

Goodfellow, P. J., Mondello, C., Darling, S. M., Pym, B., Little, P. & Goodfellow, P. N. 1988 Absence of methylation of a CpG rich region at the 5′ end of the *MIC2* gene on the active X, the inactive X and the Y chromosome. *Proc. natn. Acad. Sci. U.S.A.* (In the press.)

Guellaen, G., Casanova, M., Bishop, C., Geldwerth, D., Audre, G., Fellous, M. & Weissenbach, J. 1984 Human XX males with Y single copy DNA fragments. *Nature, Lond.* **307**, 172–173.

Keitges, E., Rivest, M., Siniscalco, M. & Gartler, S. M. 1985 X-linkage of steroid sulphatase in the mouse is evidence for a functional Y-linked allele. *Nature, Lond.* **315**, 226–227.

Keith, D. H., Singer-Sam, J. & Riggs, A. D. 1986 Active X chromosome DNA is unmethylated at eight CCGG sites clustered in a guanosine-plus-cytosine rich island at the 5′ end of the gene for phosphoglycerate kinase. *Molec. Cell Biol.* **6**, 4122–4125.

Koller, P. C. & Darlington, C. D. 1934 The genetical and mechanical properties of the sex chromosomes. 1. *Rattus norvegicus*. *J. Genet.* **29**, 159–173.

Lyon, M. F. 1974 Evolution of X-chromosome inactivation in mammals. *Nature, Lond.* **250**, 651–653.

Messing, J. 1983 New M13 vectors for cloning. *Meth. Enzymol.* **101**, 20–78.

Migeon, B. R., Shapiro, L. J., Norum, R. A., Mohandas, T., Axelman, J. & Dabora, R. L. 1982 Differential expression of steroid sulphatase locus on active and inactive human X chromosome. *Nature, Lond.* **229**, 838–840.

Mondello, C., Ropers, H.-H., Craig, I. W. & Goodfellow, P. N. 1987 Physical mapping of genes and sequences at the end of the human X chromosome short arm. *Ann. hum. Genet.* **51**, 137–143.

Mondello, C., Goodfellow, P. J. & Goodfellow, P. N. 1988 Analysis of methylation of a human, X-located gene which escapes X-inactivation. *Nucl. Acids Res.* (In the press.)

Page, D. C., Mosher, R., Simpson, E. M., Fisher, E. M. C., Mardon, G., Pollack, J., McGillivray, B., de la Chapelle, A. & Brown, L. G. 1987 The sex-determining region of the human Y chromosome encodes a finger protein. *Cell* **51**, 1091–1104.

Petit, C., de la Chapelle, A., Levilliers, J., Castillo, S., Noel, B. & Weissenbach, J. 1987 An abnormal terminal exchange accounts for most but not all cases of human XX maleness. *Cell* **49**, 595–602.

Pritchard, C. A., Goodfellow, P. J. & Goodfellow, P. N. 1987*a* Isolation of a sequence which maps close to the human sex-determining gene. *Nucl. Acids Res.* **15**, 6159–6169.

Pritchard, C. A., Goodfellow, P. J. & Goodfellow, P. N. 1987*b* Mapping the limits of the human pseudoautosomal region and a candidate sequence for the male-determining gene. *Nature, Lond.* **328**, 273–275.

Renwick, J. H. 1969 Progress in mapping human autosomes. *Br. med. Bull.* **25**, 65–73.

Rouyer, F., Simmler, M. C., Johnsson, C., Vergnaud, G., Cooke, H. & Weissenbach, J. 1986 A gradient of sex linkage in the pseudoautosomal region of the human sex chromosomes. *Nature, Lond.* **319**, 291–295.

Sanger, F., Nicklen, S. & Coulson, A. R. 1977 DNA sequencing with chain-terminating inhibitors. *Proc. natn. Acad. Sci. U.S.A.* **74**, 5463–5467.

Simmler, M.-C., Rouyer, F., Vergnaud, G., Nystrom-Lahti, M., Ngo, K. Y., de la Chapelle, A. & Weissenbach, J. 1985 Pseudoautosomal DNA sequences in the pairing region of the human sex chromosomes. *Nature, Lond.* **317**, 692–697.

Tippett, P., Shaw, M. A., Green, C. A. & Daniels, G. L. 1986 The 12E7 red cell quantitative polymorphism: control by a Y-borne locus Yg. *Ann. hum. Genet.* **50**, 339–347.

Vergnaud, G., Page, D. C., Simmler, M.-C., Brown, L., Rouyer, F., Noel, B., Botstein, D., de la Chapelle, A. & Weissenbach, J. 1986 A deletion map of the human Y chromosome based on DNA hybridisation. *Am. J. hum. Genet.* **38**, 109–124.

Weissenbach, J., Levilliers, J., Petit, C., Rouyer, F. & Simmler, M.-C. 1987 Normal and abnormal interchanges between the human X and Y chromosomes. *Development* **101** (suppl.), 67–74.

Yen, P. H., Patel, P., Chinault, A. C., Mohandas, T. & Shapiro, L. J. 1984 Differential methylation of hypoxanthine phosphoribosyltransferase genes on active and inactive human X chromosomes. *Proc. natn. Acad. Sci. U.S.A.* **81**, 1759–1763.

Yen, P. H., Allen, E., Marsh, B., Mohandas, T., Wang, N., Taggart, R. T. & Shapiro, L. 1987 Cloning and expression of steroid sulfatase cDNA and frequent occurrences of deletions in STS deficiency: implications for X–Y interchange. *Cell* **49**, 443–454.

Young, R. A. & Davis, R. W. 1983 Yeast RNA polymerase II genes: isolation with antibody probes. *Science, Wash.* **222**, 778–782.

Discussion

H. Sharma (71 *Barrack Road, Hounslow, U.K.*) Is there homology to any known protein sequence with *MIC* genes? Is it conserved in species?

P. N. Goodfellow. Outside the putative signal sequence we have not detected sequence homology between *MIC2* and any other described sequence; this is true both at the protein and nucleotide sequence level.

MIC2-related sequences are present in primates, but have not been detected by high-stringency hybridization in other animals.

Phil. Trans. R. Soc. Lond. B **322**, 155–157 (1988) [155]
Printed in Great Britain

Is *ZFY* the sex-determining gene on the human Y chromosome?

BY D. C. PAGE

Whitehead Institute for Biomedical Research, Nine Cambridge Center, Cambridge, Massachusetts 02142, *U.S.A., and Department of Biology, Massachusetts Institute of Technology, Cambridge, Massachusetts* 02139, *U.S.A.*

The sex-determining region of the human Y chromosome contains a gene, *ZFY*, that encodes a zinc-finger protein. *ZFY* may prove to be the testis-determining factor. There is a closely related gene, *ZFX*, on the human X chromosome. In most species of placental mammals, we detect two *ZFY*-related loci: one on the Y chromosome and one on the X chromosome. However, there are four *ZFY*-homologous loci in mouse: *Zfy-1* and *Zfy-2* map to the sex-determining region of the mouse Y chromosome, *Zfx* is on the mouse X chromosome, and a fourth locus is autosomal.

Studies of humans and mice with abnormal sex-chromosome constitutions have revealed the critical sex-determining role of the Y chromosome (reviewed by McLaren, this symposium). Regardless of the number of X chromosomes, human or mouse embryos with a Y chromosome (XY or XXY) develop as males, with testes, whereas embryos with no Y chromosome (X0 or XX) develop as females, with ovaries. These findings imply the existence on the Y chromosome of one or more genes whose products determine, directly or indirectly, the fate of all sexually dimorphic characters.

To facilitate discussion of these inferred but uncharacterized sex-determining gene or genes on the Y chromosome, they have been given names. Thus in complete ignorance of the biochemical nature, mode of action or even the number of gene products, one can refer abstractly to the *TDF* (testis-determining factor; McKusick (1975)) gene(s) on the human Y chromosome or to *Tdy* (Y-linked testis determinant; Eicher *et al.* (1982)), the murine counterpart.

My co-workers and I set out to identify the human *TDF* gene(s) by an approach that does not presuppose the nature of the gene product(s). We thought it would be possible to clone the gene by determining its precise location on the Y chromosome (Page 1986). A deletion map of the human Y chromosome can be constructed by DNA hybridization analysis of naturally occurring, structurally abnormal Y chromosomes (Vergnaud *et al.* 1986), and *TDF* can be positioned on such a map. By genetic deletion analysis of 'sex-reversed' individuals (e.g. 'XX males' and 'XY females'), we established that the fate of the bipotential gonad hinges upon the presence or absence of a very small portion of the short arm of the Y chromosome (Page *et al.* 1987). Indeed, testicular differentiation occurred in an XX male who carries roughly 300 kilobase pairs (intervals 1A1 and 1A2), or 0.5%, of the Y chromosome (figure 1). Conversely, female differentiation occurred in an individual who apparently possesses all but 160 kilobase pairs (intervals 1A2 and 1B) of the Y chromosome. Deletion analysis of these and other individuals suggests the following two conclusions: first, interval 1A (the sum of 1A1 and 1A2) is sufficient to induce testicular differentiation of the bipotential gonad; second, interval 1A2 contains an essential portion of that testis-determining function.

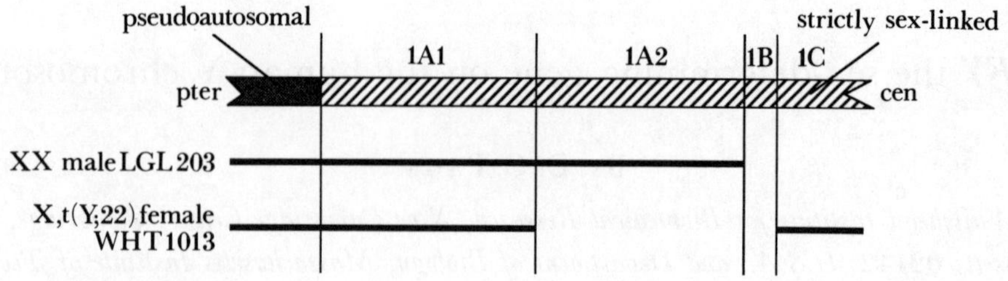

FIGURE 1. The sex-determining region of the human Y chromosome (adapted from Page *et al.* (1987)). The distal short arm of the Y chromosome is represented schematically, oriented with respect to the short-arm telomere (pter) and centromere (cen). The pseudoautosomal region frequently undergoes recombination with the X chromosome during meiosis. Intervals 1A1, 1A2, 1B and 1C show strictly sex-linked (not pseudoautosomal) inheritance, and they are defined by deletion analysis. Black bars depict the portions of the Y chromosome present in XX male LGL203 and X, t(Y; 22) female WHT1013. The *TDF* gene must be found in its entirety in intervals 1A1 and 1A2. Interval 1A2, which is present in the XX male and absent in the X, t(Y; 22) female, must contain an essential portion of *TDF*.

What gene or genes are actually found in interval 1A2, which measures 140 kilobase pairs, or about 0.2 % of the human Y chromosome? We discovered that interval 1A2 carries a gene that, based on analysis of its nucleotide sequence, appears to encode a protein with at least 13 'zinc-finger' domains (Page *et al.* 1987). The presence of zinc-finger domains, as first described in frog transcription factor IIIA (reviewed by Klug & Rhodes (1987)), suggests that the putative protein binds to DNA or RNA in a sequence-specific manner. The protein may regulate transcription.

The location of this gene in interval 1A2 – and the existence of homologous sequences in the *Sxr* region of the mouse Y chromosome, as described below – suggests that this zinc-finger protein is sex determining. However, in the absence of more direct evidence of sex-determining function (e.g. sex reversal of transgenic XX mice, or the finding of a mutation within the gene in an XY female), it is premature to refer to the gene as *TDF*. Until its biological function is determined, I shall refer to the human gene simply as *ZFY* (Y-linked zinc-finger protein).

Surprisingly, there appears to exist on the short arm of the human X chromosome a gene whose structure and DNA sequence are quite similar to those of *ZFY* (Page *et al.* (1987) and unpublished results). Until the biological function of this gene is established, I shall refer to it as *ZFX* (X-linked homologue of *ZFY*). Although it is quite likely that *ZFY* and *ZFX* are true homologues that evolved from a single, common ancestral gene, it is unlikely that either is a pseudogene, for both show a striking degree of evolutionary conservation among placental mammals (Page *et al.* 1987). If *ZFY* is the Y-linked sex-determining factor then we must consider models of sex determination that accommodate the existence of a related gene on the X chromosome (see Page *et al.* (1987) for a discussion of four such models).

It should be noted that interval 1A2 of the Y chromosome is absent in some human XX males and XX hermaphrodites, and it is at least grossly intact in many XY females (Page *et al.* 1987). Sex reversal in some such cases may be due to mutations in autosomal or X-linked genes whose products function together with or downstream of *TDF* in the sex determination pathway.

In most species of placental mammals that we have examined, we have detected two loci homologous to human *ZFY*: one on the Y chromosome and one on the X chromosome. However, mice appear to have four loci homologous to human *ZFY* (Page *et al.* (1987) and unpublished results). One of these homologues is on the mouse X chromosome, and I shall refer to it as *Zfx* (X-linked homologue of human *ZFY*). The mouse Y chromosome carries two distinct loci homologous to human *ZFY*. I shall refer to these mouse loci as *Zfy-1* and *Zfy-2* (Y-linked homologues of human *ZFY*). The fourth mouse locus is autosomal.

Adding to the evidence that *ZFY* functions in human sex determination is the finding (Page *et al.* 1987) that both *Zfy-1* and *Zfy-2* are present in XX *Sxr* male mice, which carry only a small, sex-determining portion of the mouse Y chromosome (Singh & Jones 1982; Evans *et al.* 1982). Interestingly, *Zfy-1* is present but *Zfy-2* is absent (G. Mardon, unpublished results) in XX *Sxr′* male mice (McLaren *et al.* 1984), who carry an even smaller but none the less sex-determining portion of the mouse Y. *Zfy-1* and *Zfy-2* evidently are not both necessary for testis determination.

Detailed examination of the human *ZFY* and *ZFX* genes, the mouse homologues and the encoded proteins is clearly warranted. None the less, interval 1A1 and the remainder of interval 1A2 of the human Y chromosome merit further scrutiny. The possibility that this sex-determining region contains one or more genes in addition to *ZFY* cannot yet be excluded.

References

Eicher, E. M., Washburn, L. L., Whitney, J. B. III & Morrow, K. E. 1982 *Mus poschiavinus* Y chromosome in the C57BL/6J murine genome causes sex reversal. *Science, Wash.* **217**, 535–537.

Evans, E. P., Burtenshaw, M. D. & Cattanach, B. M. 1982 Meiotic crossing-over between the X and Y chromosomes of male mice carrying the sex-reversing (Sxr) factor. *Nature, Lond.* **300**, 443–445.

Klug, A. & Rhodes, D. 1987 "Zinc fingers": a novel protein motif for nucleic acid recognition. *Trends biochem. Sci.* **12**, 464–469.

McKusick, V. A. 1975 *Mendelian inheritance in man*, 4th edn. Baltimore: Johns Hopkins University.

McLaren, A., Simpson, E., Tomonari, K., Chandler, P. & Hogg, H. 1984 Male sexual differentiation in mice lacking H-Y antigen. *Nature, Lond.* **312**, 552–555.

Page, D. C. 1986 Sex reversal: deletion mapping the male-determining function of the human Y chromosome. In *Molecular biology of Homo sapiens* (*Cold Spring Harb. Symp. quant. Biol.* **51**), pp. 229–235.

Page, D. C., Mosher, R., Simpson, E. M., Fisher, E. M. C., Mardon, G., Pollack, J., McGillivray, B., de la Chapelle, A. & Brown, L. G. 1987 The sex-determining region of the human Y chromosome encodes a finger protein. *Cell* **51**, 1091–1104.

Singh, L. & Jones, K. W. 1982 Sex reversal in the mouse (*Mus musculus*) is caused by a recurrent nonreciprocal crossover involving the X and an aberrant Y chromosome. *Cell* **28**, 205–216.

Vergnaud, G., Page, D. C., Simmler, M.-C., Brown, L., Rouyer, F., Noel, B., Botstein, D., de la Chapelle, A. & Weissenbach, J. 1986 A deletion map of the human Y chromosome based on DNA hybridization. *Am. J. hum. Genet.* **38**, 109–124.

SINGLE CELL MARKING AND CELL LINEAGE IN ANIMAL DEVELOPMENT

Developmental biology is one of the most exciting areas in contemporary science. This volume describes the results of new approaches to the embryo that have led to accurate descriptions of how, through cell lineage, the cells of the embryo produce the patterns of the adult. Results from diverse vertebrates and invertebrates are brought together for the first time.

Edited by

R.L. GARDNER, F.R.S., AND P.A. LAWRENCE, F.R.S.

187 pages 20 plates clothbound ISBN 0 85403 261 4

First published in ***Philosophical Transactions of the Royal Society,*** **Series B, Vol. 312, 1985**

Price including packing and postage

£41.50 (U.K. addresses) £44.00 (Overseas addresses)

The Royal Society

6 Carlton House Terrace, London, SW1Y 5AG